Varieties of Muslim Experience

Varieties of Muslim Experience

Encounters with Arab Political and Cultural Life

LAWRENCE ROSEN

The University of Chicago Press   Chicago and London

LAWRENCE ROSEN is the William Nelson Cromwell Professor of Anthropology at Princeton University. His books include *The Culture of Islam: Changing Aspects of Contemporary Muslim Life* (2002), also published by the University of Chicago Press.

The University of Chicago Press, Chicago 60637
The University of Chicago Press, Ltd., London
© 2008 by The University of Chicago
All rights reserved. Published 2008
Printed in the United States of America

17 16 15 14 13 12 11 10 09 08   1 2 3 4 5

ISBN-13: 978-0-226-72616-8 (cloth)
ISBN-10: 0-226-72616-9 (cloth)

Library of Congress Cataloging-in-Publication Data
Rosen, Lawrence, 1941–
  Varieties of Muslim experience : encounters with Arab political and cultural life / Lawrence Rosen.
  p. cm.
  Includes bibliographical references and index.
  ISBN-13: 978-0-226-72616-8 (cloth : alk. paper)
  ISBN-10: 0-226-72616-9 (pbk. : alk. paper) 1. Arab countries—Politics and government—21st century. 2. Arab countries—Social life and customs. 3. Islam—21st century. I. Title.
  DS36.88 .R67 2008
  909'.0974927083—dc22
                                                                    2007035706

For

Akbar Ahmed
Mustafa Benyakhlef
Abdellah Hammoudi

Scholars, Patriots, Friends

Contents

Acknowledgments

These essays have benefited from the intellectual and financial support of numerous individuals and foundations. The project began while I was a fellow at Wolfson College, Oxford, and my continuing relationship as a member of college has been a cherished association. The book was completed while a fellow of the Woodrow Wilson International Center for Scholars in Washington, D.C. The center's director, Lee Hamilton, along with Haleh Esfandiari, Lindsay Collins, Steven Lagerfeld, Michael Shank, and the center fellows and staff provided much more than an ideal working environment: they also contributed important ideas for which I am most grateful. Colleagues in Princeton—Jim Clark, Veronique Benei, João Biehl, James Boon, and John Borneman—have been thoughtful and constructive readers of portions of the manuscript, and their comments, as always, have been greatly appreciated. As the recipient of a Carnegie Corporation Scholar's award I have been free to pursue my ideas wherever they seemed most fruitful, and the corporation's confidence in my work has been enormously important to me. I am also grateful to Princeton University and everyone in the anthropology department for their ideas and encouragement. Several of these essays were presented as lectures at Oxford University, the University of Leiden, American University, Harvard University, the University of Wisconsin, and the Council on Foreign Relations; I have benefited greatly from the comments made by the attendees at those events. Special thanks are due to T. David Brent of the University of Chicago Press who, in the course of several books, has been unflagging in his support. If I have occasionally strayed to other presses I have always felt I arrived home when benefiting from David's thoughtfulness and expertise. I am also grateful to Leslie Keros for her superb editing, and to my sister Jeanne Rosen for her many helpful suggestions.

I have long benefited, too, from the generous help of the government of Morocco and the city and province of Sefrou in carrying out my research, while comparative work in Tunisia and Malaysia has also been aided by various agencies and grants. To all I am most grateful.

The spelling of Arabic terms broadly follows the style of the *International Journal of Middle East Studies*. Variations will exist where a colloquial term is used, and words that have gained currency in Western publications will be rendered in those more recognizable forms.

Finally, I have dedicated the book to three colleagues and friends who over the years have enriched my understanding of Arab and Muslim thought beyond any capacity for measurement. Akbar Ahmed embodies all one could hope for in a man of ideas and a guide in matters both academic and moral, and his heartfelt attachment to interfaith dialogue is matched only by his unrivaled generosity of spirit. Mustafa Benyakhlef was my first teacher of Moroccan Arabic, and his love for his country and for scholarship has been a precious gift, for more than forty years, to his people and to me. Abdellah Hammoudi, my colleague at Princeton, has kept me thinking about the smallest details and the largest ideas for many years, and his commitment to grasping the unique and the general at the same time has been, for me as for so many others, an endowment of incalculable value. Their institutions have in each of them the most marvelous of scholars; their nations have in them the finest of patriots—and I have the privilege of having in them the dearest of friends.

Introduction: Presenting and Re-presenting Islam

Ethnocentrism is a dirty word—as well it should be. To approach another culture solely from the judgmental perspective of one's own is both unwise and immoral. But (to paraphrase Lucretius on nature), one cannot throw context out the door and not expect it to rush back in through the window. Indeed, once we recognize that it is from some particular place that, in the best of circumstances, we try to make sense of other cultures, we can actually use that stance to advantage.

The essays in this book start, for the most part, from the perspective of someone from the West who may be struck by certain features of an Islamic culture that appear particularly curious. Whether that curiosity concerns the belief in genies or how a scientist can be a fundamentalist, whether one is struck by the ostensible prohibition on human images or wonders whether something did indeed "go wrong" in Arab political development, the Westerner who is sincere in understanding something about Islamic cultures—even to the point of asking if such a classification is itself helpful—needs responses that account for his or her own cultural background. It is not a matter of raising one's Western values to ethnocentric certainty any more than it is about reducing differences to claimed universality. And it is certainly not about securing enough data to validate one's own judgment of other cultures. Rather, realizing that the reader does indeed come at issues with questions and interpretations influenced by a particular background and experience, it is necessary to render explanations that take these influences into account. Thus without in any sense avoiding the task of any scholar—to make the best sense possible of the subject involved—these essays attempt to address questions in a way that acknowledges some of the starting points from which the sympathetic Western reader may approach the variety of Muslim experience.

Where you stand affects many aspects of the way you interpret another culture, not least when it comes to issues of gender. For purposes of readability, no less than accuracy, I generally employ the male pronoun when referring to activities, such as the intense negotiation of political relationships, that are more commonly practiced by men than by women, and I refer to both men and women when I want to suggest that the activities involve both men and women. When words like "he" and "him" are employed, readers should not read too much into them unless specific issues of gender difference have been highlighted as crucial to the purpose of a given chapter.

It was, I believe, Octavio Paz who once said that there are two kinds of people in the world: those who divide everything into two kinds of things—and those who do not. Without betraying my deep attachment to the latter approach, I would just add that there are indeed two kinds of people whose roles continue to be critical to the sociology of knowledge generally. These two groups (to borrow the language used to describe their history in biological studies) may be referred to as the lumpers and the splitters. The former see similarities and classify things as members of the same group that the latter, seeing differences as more self-evident, would use to separate items into discrete groupings. Indeed, the history of certain disciplines has been characterized, in no small part, by the struggle between these orientations, even to the point where the ascendancy of one over the other has come to define the entire discipline. In physical anthropology, for example, lumpers and splitters have lumped and split entire academic departments; in other fields—such as American, African American, or Women's Studies—the splitters have used their arguments to consolidate the field against those who might deny them their identity by characterizing one area of study as solely a subset of some other. For students of Arab thought and culture—whether they come out of departments of Oriental Studies or particular social sciences—the tendency has also been toward splitting, and with it has come one of the more peculiar failings of scholarship on this critical region. This propulsion toward legitimization through differentiation manifests itself in numerous ways.

Every discipline or craft has its mysteries, indeed its mystifications.

Elongated training, rites of professional passage, obscure jargon, and in-group gossip may all serve to solidify identity. In the Western study of the Arab world this process takes several distinct forms. The first has to do with the Arabic language itself. Orientalists would often have one believe that Arabic is among the most difficult languages to command. An extensive vocabulary—ranging from the ninety-nine known names of God to the elaborate catalog of a camel's delights—combined with poetic virtuosity, intimate knowledge of how Arabic words often imply their opposite, and practice in the hierarchies of pronunciation that would make a French academician or British snob blush, all contribute to the Arabist's special claims. The mentality of the splitter supports this orientation, which not only claims a need for extensive preparation and pressures toward very limited interpretation but divides the pursuit of knowledge about the Arab world from the very comparisons that have vitalized so many other studies of area history and culture. The result, quite commonly, is to have it said of any part of the Arab world or any moment in its history that it is unlike any other part or time: "the Lebanese are nothing like the Saudis"; "the present is completely different from the medieval period"; "the guys on that side of the hill are not at all like the guys on this side." While such splitters highlight the range of differences, they fail to grasp that it is precisely a range of variation that is indeed being observed. Just as in biology, so too in social and cultural life it is variation that is key, and anyone who is set down in any part of the Arab world and thinks they are among the Eskimo or Hottentots has simply failed to get the point.

The relevance of this for the current study is quite simple: the issues explored here must be addressed in a theme and variation context. Of course, every element is not replicated in every part or moment of the Arab world, and of course the idea that things have remained unchanged for ages simply because they bear attachments across time would be a distortion of the argument. Variation, too, is not essentialization. There are no pure types or irreducible essences to Arab life or language, any more than of any other set of related cultures, and hence no indispensable feature without which the Arabs would cease to be Arabs. Terms such as "Arabs" and "Muslim" are, of course, not without their problematic aspects. If by the former one means not only those who speak a dialect of Arabic but partake of many of the cultural features pointed to in this book, then one may properly speak, as scholars often do, of Arab Jews and Christian Arabs. The characteristics of the latter groupings will, in quite variant ways, be modulated in turn by the orientations reinforced by beliefs and practices associated with these religious affiliations. While both "Arab" and "Muslim" will be used in broad terms, by and large where there are concepts and resonances in sacred sources reference will be made to Islam as well as Arab cultures; where the ideas or institutions arise more from nonreligious bases the tendency will be to speak in terms of Arabs. In each instance, it is important to remember that throughout the Muslim world it is common for local practice to be regarded as Islamic rather than something set alongside Islam and that, to drive the point home, variation is not essentialization but its very opposite.

Similarly, to say that some of the features discussed are found in other cultures outside the Arab world is to carry particularism to an absurd conclusion. What is being asked of the reader, therefore, is a twofold task. One is to think of the ways in which the themes addressed vary across a shared cultural base. The other is to appreciate that whatever insights these essays provide stem partly from a fundamental anthropological assumption: what binds a culture together is the resonance across such diverse domains as the religious, political, spatial, familial, and legal of features that, for all their variety, partake of shared orientations toward the world of everyday experience.

It is in this respect, too, that I will frequently refer to Islam and Muslims rather than just Arabs. For even though the main examples are drawn almost entirely from that 25 percent of the Muslim world composed of Arabs, and even though Islam is by no means the be-all and end-all of these cultural variants, it is also true that the themes that pervade multiple domains of Arab life find deep and often propelling expression in the context of religious thought. Rather like genetics, one cannot understand Arab societies or polities without recourse to the religious involvement of any concept even though one cannot explain many aspects of Arab, any more than of human, action by means of religion or genetics alone. Because these essays are intended as a point of entry to many features of Arab cultural life as well as an invitation to those familiar with non-Arab Muslim societies to think about the ways they may apply in their realms as well, the title is meant to urge one to think in terms of variation and about the role of religion as a vital ingredient in any observable array.

That said, common themes pervade these essays in much more substantive terms, even when the propositions may appear to be rather generalized. Specifically, I argue throughout that Arabs place great emphasis on the relationships people forge with one another, a point that may hardly seem to distinguish them from many, if not most, other people in the world. But the differences make all the difference. For there are distinct ways in which these relationships may be formed: some are as unusual as offering a sacrifice at another's door to conduce aid in some enterprise or as common as constructing a friendship that may be called upon later at a time of need. Some appear obvious to the Western eye—like focusing on the individual rather than solidary groups—only to have the Westerner's perceptions troubled by discovering that statements about relationship require some additional action before they can be appraised for their truth-bearing quality, or that causality may take a different course of implications than that found in Western cultures. To suggest that Arabs see bonds of obligation as interchangeable is no more to suggest that they are merely instrumental in their ties to others than it is to claim that underneath a world of differences all people are really much the same. To the contrary, it is by attending to the distinctive ways that ties are formed, the distinctive implications they possess within an overall orientation to the world, and the distinctive differences these orientations make to the way new experiences are created and categorized that my approach to Arab culture may help make sense of practices that elude easy characterization.

Each essay, then, shows another aspect of these common themes. Often, as in the first section of the book, a story helps to situate the problematic elements of Western encounters with Arab culture. Through the story of a dispute on my block between a Middle Easterner and the other neighbors one begins to see how different orientations to relationships may affect cross-cultural communication. Looking at the larger context of Arab culture, the question "what went wrong?" (popularized by the title of Bernard Lewis's book) can be transformed into a question of how the diverse aspects of Arab culture form a coherent vision of life that centers on the ties people negotiate with one another and the implications of a vision of the self as not readily segregated into potentially discordant roles. In this context one may even be able to understand why, when a terrorist kills himself, he may actually be trying to establish the network of relations that is crucial to defining a man and solidifying that web of indebtedness beyond risk of revision. Property, too, can be seen as less a question of one's relationship to things than to others, and with it some suggestions present themselves as to why attachment to particular territories may vary in intensity across the Arab world. Similarly, the emphasis Arabs place on ideas of "justice"—rather than, say, "rights" or "liberty"—also becomes more comprehensible as we grasp that for them justice actually implies equivalence rather than equality.

The second section of the book addresses several matters of literary, visual, and historical representation that Western readers often find curious. What is it that makes reading the Quran such a difficult and even boring prospect for most Westerners, and how should Westerners understand some of the themes that appear to leap out from this seminal text? Portraiture is often thought to be forbidden by Islam, but that is not strictly true. Why then might Arabs find little or no meaning in such images when Westerners commonly imagine them as revealing important insights into a person's character? When we look at conflicts between Western styles of critical speech and the sensibilities of affected Muslims, as in the Danish cartoon controversy, we see that it is necessary to understand the meaning of prophets—and particularly Muhammad—if we are to fully understand why believers feel so great a need to protect the Prophet from insult. And if a scholar like Ibn Khaldun is held up by Western historians as an example of either the first true sociologist or the first to grasp key universals of human history, how does reading him as a distinctly *Arab* scholar alter our view of his contributions?

The last section of the book raises several aspects of political culture. Why some Arabs with training in science would be attracted to fundamentalism is, of necessity, a speculative issue. But we can hypothesize several reasons, missed by commentators, that are based on the implications of an intensely relational view of the world. Indeed, through such a relational focus we can even speculate as to how a particular social focus may have contributed to the decline of Arab science in the medieval period. Likewise, if one thinks about the relation, say, of Islam to democracy, one must consider what assumptions may underpin Arabs' ideas of society and hence what freedoms might have to be addressed by any reconstituted governmental form. And finally, if one is to think about human rights in universal terms yet respond to local conceptualizations, one should ask how history suggests that the movement from the local to the universal takes place, and why any such development might raise particular issues that affect the prospects, or indeed the desirability, of applying such universalizing norms in the Arab world.

At times these essays may suggest that it is easy to think of the range of Arab cultures as diverging from those of the West by only a few degrees. Similarities can be mistaken for the intimately familiar, yet as Western and Arab cultures continue to follow their own paths, differences may appear more pronounced. "A difference is not a distinction," say the Arabs, and certainly to underscore divergence is not to imply any judgment of superior and inferior. Indeed, as Westerners try to understand what is different about Arab cultures from their own, they—we—may perhaps appreciate all the more that statement by God transmitted in the Quran, that "had it been Our intention We could have made you all the same." Mutual comprehension does not require that we all be the same, any more than mutual misunderstanding must necessarily result from differences. To the contrary, it is our difference, both in what we are and in how we come to view one another, that opens the possibility—the far more realistic possibility—for creating mutually enduring ties as well as the local emphases that give meaning to our separate ways.

PART ONE

Just and Not Just

ONE

Junk Democracy: Middle
East Meets Middle America

The noise was driving everyone crazy. At odd hours of the day and night, as well as on weekends and holidays, sounds of machinery and crashing metal emanated from the junkyard with mind-jarring irregularity. The problem was not the junkyard itself; we had all bought our homes knowing of its presence. But for the quarter-century I had lived on the street the man who owned and ran the junkyard was an excellent neighbor—thoughtful, quiet, clean, and helpful. Indeed, Tony had described his place, when I was first contemplating buying there, as a "Hollywood junkyard," and seeing Tony in the summer in his porkpie hat and tank-top undershirt, or having him use his plow to dig us out of the snow when the city had not yet gotten around to us, just added to the slightly eccentric nature of the place.

The street and the people living on it had long been a mix of categories and ambiguities, best symbolized, perhaps, by the fact that the post office calls the little dead-end street by one name and the town calls it by another. Located at the edge of a well-to-do commuter community, surrounded by institutional land and composed of six houses and the junkyard, it is also a designated historic district and close to a scenic towpath and bird sanctuary. Several of the houses were projects of the local historic preservation society: my own house, built in the 1830s, had been moved twice, once in the 1870s and again a century later. My neighbor's house had, over the years, been a warehouse and a glass factory, a hippie ashram and the home of a famous jazz critic and radio host. In my own years on the block the neighbors had included a cop, a janitor, an economist at the Federal Reserve, several university faculty and staff, and residents of the one rental house on the block. And, of course, Omar.

Omar appeared rather suddenly. He came from the Middle East and had been living in the area for some years when Tony decided to rent the junkyard to him. The property included a house, but when the wife of the cop who had lived next to the junkyard for forty years died and her husband moved out, Omar bought that house and moved into it. At first we just assumed that, as Tony was getting on in years, the junkyard was becoming too much for him and that he had found someone who would continue to operate it in the same manner he had. That was our first mistake. Our second may have been in the way we spoke with Omar when he began to make a nuisance of his operation.

Conversations with Omar seemed to most of my neighbors to follow a rather peculiar form. All smiles and warm gestures, Omar would tell us how he was going to make the junkyard a state-of-the-art operation, how he was not really engaged in a business but a service to the entire community, how he wanted us to be "his very good neighbors." "But Omar," people would say, "the noise is outrageous. We can't work, we can't sleep, we can't have friends over." "Oh," he would say, "I will stop that, don't be worried, don't be concerned"—and the next day, if not the next moment, the noise would resume. In the past all the junk metal was kept in the back of the property well out of sight, but now piles of scrap and rusting appliances overflowed to the street and onto the property in which Omar was living. He even put out a flyer—on recycled paper, of course, and with a lovely photo of the planet earth, all green and blue and pristine, as seen, rather significantly, from outer space—that urged potential customers to "save all the scrap papers, metals—save the earth," but concluded with the bone-chilling words, "open 7 days and nights." "Nothing to worry about," said Omar, when told that by remaining open all hours of the day and night he was violating zoning laws, noise laws, God's laws; "I'm going to make it all beautiful. A real service to everybody." It was here we may have encountered our third difficulty: we tried explaining to Omar our understanding of the meaning of law.

I like to think that the folks who were living on the block were not at all unusual in their understanding and attachment to the rule of law. And, like people generally, the more distressed we became, the more we cleaved to idealized forms and standard phraseology. "The law exists for everyone alike," we would tell Omar. "If we don't have law we can't have any order." At the same time, we were not unmindful that, in our own area, to say nothing of the world at large, those with greater influence not infrequently got treated a little more equally than others. When, for example, I would say, "Omar, it's against the law," he would respond with an indulgent smile, "I'm just trying to make a living, and all those laws make it hard for a little guy like me to succeed. The law," he would conclude with a rather obsequious shrug, "exists to be broken." "No, no," I would insist, "you can't choose which laws to obey. What if some people stopped for the sign at the end of the street and others chose not to?" "Oh, doctor," he would continue, as if to a child, "the law is just what the rich people get passed for themselves." "No, no," I would again insist, "the law applies to everyone alike." And as I would carry on with my high-minded principles, my irrefutable arguments, my ever more patriotic and law-abiding arguments, Omar would look at me as though I was really quite simple.

At one level, of course, we understood each other perfectly. No one on the block would have been surprised by the idea that those with access to power were listened to more readily than those who had no such entree. Indeed, at the very time the junkyard dispute was raging we were also attending meetings of the local city council, which was considering a new construction project near our properties. Since access to the facility could be routed in one of two ways—through the street adjacent to our own, past some high-density residences and a low income housing project, or around the other side, through one of the most exclusive neighborhoods in town—the dispute seemed to pit the haves against the have-nots. When we learned that the main opponent to the road traversing the richer area was a major contributor to an important local politician and that he also had enough political influence to block a back road that traversed both areas, people on our street were eager to confront the matter head-on. At a city council meeting, our opponent and one of his neighbors claimed that there were children in their neighborhood who might be endangered if access to the new project came through their area. When several speakers pointed out that the children of the poor were at least as important, the elected officials present appeared sufficiently embarrassed to gracefully distance themselves from their more affluent backers. Our faith in the system confirmed, I cited the outcome to Omar.

But Omar was not impressed. He knew that the fight over the project was far from over and that use of the back road we all used to avoid heavy traffic was still blocked as a result of one influential man's efforts. He saw the various meetings and phone calls as our attempt to get into the game: whether we succeeded or failed would be a function of our ability to play it well, and that in turn would depend on who we knew and probably how deep our pockets were. For all my assertions that the law was the vehicle for settling such matters, Omar was unconvinced. Thus when I said that if he wanted the applicable zoning rules changed he should do so through the established legal process, he shrugged, smiled, and said that that was just the way the rich got what they wanted. Like a psychoanalyst who tells you that every argument you make is simply a displacement of deeper anxiety, or a true believer who always finds a way to confirm scripture in the face of scientific evidence, Omar could divert every argument by playing on our own sense that indeed it was not always the case that the rule of law was the deciding factor.

Indeed, to many people it seemed as though Omar was simply unwilling to distinguish truth from lies. After all, he kept telling us he would do things that he did not, or would seem to accept our statements of certainty for their face value and then not abide by the terms. But if, for Omar, truth is not a point but a process, if a statement of certainty is more like a price suggested in the marketplace than a sum that is fixed, if indeed he envisions a statement of absolutes as a structure within which one searches for what part of that statement really matters to the person you are forming ties with, then truncating the process by not having any ongoing ties that turn on its implications could lead only to misunderstanding. There is a saying in the Middle East: You tend to ignore many truths from a liar. Perhaps there was a question, then, that we needed to ask. Had we been ignoring Omar's idea of truth as something that needs to be validated by the actions taken on its basis, and thus thrown out elements of that truth just because some of his utterances seemed to us to be self-evident lies?

Omar was clever enough to call a local newspaper about what was happening. The reporter portrayed Omar, as our neighbor portrayed himself, as a hard-pressed little businessman up against the powerful, who, Omar insisted, were really trying to take over the junkyard and force him out. This cabal of the rich and well connected had even led Omar to present himself at several offices in a manner that was regarded as so offensive that a restraining order was issued barring him from those premises. The other residents, perhaps fearful for their property values, were less than eager to go public with the dispute. So the reporter never learned of the restraining order or that the whole matter had been set in motion by Omar's repeated violations of the nuisance law.

For those living on the block, of course, the explanation for Omar's behavior tended to be quite simple: Omar is cunning, Omar is crazy, Omar is evil. And, as events began to unfold, there was reason to think that none of these theories was entirely without merit. After numerous contacts with public health and zoning officials Omar was cited and fined for violating various statutes. When he persisted he was hauled into municipal court. Confronted with his pattern of violating court orders he was even put in jail for several days and threatened with further fines. In addition, Omar was far in arrears in paying rent to Tony and, following still further court proceedings, he was formally evicted from the property. In turn, Omar filed suit claiming that Tony had polluted the junkyard, thus endangering Omar's health when he was still renting the junkyard, as well as polluting the adjacent house in which he was now living. This claim engendered a whole new set of delays and legal complications. Omar told people that he thought Tony would settle with him and that he would get to buy the junkyard outright. So little regard did he have for the process he had himself initiated, however, that when Omar refused to allow soil tests on his property to evaluate his pollution claim the judge once again had to intervene and order him to allow the sampling to go forward. The tests eventually proved there was no significant pollution on either property. In the meantime, Omar was also found to have defaulted on a major bank loan.

That winter Omar lived without any electricity, heat, or water; Tony even caught him trying to take service from the junkyard's lines. The neighbors wondered how Omar could use his toilet without any water. When the local officials were apprised of the situation they moved to check the property for violations, but, except for requiring him to remove all the junk from his yard, they were powerless to make Omar reinstate his utilities. Throughout that winter we would see Omar, now rather glum and disheveled, chopping wood, and propping open his front door on the occasional warm winter day. For many months, too, we saw an electrical line snaking from his house to his car. We assumed he was charging the car battery until we realized it was the other way around—he was actually running his lights and TV, as I had so often seen people in the rural areas of the Middle East do, from his car. Any sympathy these circumstances may have engendered was, however, quickly dissipated when Omar was observed stopping prospective buyers of another house on the block and telling them—as he had others before—that all the properties on the block had been polluted by Tony. Threats of a suit for slander of title had little effect. Omar's own attorney even grew exasperated by attempts to control her client's behavior, and when he failed to pay his legal bills Omar continued the pollution suit as his own lawyer.

To almost everyone involved, then, the dispute was explainable in terms of Omar's personality or financial circumstances. "Liberals" all, no one wanted to suggest that Omar's cultural background was responsible for his behavior, much less stereotype or denigrate Omar in terms of his origins. Indeed, one of the other homeowners on the block was himself from the Arab east while a second house had previously been rented by two different Muslim couples, and none of them had ever had any difficulty in coping with American life. As a result, it was, perhaps, relatively easy for various people, including the local newspaper, to miss the real story—that at least in this particular instance Omar and the rest of the participants were operating with somewhat incompatible views of the order of things. For even if Omar, unlike the other highly educated Middle Easterners who had lived on the street, was unusually obtuse or difficult the question nevertheless arose whether his behavior derived at least in part from cultural experiences that affected the meaning of his acts. If, given his background, he imagined the world quite differently from his neighbors, then the failure of those now living on the block to attend to his concepts and concerns could not be ignored. The possibility certainly existed, then, that this really was as much a clash of orientations as of interests, one in which, personality quirks aside, Omar's cultural image of power and society came up against the very different images of relationship, law, and politics that informed the views of others on the block, in city hall, and at the local court. To me, after forty years of study of the Middle East, there were familiar reverberations that fit with my own understanding of Omar's origins—reverberations that have a great deal to do with culture and history and that, in the context of systems that sustain these orientations, I have always regarded as enormously sensible and realistic.

To people from Omar's homeland interpersonal relations are at the center of human life, and the ways in which those ties have been arranged by those with the resources—financial, familial, political, oratorical—to make their view hold sway are simply performing in the world as it really is. Law, in this schema, is never simply impersonal: the idea of a rule of law and not of men would no doubt seem to Omar internally contradictory. For while regularities may indeed develop and broad willingness to abide by the same precepts apply, it is only through constantly testing the limits that one establishes the contexts that give principles their meaning. The image of the stop sign—particularly since everyone tends at times to slide through one—was, therefore, a poor choice of analogies with which to persuade Omar of the merits of institutions that, by definition, do not depend on those who inhabit them. Once, standing beside a road in North Africa with a young lawyer, I asked about his view of law in general. He pointed to the heterogeneous array of cars and buses, donkeys and horse carts, wandering pedestrians and ambling hawkers. Law, he said, never works to get people to do the same thing in the same way; it can only delineate some rough boundaries, like the edge of the road or the line down the middle. People always press to advantage, and if they can make their way stick, they are "right." The pressure to adhere to the limits of the acceptable, he seemed to be saying, is more a function of process than of prescribed result. Law, for this attorney, as for Omar himself, is therefore not an end in itself but part of the process of negotiation. Within the broad rules of alliance formation and divine implication, whatever the traffic will bear is, particularly if enforced by a big man at the center, the reality of law for that particular moment.

Similarly, Omar's ideas of public goods and of justice itself may well have informed his actions. For many Arabs, as we shall see in chapter 4, the concept of property is defined primarily in terms of the relations formed in connection with it: one's identity is borne along not by the things one possesses but by the populated world those relations represent. "Public" property is without identity—it is something unpeopled, something over which no one has responsibility since no one's social identity is conceived through it. For Omar to spread junk out to the street was not to invade a territory over which everyone has obligations but, perhaps, to test whether he could form ties based on that use—and if he could not, then by definition it was, as yet, not identified with anyone. Justice is not, as some Western commentators on the Middle East would have it, a matter of blaming others for one's own failings. Quite the contrary, it is a matter of others having such interpersonal and reciprocal ties of dependence that no individuals, in the process of gaining advantage, will fail to share their largesse with those in their network of obligations. Omar may have been quite sincere, therefore, in his assertion that he was doing a public service with his junkyard and that he did indeed want us all to be "his very good neighbors." But neither he nor we were playing the same game. We could not look to one another for interchangeable obligations—of political support or marital alliance or financial partnership—and hence the bonds of reciprocity necessary to such a relationship could not come into effect. For Omar justice might lie in our negotiated interdependence; for us it lay in our mutual separateness.

Because we had none of the interdependent ties that neighbors might possess in Omar's homeland, none of us could draw on those go-betweens who would likely have been brought into the matter long before our dispute became public, much less a formal lawsuit. When I suggested to my neighbors that we might see if the imam of the local mosque might bring some pressure to bear on Omar, I got no support. When I thought how often I had heard people in the Middle East say that "your neighbor who is close is more important than your kinsman who is far away," I almost rued the fact that being neighbors for us simply meant living adjacent to one another, without any involvement in one another's lives—yet reveled in the fact that I had no other obligations to Omar even as I realized the price to be paid when problems arose. To some Middle Easterners—particularly from older families or higher economic strata—there is some shame in going to court about a dispute, but for many others the legal process is just another aspect of the total engagement in one another's affairs and carries no stigma. In our case, however, the absence of society left only the presence of law.

Omar's view of the way politics works was, of course, not entirely foreign to the Americans on the block, political skeptics all. For we were not unaware of the power of the purse or persuasion in the law, however much we may also have believed in the impersonality of the legal system at large. Oddly enough, we were in exactly the same position as Omar: we lacked the interpersonal connections or financial entanglements to have access to those with discretionary power, just as Omar could not turn to family connections or political patrons who might need his dependence to build their own power base. If his support system was not there, his resort to seemingly outrageous behavior may have been his reaction to a situation of relative anomie and disorder; if our political wisdom could find no traction in the interstices of local politics, we could only assert our idealization of the law. It was not that people like Omar, who have emigrated from the Middle East, adapt poorly to life in the West; the very opposite is much closer to the truth. The Arabs who had lived on the block were extremely cosmopolitan, and (the difficulties of many Near Eastern migrants living in Europe notwithstanding) others with far less education commonly accommodate themselves to the host culture. But however well people adapt to a new culture, they usually tend to do so in ways that resonate with the assumptions and orientations they have come to accept in their lives. Omar may have failed to grasp the way things work in America—or he may have grasped them all too well. But whether his was an act of personal malevolence or an oddly misplaced attempt to be "our very good neighbor," his possible expectation that matters should be conceived in terms of interlocking obligations may have deeply informed his approach to our mutual situation. Neither Omar nor we his neighbors were entirely at home in the world we articulated; neither of us was able to move to effect in the world as we would have liked it to be. The fact that our views of law and order simultaneously intersected and diverged may only have heightened our respective lines of argument. But the result, like paths that gradually diverge by even a few degrees, is that eventually the two groups may wind up very far apart indeed.

To a certain extent we may also have approached law with quite different social expectations. People in the Middle East are frequently involved in lawsuits that go on for years, whereas the image of people in this country as highly litigious is actually quite misleading. For most of the Arabs whose legal relationships I have studied, lawsuits do not simply represent a breach of relationships. Rather, they are often part of the pattern of creating and servicing such connections. As a vehicle for marshaling allies and fabricating new forms of mutual indebtedness, as a way of demonstrating one's position or influence, as a way of testing whatever the traffic will bear and creating new spaces for interpersonal maneuvering, such cases keep open the boundaries of both persons and institutions. Perhaps Omar thought that he really would be "our very good neighbor" if even a lawsuit demonstrated his contribution, his connectedness, his place as a man, if his actions would forge ties, rather than ruin them, or simply shake them up, or cultivate new ground for a new place in a new social order. Perhaps for him, law, like so many other domains of the cultural life to which he was accustomed, could not be rendered separate from the world; perhaps he was unprepared to grasp a world ordered by principles that can appear so impersonal.

"The law exists to be broken," Omar had said. But of course for most Muslims the idea of law as a thing to be broken is contrary to their deepest beliefs. Islamic law, both as a set of legal postulates, however locally variable, and as an embodiment of common sense, however connected to divine ordinance, is central to their conception of an orderly world. And local custom, which may even take precedence over the sacred law itself, is a vital part of the relations that structure society. But perhaps, as Jessie Allen suggests, the idea of law as something to be broken implies a larger truth in any culture.[1] For if law and its ritual enactments have the capacity to stand outside the normal flow of time, to create a sense of the orderly out of the disordered events of everyday life, and to displace the uncertainties of the quotidian with metaphoric extensions that link the known with the uncertain—if, in short, the breach of law is both expectable and ironically valuable for the creation of orderly relationships, then Omar's attitude to the law may not be so far from its common function. That merger of chaos and order, or the very rage for order and its ever-present twin, the rage for chaos (as a challenge to existing categories), may, for all its distinctive qualities in any cultural system, be closer to the core of any society's fears and ambitions than many of us are willing to acknowledge. Even if Omar relies on such notions to exaggerated personal effect, it may well be that the approach of many Middle Easterners to law, as to other aspects of social relations, is more direct and consistent given the ways in which interpersonal relations order the world as they see it. Whether he needs a partner in this process or one over whom he can, for the moment, seek an advantage is an open question. But that a distinctive style of reciprocity may underlie his vision of law as an aspect of social life may be one of the crucial differences that separates Omar's worldview from that of his neighbors.

Another winter came, and the electrical cord snaked through the snow to Omar's car, a faint light shining in the house in the evening, the back end of the structure relentlessly falling apart, the uncut wood and chopping block on the front step a parodic doorknocker. The court had dismissed Omar's pollution suit against Tony, and Tony was about to win a suit of his own against Omar for back rent and expenses. Was each entrenched in a situation from which neither could comfortably retreat? Had both reverted to a pattern of endless litigation because they simply had no other alternative, no respected intermediary, who could bring the world back together again? If so, theirs is not alone a story of those caught in the middle, trying to make their way when there are few if any social constraints on behavior, when the price one may have to pay in reputation is low, or when there is little need for mutual reliance in other circumstances. Perhaps, too, theirs is a story of the frustrated exploration of possible relationships, an example of an emotionally provocative encounter between the felt sense of injury and the felt sense of injustice.

The junkyard is gone now, its outbuildings leveled, its long history in the town a thing of the past. For a while Omar was using his place as an auto repair shop, further violating local business and zoning laws. But that winter a chimney fire damaged the house, and local officials refused to allow him back into the building. Soon afterward the bank foreclosed on his loan, and the court formally evicted him from the property. Omar was seen trying to sneak into the house after it was posted as uninhabitable. The police mounted a watch to keep him out and even towed away his backhoe after he left it parked on the street. Barred from the property, Omar was observed sitting in his car through the cold winter night outside his former house. A few neighbors felt a twinge of sympathy for him, a homeless man sleeping in his car—but when they recalled how badly he had conducted himself their sympathy soon dissipated. Omar told some people that he was heading off to New Orleans, where, in the aftermath of hurricane Katrina, he would perhaps find his ultimate junkyard. But through the spring he was seen, from time to time, just sitting in his car in front of his former home, barred by a court order from trespassing on the property and by whatever private demons touched us all from talking to others on the block.

The story of Omar and we his neighbors may underscore a broader theme in Western encounters with the Middle East—that so much of each other's behavior may seem no different from that of family and friends who also think that those who can manipulate the system usually get their way despite the formal law. Tony certainly sees the world that way, and so do most of us at various times. To exoticize Omar, to say that he has a totally different vision of the world, would be to distort him into a far more unfamiliar figure than he is. Perhaps if Omar had come from New Guinea or Mars we would have regarded him as so obviously different that we would have been less exasperated simply because we would have had to find a completely different way of relating to him. Indeed, the fact that Omar's cultural approach was really quite close to that of his neighbors may have been a source of the shared frustration: being just different enough, as time and distance pass, all that appears shared becomes increasingly divergent, until one winds up—as in the dispute, say, over the publication of the Danish cartoons satirizing Muhammad, or when one simply does not believe that institutions can have an independent existence—at a point where one is confronted with the difference between a looming rock and a safe way around. If Omar is the stranger he is that most subtle of strangers, the one we recognize so easily in ourselves in certain contexts but who, when we suddenly encounter him in numerous and unfamiliar domains—like seeing the waitress as the lay pastor or the strong parent as the meek employee—we may be surprised to find we have not credited with his own distinction. Finding similarities is not enough: as one follows the traces of Arab culture through a number of different contexts in this book it may be precisely the tiny differences we discover that make all the difference to our mutual comprehension.

Omar's place on the block has come to an end. One day he was simply gone. I never did succeed in convincing him of my idea of a thoroughly impersonal rule of law, nor did most of the people on the block relinquish their view that Omar was not embroiled in a conflict of cultures but was simply crafty or mean or nuts. Once matters got involved in legal proceedings we all stopped speaking to Omar. We no longer even waved at him as we went past his house. For each there may have been a sense that, having reduced matters to one aspect of the interpersonal, we had in fact made things all too personal. Perhaps, as so many people in the Middle East have confided in me over the years, if we were more entangled we might, in truth, have felt that our individual freedom might be hampered by our mutual indebtedness. Whether it is our differences or our similarities that bear emphasis, though, it is difficult not to feel that our engagement across interests, across cultures, across truths will continue to elude our comprehension just so long as our respective need for certainty raises far fewer questions than our common encounter demands. Nowadays, in the post-9/11 world, there is the possibility, I suppose, of a virtual Omar on every street in America. But if Omar and we his neighbors really do have somewhat different orientations to the world—different views of human nature, society, and the forces that keep it working—then the legal victory of one and the isolation of both may have poignancy that extends far beyond our little dead-end street.

TWO

What (If Anything) Went Wrong? Personalism, Institutions, and the Unfractionated Self

Personalism and Its Discontents

A Man in motion has a chance

NORMAN MAILER

Two recent studies attempt to account for the Arab world's apparent failure to keep pace with the economic, political, and scientific innovations of the West. Bernard Lewis's *What Went Wrong?* focuses on Muslim fears that foreign contacts and governmental entanglement lead to a loss of faith and self-pity, while the United Nations' annual *Arab Human Development Report* emphasizes the lack of individual freedom and the Arabs' fear that social chaos may result if their basic assumptions are called into question.[1] Whatever the merits of these studies, neither focuses on the deeper cultural factors on which any assessment of the ostensibly self-defeating nature of Arab society must be grounded.

Three concepts in particular may be crucial to the resistance of Arab culture to engage in Western-style reform. First, by contrast to the West, in the Arab world the "self" was never rendered divisible. In addition, doubt about fundamentals has always been equated with unbelief and premonitory chaos. And, finally, owing to the Arabs' intense form of personalism, political institutions have never been separated from the individuals connected with them. Together these factors form a cultural fabric of enormous resilience and durability, one whose very success may also account for its resistance to Western ways of viewing the world.

The idea of the self in Arab culture is fundamentally relational. People are known, to themselves as well as others, in terms of those with whom connections have been formed. Kinsmen and neighbors, fellow tribesmen or religious confederates are not, however, ready-made; the content of one's ties is not prescribed by necessity, expectation, or the sanctions of an all-observant community. To the contrary, choice about how to relate even to kinsmen is constantly at work as one exploits the possible array of associates and engages them—through an unending process of ingratiation and maneuvering—in relationships that grant some measure of predictability in a constantly fluctuating world. In the course of this book we will see how this relational view of the person manifests itself in numerous domains. Property ownership is thus envisioned not as a statement about one's relationship to particular things but as a statement about one's ties to others as they concern such things; unoccupied space—space that defines no relations—implies neither collective nor private responsibility for its care; intentions can be read directly from actions, and there is no point in seeking a person's inner thoughts in order to discern their social or legal implications.[2] Even portraits that render a person's distinctive features in highly individualistic terms are spurned not because of some religious prohibition on human representations but because such pictures do not show what one really needs to know about another—the living nature of one's negotiated ties to other people. Within this cultural system it is a person's worldly consequent acts that make him— or, in somewhat variant ways, her—a reliable witness, someone whose word is more meaningful than material proofs. Even time is seen not as a medium that reveals the truth of persons but as sets of relationships categorized by whether they have a continuing effect on current associations. Whether it is in the simultaneous danger and allure of the poet as one who may challenge established categories through the new relationships conceptualized in his terms, or the open-ended logic of connections that constitutes a framework for everything from architecture, music, and mathematics to science and storytelling—a logic that envisions existing connections that may be precipitated into an actual array, an orderliness that has the capacity for being added onto without felt constraint—the ability to play the relational game in ever new and fascinating ways reverberates throughout every aspect of Arab culture.[3]

The individual, then, is defined by the sum of these relationships rather than by any purely internal construct or moral innovation. Social consequence is crucial: "God loves those who hide their sins," says the Prophetic Tradition, not because Muslims favor hypocrisy but because they believe that actions that are harmful to the social order are more dangerous to a community of believers than are personal failings.[4] Moreover, it is inconceivable that a person could encompass multiple, and indeed contradictory, aspects of himself at a single time. A story may help sharpen the contrast to the West. I have often mentioned to Arabs the decisions by two U.S. Supreme Court justices in which each expressed his personal objection to the death penalty but felt called upon by his judicial position to enforce the existing law.[5] In every instance my Arab interlocutor responded with a series of rhetorical questions: Who is this man? Where is he from? Who is he connected to? Has he or one of his dependents ever been attacked by a criminal? Since Arabs assess persons by inquiring about their connections in many contexts, the point of their questions was clear: if only I knew enough about these men, I would see that there was no contradiction between their personal beliefs and their professed role. Put in my own terms, since the self is always a concatenation of negotiated traits and ties, and since one is always identified by these connections to others, only my own imperfect knowledge of the judges' networks of obligation could account for my misguided view of their split selves. People are a unity of relationships, these Arabs seem to be saying, and the idea of segregated roles is a sign that I am the one who needs to learn more about how to appraise the necessarily interconnected contexts of any man's life.

The contrast to the West, of course, could not be sharper. Where Judaism underscores the distinctive components of the self by separating the qualities of God from those of humans except through metaphorical linkages, and Christianity underscores the inevitable separation of aspects of the self by their unique unification in Christ alone, Islam offers unity as both the given of this world and its perpetuation into eternity. Each moment, in the dominant philosophy of Islam, incorporates the whole creation of the world rather than, as the losing philosophers of the medieval period held, a fractionated set of creations that might seem to undermine the unity that suffuses every level from the self to the community of believers to Allah himself.[6]

Additional contrasts to the West abound. From Greek representations in tragedy and comedy of the multiple roles an individual may play, to the twelfth-century "discovery" that we have internal states that are so separate from our overt acts and utterances that God may even reward us for having the right intent though we perform the wrong act, through to the Enlightenment idea that we actually have the capacity to fashion our own moral selves, Westerners have accepted as obvious that the self is indeed divisible. Theatrical presentations encapsulate this sensibility. The actor separates his private self from his theatrical roles, just as ordinary behavior reveals conscience and morality through these very multiplicities. But for Arabs the idea of a fully divisible self does not accord with their sense of human nature and society. We are our embedded relationships, they are saying, and the knowledgeable observer is the one who discovers all the attachments that make a man whole. What varies is not the role but the context; to know someone is to see him or her in multiple contexts of relationship and thus to comprehend the way that person acts in different situations. Arabs are cultural particularists: terms do not stand still, and the tension between the particular and the universal appears as a tension between the desire for communal and personal unity. Emphasis is therefore placed on the realization that human nature implies a constant quest for the fabrication of situated distinctions. To suggest that the different aspects of our connections to others are fractionable, rather than instances of a unitary self reaching out in diverse and flexible ways, is to fly in the face of revelation and common sense alike. Indeed, to the extent that it is imaginable, the division of the self—like the splitting of an atom—might risk the release of unknown and uncontrollable forces.[7]

The repercussions of this idea of the undivided self are immensely important. Without in any way passing judgment on it, we can see that the absence of a divided self means that a person may not wholly segregate his diverse functions. The occupant of a political or legal position does not set part of himself aside in order to emphasize some impersonal role. Institutions are inseparable from those who occupy them, hence at any given moment the full implications of one's webs of indebtedness are actively in play.[8] If Allah is one and He endowed humans with reason to better themselves and their dependents in a life that the Quran itself describes as a sport and a game (6:32 and 57:18), then there is no sense to the idea that anything less than one's full, relational self is involved in every circumstance of that life. Like that most theologically correct of pastimes, we are all involved in a kind of chess game that requires no new pieces or changes in the board to be endlessly fascinating and revelatory of what is, quite simply, true.[9]

Thus, to take but one example, the American occupation of Iraq in 2003 did not destroy "the game." Initially, at least, it did something worse. It froze the game, rendered it unplayable, and did so without supplying any alternative. People could not start rebuilding alliances and debts because the United States had interfered with the resources needed to do so. The American occupying forces were not in the same position as an Arab leader building his networks from within the culture—and when they tried to act as if they were, they did it very badly. Indeed, in the absence of "the game" many Iraqis began to lose their sense of order and identity, so that it was small wonder that they wanted us out. The claim that Iraqis really favored the American presence, but were just too scared to speak up, is misguided: by not allowing the Iraqis to maneuver in the world as they understood it, and by assuming that the former way of building ties simply produced tyrants and not "legitimate" leaders, American forces showed their lack of understanding of the culture into which they had so forcefully inserted themselves.

Arab concepts of causality also play a role here. If, from their perspective, the social world is composed of entangled relationships possessing an implicit set of connections that a clever or wise man can envision and bring about, then the world can seem, despite its surface messiness, to always have an open-ended logic that is in no way undercut by a certain random and even arbitrary nature. What one looks for are the ties among sentient beings—people, God, genies, or angels—that account for people's actions toward one another. Like chess the strategies are infinite and varied even though the framework is organized by recognizable moves and what the Quran calls "the bounds of God." Like that most Arab of inventions, the zero, a person acts like a placeholder, the center of an open-ended array, whose particular unifying possibilities are immanent and can, by clever negotiation, actually be made manifest. If Talmudists must test their categories by exploring the excluded middle and Christians by exploring an implied morality, Arabs cannot imagine genuine disarticulation: people and things can take on any number of attachments, but one cannot simply leave the pieces scattered over the landscape. What appears to some as an Arab penchant for conspiracy theories may perhaps be better understood as a constant quest for causes that can be traced back to some person; from the Arabs' perspective it is sentient beings, not impersonal forces, that move events.[10] Indeed, from such a stance even biological evolution, at least of humans, seems literally unreasonable. Randomness that cannot be redeemed by humanity's God-given task of finding and servicing an orderly community of believers violates the first premise of humanity's purpose and ability.

The pattern that emerges, then, is neatly captured in the idea of the Arab frame tradition. This idea suggests that many aspects of Arab culture employ a mode of organization in which each interior portion of a given design embraces the totality of the structure's critical features. An overarching design does not govern the internal pieces; instead, limitless chains can be attached to the structure such that each part possesses a greater degree of equivalence and independence than a rigidly "organic" design would entail. So, for example, a poem can have any number of couplets added on over time, yet each mirrors the crucial features of the whole; additional rooms can be added to a building, without the initial design constraining the subsequent possibilities; the arrangement of musical phrases can remain extremely loose, and, as in poetry, no one phrasing should be constructed so as to be dependent on any other. It is the speaker or the participant in the structure who constitutes the central focus, a figure who personally witnesses and authenticates the meaning of the entity. Characterized, as Katherine Gittes says, by "an inherent sense of boundlessness," all the cultural manifestations of this paradigm—from infinitely variable arrays of social relationship to the structure of the Quran or ordinary tales—allow for constantly exploring all sides of an issue, for appreciating the "structural elasticity" in which "each unit could exist alone or as a cell in a larger work." It is a world-orientation that "emphasizes the separate unit and does not allow the open-ended and inconclusive overall framing structure to determine the nature or construction of its parts."[11] Being cast into multiple domains the framing tradition reinforces the sense of each aspect of the culture as both natural and true. It is a worldview in which a very wide range of practices, including (as we shall see) the meaning of martyrdom itself, come more sharply into focus.

For Arabs, then, the social world is composed of a running imbalance of obligations, constantly fashioned and serviced, constantly in need of reciprocation. Like an electrical system it is precisely the difference in the charge—what, at a given moment, someone owes to another—and the constant involvement in ingratiation, one-upmanship, and the discovery of others' networks of obligation that bind society together. Cancel the relationship, and everything could fall apart.[12]

This orientation is wonderfully captured in a typical encounter, one involving the anthropologist Steven Caton and a Yemeni shopkeeper with whom he dealt, when the latter asked him one day:

"Don't you trust each other in America?"

"What do you mean?"

"You buy my stuff, but you always pay for it immediately. I thought we were friends."

"We are friends, Muhammad. I show my respect to you that way."

"No, you don't. You show me that you don't trust me to be generous and understanding when you fall behind in your payment."

"I don't want to end up like that young man you had a fight with [who never did pay you], Muhammad, and have our relationship spoiled."

"You're different, you wouldn't try to take advantage of me. I know that because I know you, and it's because I trust you that I don't ask you to pay for your purchases immediately. Otherwise, I hurt your feelings, and you mine." [13]

One has only to imagine how a merchant in the United States could possibly be offended by a customer who pays cash immediately to grasp the relational emphasis of this conversation. True, Arabs often chafe at these obligations. "A favor comes on a donkey but returns on a camel," say the Bedouin, emphasizing the expectation that the recompense must be greater; "there is no measure for weighing a favor," they say, knowing the uncertainties that may await repayment.[14] Enmeshed in the need to form debts and the desire to be in an advantageous position, Arabs know that the cloying nature of their networks is synonymous with their security. And if building networks of indebtedness is vital to the fabric of Arab social order, the individual quest for such an embedded place in a skein of reciprocities may be crucial, as well, to the understanding of how, when such a place is hard to find, things may head in quite a different direction—even, as we shall see in the next chapter, for a few to self-destruction.

No Doubt: Men, Women, and Legitimate Power

To consequence no limit can be set.

LEGAL MAXIM

It is here, too, that the fear of doubt plays an important role. From its earliest years Islam equated doubt with unbelief. While at one level there have always been debates and skeptics, such alternative opinions and diverse interpretations never go to fundamentals lest the individual risk falling into unbelief. Thus to question the unity of Allah or the place of Muhammad as the last of His prophets is to risk not just personal condemnation but the orderliness of the community of believers that makes possible the world created for mankind. Whereas in the West doubt became for many a test and avenue to faith, in Islam it became the primary threat to social order. "He who believes, believes," says the Prophetic Tradition; "he who does not believe, disbelieves." Even doubt about nonfundamentals could become a habit whose scope might be hard to contain. The idea of probability—the Western term itself having meant "authoritative" until, in the sixteenth to seventeenth century, it came to represent gradations of moral certainty—has not come to pervade Arab culture, hence the continuing dichotomy between inviolable and mundane opinion.[15] On those rare occasions when people have confided to me that in their youth they expressed some doubts about God to their Quranic teachers, they say they were invariably told to keep these thoughts entirely to themselves, for to do otherwise would be to risk both the loss of salvation and the coherence of the world of relationship. Indeed, the great threat of Salman Rushdie's book *The Satanic Verses* may not have been so much his portrayal of the Prophet's vulnerabilities but the author's attempt to introduce a concept of doubt into a religion that views it as destructive of social order.[16] In the present climate of religious ardor and disruptive globalization it may well be true, as Akbar Ahmed has said, that "fundamentalism is the attempt to resolve how to live in a world of radical doubt."[17]

This idea of social disorder is vital to the Arab concept of history and reality. Suzanne Langer has said that "man can adapt himself somehow to anything his imagination can cope with; but he cannot deal with Chaos."[18] Yet chaos, and the response to it, is itself a construct of the imagination. Whether it is among the Russian revolutionaries, the Ranters of seventeenth-century England, or European anarchists in the years surrounding the First World War, chaos always has a definite cultural shape and meaning. The Arabic term *fitna* translates well as "chaos," but its resonance goes in rather different directions than the English equivalent. The Arabic word comes from a root meaning "to tempt, fascinate, seduce, and enthrall." It portends all those enticements of political alienation and worldly allure that may lead the Muslim community to doubt and disbelief.[19] It calls forth the dissolution of all relationships, the testing of a soul (like its added implication of testing metals in the furnace) in the fire of divine justice; it implies the fabrication through words of a reality that may be entirely delusional. Fitna is the proof that words are always actions, that relations can be ripped apart, and that, as the Quran says (64:15), even "your wealth and your children are a fitna for you" since they may draw one away from God. Fitna, as Stephania Pandolfo notes, is a "flirtation with the unknown, with the insecurity of novel paths, that taste for dissent, dispute, and hazardous games."[20] Yet, like so many Arabic concepts that imply their opposite, the threat of chaos also entices renewal precisely by upsetting social arrangements that may work too long to the benefit of too few. So, following the defeat of Saddam Hussein's regime in Iraq, what most Westerners took as examples of looting, mayhem, and anarchy may have held quite a different set of implications for many of the Iraqis themselves. The apparent lawlessness may have signaled one of those moments when, after a big man falls, everyone scrambles to reconstruct bonds of indebtedness that alone may yield new patterns of predictability and safety. Such moments pose exceptional dangers, since chaos, not freedom, is seen by Arabs as the real alternative to tyranny. "It is worse to make a man live in chaos than to kill him," goes one saying, based on the Quran; "better to live in tyranny than chaos," goes another.[21] Just as the Quran repeatedly warns against social disorder, so too common sense urges one back into the game, into keeping the flow of mutual indebtedness alive rather than risk neutralizing all obligations and having the system itself fall to pieces—like that electrical network whose unifying positive and negative forces are removed when the plug has been pulled.

Women are a special threat to orderliness. Whether it is their irrepressible sexuality or men's vulnerability to it, women, as holders of men's good opinion of themselves, threaten relationship itself by confuting particular ties.[22] Lacking an indispensable ritual place in the practice of Islam, they nevertheless test the central requirement of Islam—the maintenance of a solidary community of believers. To bind women to established social roles is therefore not merely to express male dominance but to highlight one of the central sources—along with ignorance and irreligious passion—of societal disruption. However, there is a second cultural proposition in conflict with this one. A basic precept of Arab culture is that particular individuals may rise above the natural tendencies of their category; thus (to use their own rhetorical form) *even* a woman, if learned, may be wiser than many men or, contrary to the usual formula for awarding custody, may be the better parent for a child. It is the probing of these boundaries, when brought about by changing conditions and exacerbated by implications not of the individuals' own making, that leads many Muslims to equate Westernization with the breakdown in boundaries. That fear of social chaos is often brought into focus by the changing roles of women. As one Moroccan judge put it:

> Civil society is chaos itself because the frontier between private and public spaces vanishes. If women cross the line to the public space and start speaking as if their opinion matters, it is the end of the *hudûd*, the sacred boundaries of authority. If women do not obey authority, no one will. As a judge I call that chaos; in the West, they call it civil society.[23]

Politics, then, is intensely personal. Power is accumulated by building alliances, trading in information and obligations, and conducing others to choose to rely on you rather than another. In such an environment institutions—in the sense of political or religious forms that have a high degree of constancy regardless of who occupies positions within them—contravene the common sense of those who would pay them heed. Whereas in the West Suetonius could argue of Caesar, or Einhard of Charlemagne, that institutions arise naturally out of the extraordinary personality of the great leader, in Arab political culture neither dynasties nor governmental structures are secure beyond a leader's lifetime, at which point networks fall apart and another must demonstrate leadership through the fabrication of his own set of dependents. This personalism is evident in all domains. Corporations were unknown in classical Islamic law, education was the transmission of knowledge from one authority to a disciple, and Ghazzali's triumphant vision of divine causality as utterly separate from human causation effectively precluded human reason from establishing universal principles. Whether it is a legal proceeding or a political election, the credibility of a religious scholar or the reliability of a trading partner, the crucial questions are always, who is this person, who owes him what, what kind of reciprocity is possible with him? When, for example, people have sought to codify customs in some Arab countries, they have often found that informants did not comprehend the project. How, those approached would say, do you expect anyone to decide a legal case without emphasizing who the person is that's involved? When it comes to court proceedings, the first question is usually about who each party is connected to; when listening to news broadcasts, listeners commonly ask to whom the speaker is obliged; when hearing a recitation of poetry, they ask how the poet has envisioned repercussions among people such that his terms have effect in the world. And it should have come as no surprise to him—though it clearly did—when an Iraqi asked Noah Feldman, who was in the country working for the American authorities to develop a constitution following the war, "*who* is the government?" To Feldman this emphasis on the person demonstrated how much the Iraqis had suffered from Saddam's political brutalization. To anyone who has lived in the Arab world, it is immediately recognizable as the way one always inquires about centralized authority and its consistently personalistic focus.[24]

Legitimacy, then, is an attribute not of the office but of its occupant. As one builds up dependents in recognizable ways, one begins to be regarded as possessing the qualities and powers associated with a given position. If a political figure can capture a given office, he is ipso facto legitimate. It is, therefore, a grave error of Western commentators to assert that the regimes of the Arab world are not legitimate in the eyes of their citizenry.[25] To the contrary, they may be highly legitimate—in the sense that the leaders have arranged dependencies in culturally recognizable ways. What is also true, however, is that any successful contender will be just as legitimate as his predecessor. Thus, it is seriously misleading to suggest that those who have come to power by building networks of dependents, rather than through democratic institutions, are illegitimate and that once the political culture changes, only those who rely on impersonal institutions will be regarded as truly legitimate.

The flip side to this culture of legitimacy is the vulnerability and transience of any leader's network. The pattern was, in a sense, set by the Prophet himself: by not designating an heir, he left matters, albeit within the context of an altered concept of human attachments, for those who followed to sort out. The fact that in the years after the Prophet's life (632–61) three of the first four caliphs were assassinated only underscores the problem. Then as now, succession to leadership is not readily inherited. Rather, like any paramount chieftain/warrior, one has to demonstrate the construction of personal dependencies in order to claim preeminence over others. Validation through worldly consequence is expressed in a common saying: On the third day after his death, his properties divided, his power dispersed, a man ceases to exist. This emphasis is reinforced throughout the culture. Thus, as we have seen, time is envisioned as packets of relationship, and relations that no longer affect current ties are placed in a kind of attic of memory. Since the relationships that affect ongoing alliances do not necessarily accord with chronological ordering, people will speak of "current" matters that may long precede more recent but no longer effectual ties.

33

Memory, like a stone cast at the waters, seems to skip about, support being found in those situations with a continuing impact on relationships wherever they may fall in time. And since, at every point, choices are being made among those with whom one can form interdependent ties, repetition—whether in story, ornament, or music—is seen not as mere redundancy but as creating and facilitating the opportunity to exercise the capacity for choice at every juncture.[26]

The Tribal Ethic and the Spirit of Reciprocity

He belongs to a tribe whose fathers have laid down
    For them a way of life.
Every folk has its own traditional way of life,
    Every folk has its objects of imitation

LABĪD B. RABI'AH (ARAB POET, SEVENTH CENTURY)

In the West, thanks to Max Weber, we speak of the Protestant ethic, the idea that we work hard in order to demonstrate our own sense of moral worth—now often detached from its implications of salvation— rather than for strictly hedonistic ends. In the Arab world one might, by contrast, speak of the "tribal ethic." This does not mean that all Arabs belong to actual tribes any more than only Protestants are affected by the Protestant ethic.[27] Tribes themselves, though, have certain characteristic features: they can take on a number of organizational forms, variously emphasizing genealogical descent, residence, marital affiliation, or interest in a common resource. They can also lie dormant— their members' identity as fellow tribesmen set aside in favor of other grounds for recruitment and distinction—as they adapt to changes in the political surround. Tribes also have mechanisms for redistributing power when major figures leave the scene and ways of counterbalancing it during the leaders' lifetimes. And it is a vital aspect of all tribal forms that they treat members of the tribal society, regardless of other differentiating factors, as morally equivalent.[28]

Transformed into a general ethos these factors remain prevalent in contemporary Arab culture. Thus, there is considerable ambivalence to power even though any given figure may gather the reins of obligation in his hands for a time. Each person is thought able to choose those upon whom he or she will depend. And each person regards himself or herself and others as morally equal notwithstanding the differential in worldly influence. All these factors contribute to a political culture that is, in turn, founded on a naturalized view of humankind and its capabilities.

Concepts of human nature and political power are mutually reinforcing. For if it is vital to a man that he be able, quite literally, to move about freely in the world, then to be bound up by a superior power is to risk the loss of one's very identity. If reason best controls passion through attachment to strong leaders or teachers, then it is an act of moral control to depend on one who has proved his ability to forge connections, even though a man will chafe in his weakness, indeed his symbolic effeminacy, while serving as the leader's disciple. Similarly, to be restricted to a given territory, unable to forge ties freely with others, is for an Arab an attack on his most vital ability. Just as chaos is seen as the antonym of tyranny, so the opposite of freedom (*huriya*) is not tyranny but *rbeṭ*, literally to be tied up, constrained, and more particularly to be unable to move to effect in the forging of relationships in the world.[29] To regard women as less able to exercise self-control is to assert priority against those whose powers threaten the order of the game. Ambivalence to power—whether expressed about a saint, parent, politician, or mate—thus generates the capacity to build alliances even as it replicates society's limitations on the acceptable means of their construction.[30]

Democracy, too, must be viewed in light of this political culture. If the tribal ethic is one part of the Arab's Weberian equation, the other might be denominated "the spirit of reciprocity." The interchangeability of obligations—where an economic tie may be called up in a marital alliance, or access to an opportune connection as a political debt—suffuses and knits together Arab upbringing and society. But if the ability to conduce obligation lies at the heart of relationships, then to the extent that persons cannot be separated from roles it is understandable that the state, as an impersonal entity, be seen as incapable of genuine reciprocity. Occasionally one even hears people say that "bribery is our form of democracy," a comment they elaborate in the following way: if a big man says do such-and-such a thing but I can bribe a lower official not to do it, then I can exercise some restraint on the big man's power—and is not democracy really about limitations on power? Again, whereas in the West these restraints are conceived as being built into the institutions—and the ability to fractionate oneself sufficiently so that one can set aside personal disposition—in the Arab world the separability of person and position runs contrary to the perception of reality.

Many analysts have argued that in order to develop democratic institutions it is vital that there be an established middle class. But, it could be argued, there is no middle class in the Arab countries.[31] Such a "class" requires not just consciousness of its separateness but a significant degree of institutionalized continuity—of family fortunes and attitudes, of education and income—as well as acceptance of certain depersonalized organizations, legal mechanisms, and a stable group of power brokers. In the Arab world, depending on the country and period, one could identify upper classes, royal classes, and haute bourgeoisie who remain close to power and, on a sliding scale, have a relatively high degree of continuity across generations. But the middle class is not a perduring group; rather it is, like all other matters, an aspect of the self. It would be as if one said not that a person is a member of the middle class but that he is a middle-class person: the significant feature is a quality of the individual rather than the persisting status of a group. Indeed, it is very difficult for parents to pass along the success they may have had in this middle range since so much depends on force of personality and personally fashioned connections. This may be another aspect of the tribal ethic—leveling through personalism, undercutting institutions through personal servicing, undermining the ability to correlate moral superiority with worldly success.[32] Whatever its sources, its frustrations cannot be underestimated.

To ask, then, why the Arabs have not developed in the sciences or the arts of government when once they led the world is itself a misplaced inquiry: it assumes that the indicators of a "successful" culture point in only one direction, that success can be measured only against the professed accomplishments of the West. But even if we set aside for a moment the question of judging other cultures, some alternative explanations may be worth considering. In chapter 10, for example, we will take up the question of scientific investigation. There it will be suggested that in the Arab world science proceeded as far as it did when research and theorizing could be viewed as affecting the world of relationships. Thus, the discovery of various mathematical propositions or chemical compounds, the development of engineering skills, medical cures, and architectural insights all served, given their conceptual emphasis, to create new or intensified relations among men. Like poetry and politics, science may have been measured by its influence on the broader sphere of human interaction. However, once science began to move into realms where its effects on relationship were, in terms of Arab culture, neither credible nor commonsensical—where inquiry approximated doubt and "pure" experimentation was not clearly connected to something affecting human ties—such science could not

garner sustainable interest. The differential acceptance of outside technology underscores this emphasis. Movies, cell phones, and modern
transportation fit immediately into existing meanings—film because
it shows "living" people relating to one another in multifarious ways,
cell phones because they serve the connections people are constantly
negotiating, transportation because it enhances the mobility necessary
to forge bonds of dependence. By contrast, musical comedy, Freudian
psychology, and moral speculation convey no significant meaning, the
first because people do not "really" start singing and dancing at the
spur of the moment and the others because they suggest either a lack of
freedom or the wrong sort.

But the West's assertion that something has "gone wrong" in Arab
culture may be more than a mere expression of self-congratulation,
for it obscures the accomplishments—and the criteria for assessing accomplishment—of another culture. When President Bush says of the
terrorists and their supporters that they hate us because they hate freedom, he misses the point. Most Arabs see themselves as far more free
(to build relationships) than we who are constrained by material objects and impersonal institutions. (Indeed, would we say, for example,
that someone who defers to the authority of the Catholic Church or a
noted rabbi hates freedom?) Moreover, the Arab view of human nature
is not without merit. Instead of focusing on suffering or sinfulness, a
hierarchy of being or moral self-fashioning, Islam views humans as maneuvering to advantage in a world whose constant probing for the new
must be kept within bounds if the socially detrimental is not to outweigh the collectively advantageous. It is not equality, then, that constitutes the basis for justice but equivalence—a recognition that people
are not all the same, that to treat others true to their nature is fairer
than to treat them as if they were identical. Rather like those Western
religions in which women may not be allowed to serve as priests or rabbis, the measure of worth is not identity of tasks but replicating society
through the positioning of each sentient being according to its nature.
At the same time for Muslims there is no feature of a person that is
so constrictive that it may not be superseded by the development of
one's knowledge and one's contacts in the world of others. Freedom of
choice, therefore, may take on different meanings given the differences
of history among the Arab nations: for Moroccans it may imply relative
ease of movement owing to the brief period of colonization, for Egyptians the imagined license of irony and political humor, for Iraqis the
tightly circumscribed demands of kin and territory, and for "suicide"
bombers the recapture of order through visible martyrdom.

There are no prerequisites for democracy, no preconditions for freedom. For better or for worse, Arab politics and culture have their own ways of managing power, and of suffusing time and circumstance, person and place, advantage and attribute with local import and consequence. The question is not whether anything "went wrong" but whether, by withholding judgment long enough to grasp the Arabs' own sense of meaning, we in the West can come to terms with our own understanding of this crucial part of the world.

THREE

Why Do Arab Terrorists Kill Themselves?

When Westerners attempt to explain why Arab terrorists engage in acts of self-destruction, their arguments usually emphasize religious devotion, unspecified anomie, solidarity with their fellows, or nationalistic fervor. They correctly note that most Arab "suicide bombers" are young men from a full range of economic and educational backgrounds, sometimes with experience living abroad but more frequently home grown. In attempting general explanations for all such acts or a very limited range of them, however, few of these accounts adequately consider how such individuals envision their world and enact that vision through self-inflicted death.[1] Whatever the roles of "unit solidarity," social disaffection, or otherworldly promise, Arabs who kill themselves in terrorist acts—as opposed to those who send them out on such missions— may actually be trying to hold the world together, to confirm by their acts, with a certainty and permanence not normally available, that they have created a network of relationships that alone assures a mature person's identity. In a social world in which all relationships imply the need for reciprocity, in which one must constantly negotiate a web of indebtedness in order to gain a foothold in life, and in which such relationships are open to constant reconfiguration and dissolution, the terrorist may be able to render his attachments both manifest and irrevocable by his own act of self-destruction.[2] To see how this may operate we need to review a range of interconnected factors.

If one looks at a group of related cultures as embracing a set of categories through which the world of experience is organized and made meaningful, several themes appear to vitalize Arab social life. First, each individual, seen as endowed with God-given reason, is expected to construct the relationships of mutual indebtedness that afford a measure of orderliness and predictability in an ever-changing world. A wide array of resources—kinship, money, eloquence, sheer force of personality—exist to fabricate the ties that define one in a world of others, and so long as these alternative avenues remain available, the sense that "the game" is afoot validates the meaning of both freedom and self-worth. As a result, a person is culturally envisioned not as a series of compartmentalized roles—where, for example, one might be expected to set aside personal beliefs while executing the powers of a given position. To the contrary, a person is always the totality of his traits and ties, themselves always implying some form of expected reciprocity. To know another thus requires knowing as much as possible about that person's own web of obligations.

Moreover, these interdependencies require constant servicing; they come into existence and remain potent only through one's acts. An Arab Cartesian, it has been noted, might say: "I act, therefore I am." Indeed, it is the possibility that society may fall into chaos and disunity (*fitna*) that must at all costs be avoided—particularly when it involves disruption to the creation of bonds of mutual indebtedness. To recycle an earlier image, it is the running imbalance of obligations, like an electrical system that works only through positive and negative charges, that holds society together. Pulling the plug on mutual indebtedness threatens the destruction of the entire community of believers (*umma*). These same relational factors also inform the meaning of violence and self-destruction.

There are, of course, many issues that may form the backdrop to a terrorist's sense that social order can indeed be reconstructed by his (or, rarely, her) willed death.[3] He may feel the strangeness of his younger generation moving ahead of its elders to take charge—an ambiguous feeling, shared with the parental cohort, that the world of authority has indeed been turned upside down and only the reverence for religious figures of a grandparental generation can assuage the sense of generational disorder.[4] Or he may feel that being ignored, even by enemies who refuse to engage him in the give and take of the world, denies him the ability to create a person-centered universe out of the sociological pieces he knows a man is expected to assemble. Whether it is in personal or international situations of dispute, an individual may strike out if the other turns his back and thus indicates that no reciprocity exists between them or is even possible. Such unpredictability of relationship goes against the very nature of identity: it increases the fear of chaos that comes from not being a man who can see or gather together that unifying array of ties necessary for having an effect in the world. In such circumstances, violence, however much it seems to distort the creation of order, may be felt as the surest means to demonstrate that one is indeed capable of reconfiguring an array of otherwise disarticulated parts.

Western commentators, then, misconstrue the acts of terrorists who kill themselves as being a form of suicide. Indeed, since all schools of Islamic law (following a clear Quranic injunction) regard suicide as impermissible, it has been suggested that it was the Egyptian doctor Ayman al-Zawahiri who had to convince Osama bin Laden that suicide bombings were "martyrdom operations," over the objection of many Islamic scholars and leaders who, before and since 9/11, have condemned such acts.[5] But if, instead of limiting analysis by applying the label of "suicide," we see this self-destruction through the categories available in Arab culture, quite a different ordering suggests itself. Two elements may be important here: the idea of sacrifice and the idea of reciprocity.

Sacrifice has at its heart the giving over of a life that cannot be reinstated in the same form. An animal sacrificed to God or a Muslim saint is invariably accompanied by a request for some alternative form of life (the birth of a child, good health, a change in vitalizing circumstance), but the life given cannot simply be restored. Sacrifice is an act that simultaneously invokes reciprocity and negates it: it broadly constrains the recipient to answer one's request and, in the case of a sacrifice to God, it reverses reciprocity by conducing—indeed all but compelling—a life-enhancing response. Like any ritual reversal it therefore reasserts the norms, in this case of ingratiation and reciprocation, by momentarily turning them on their head. The sacrifice is a "gift" that nevertheless assures a favorable return. Similarly, for many Arabs the destruction of others and oneself may possess some of the defining elements of sacrifice. We know, for example, that Algerian terrorists often uttered the prayers for sacrificing an animal while cutting the throat of a woman or child. And bombers who blow up others may also think that what they are doing is like a ritual sacrifice. But it would be quite wrong to say that the terrorist obliterates *his own identity* by sacrificing himself for the group.[6] To the contrary, through his own death the martyr's personal identity is presented as complete, for by his act he

proves his claim to be seen as a full person. Like one who makes a sacrifice or forges ties through hospitality and strategic "favors," he forces
this recognition on both the community and God. Because he is proving the existence of his own network, he is, in a sense, also proving the
truth of the proposition that the community of believers is composed
of individuals whose interdependent ties create collective security.

In such an economy of reciprocity, the martyr's death is a condensed
and fixed microcosm of an idealized social system in which a person's
effectiveness is marked by his actualization of potential relationships.
The "suicide" ritual—from a filmed statement of faith to the last cry of
God's greatness—thus becomes a form of ceremonial exchange, similar
to that described by anthropologists in numerous other contexts, one
that displays and activates the network of latent relations envisioned as
central to the community of believers. Moreover, this ritual exchange
of personal life for communal existence may, as Marilyn Strathern suggests in other situations, anticipate the impact of one's acts on the exchange relations of others, such that "each person sees him or herself
from the perspective of the other."[7] Self-destruction in this context
implies the validation of all modes of building relationships—indeed,
all those legitimate relations that render death itself amenable to salvation. Taken as a form of exchange by which one becomes linked to
others as if bound in face-to-face contacts, the martyr simultaneously
reinforces shared perspectives and proves others' attachments to him
as if their ties had moved from the ineffable to the inviolable.[8]

To this emphasis on creating social networks, however, a second
element must be added, one that bears on the way in which categories possess a cultural logic even when they may appear to outsiders to
combine incompatible elements. This process is familiar to every time
and place. To take an example from our own social history, consider
how the category of the "insane" changed over time. As Michel Foucault has shown, with the florescence of commercialism and the Protestant ethic in seventeenth-century Europe, the medieval sin of pride
was replaced by that of sloth, and with it a new category of previously
distinguishable persons—the insane, the unemployed, and the impov-
erished—could be grouped together as idle regardless of their reasons
for being so. Each could now be incarcerated, too, lest their idleness
remain visible and set a bad example for others.[9] Similarly, to understand the place that martyrs occupy for many Muslims, one must grasp
the category into which they are placed and the implications of that
grouping.

The martyr is regarded as someone who, by that act alone, automatically enters Heaven. Given this assurance of paradise, there is no need for prayers by the community of survivors. The important question to ask, then, is this: who else falls into the category of those for whom prayers at death are unnecessary, and what logic places them all within a single category? The answer Muslims commonly give is that there are three types of person that make up this category. In addition to the jihadist who dies in a holy war there is the person who dies in the course of the pilgrimage to Mecca (*haj*), and, quite intriguingly, the individual who, as the result of accident or illness, dies in a particularly gruesome manner.[10] What unites these types of individuals is that their bodies have been destroyed in life or rendered odious or inaccessible to their survivors, and they are thereby regarded as having transcended reciprocity. They have experienced the sharpest break with their society while alive. Having had the full measure of their failings exacted as they died, they are beyond that weighing of their souls for which, as the Quran says, even a mote of difference could otherwise condemn them. For all those who fall into this category, justice can be rendered only by taking into account, in addition to all other features of their identity, the circumstances of their death, whereas for all others it is only their lifetime of action that will be weighed on the Day of Judgment. Indeed, the martyr and his category-mates are now beyond the need for human reciprocity. Since the point of saying prayers for the dead is to exchange one's acknowledgment of God for mercy on the soul of the deceased, instances in which such prayers are unnecessary become a crucial indicator of the class to which the deceased belongs. The angels will pray for the one who dies in a holy war, and God will sing his praises, so human prayers are irrelevant. Those who die a violent death occupy a similar position. God, people say, likes us to die quietly, peacefully, surrounded by our families, lying properly in bed. By dying in a way in which the body becomes extremely unpleasant—through drowning, a fall from a great height, or a disfiguring disease (to use some commonly mentioned examples), God may erase one's record of misdeeds and assure one of Heaven. But reciprocity—both in the sense of engaging the body of the deceased in various rituals and in praying for that person's salvation—is no longer required. Similarly, the third member of this category, the pilgrim, has also broken with normal reciprocity in various ways. The white shroud worn by male and female pilgrims alike symbolizes the erasure of normal personhood—even to the point of setting aside during the haj such distinctions of gender as the wearing of a veil—and the pilgrim is really in a somewhat unearthly state that carries over to a Heaven-assured death. In each instance, therefore, the relevant categories are those of a negation of ordinary social reciprocity and with it the irrelevance of prayer on behalf of the deceased.

Even the seeming differences among the members of this category confirm the underlying theme. For the pilgrim and the one who dies a gruesome death carry their networks into the next world—indeed they are often spoken of as being surrounded by their loving kin and friends—whereas the martyr leaves his network behind in this world and moves to a domain of hedonistic, rather than sociological, delights. These two modes of afterlife existence, which may seem quite different, are structurally linked and mutually confirming: they both demonstrate that it is one's social network, immortalized for the one by being transposed to Heaven and for the other by being permanently implanted in the world left behind, that is common to the reward accompanying the form of their dying.

When a terrorist kills himself, then, it is like an explosion, in which two otherwise nonlethal forces are slammed together to produce a deadly combination. The first of these factors is the one we have already noted—the array of affiliations that are known to exist only by being manifested through open display. Thus, when the bomber kills himself he both demonstrates and attempts to provide a freeze-frame vision of the network that purports to define him as a person. Those who actually have such networks—more established, usually older men—are far less likely candidates for self-destruction precisely because their arrays of attachment are more visible and real, whereas younger men who have no such ties can claim them and render them beyond change through the enforced reciprocity of their own self-destruction.[11] Indeed, the permanent payments that may be made to their families by Islamic charities solidifies the irreversible sense of obligation owed them.

But there is a second, seemingly incompatible factor that must also come into play, namely the submerging of the self. This may seem an odd claim since, in a system of constant personal maneuvering, the self would never seem to be truly submerged. But in certain very important ways this is precisely what does occur. It is evident in the master–disciple, father–son relationship when the acolyte or offspring, at least initially, lacks a social personality of his own. It is evident in prayer, when the entire community pauses from interpersonal maneuvering and bows in utter, individual obliterating surrender (the meaning of the word *Islam*) to Allah. It is evident in some marriage rituals, when the groom is actually dressed like a woman and even physically constrained only to be freed and made a man at the ceremony's culmination. Such submission is enormously powerful, for while it seems like the overshadowing of all personal power it is actually the very opposite, both psychologically and sociologically. It is the burial of one status awaiting the empowering renewal as another.[12]

In Arab cultures, which have very few rites of passage for men, where the average age of male marriage has climbed to the late twenties (just short of the average age of most martyrs), and where unemployment even for educated men often tops 40 percent, there are few markers for manhood available to assist the fabrication of a personal network.[13] Joining the need to demonstrate social connection with the ritual submission that promises social renewal may, then, produce a culturally explosive force, one in which the martyr simultaneously demonstrates that he is a person with a network that need not be proved by further reciprocity (as symbolically displayed by the absence of prayer for him) and ritually submerges his own negotiating self. Through such self-immolation he asserts, as in any ritual reversal, a vision of society as one that avoids social chaos through the constant bonding that occurs in those interpersonal negotiations that are, in the martyr's case, now fixed beyond risk of revision.

Seen from this perspective, it can be argued that people who kill themselves in a terrorist act confirm the social order through their own self-destruction. Their deaths merge the standards by which society ought to be composed with the judgment that will be made of them individually. Part of that judgment is to leave behind an array of attachments, centered on their social persona, which by their death they have precipitated. It may be a set of associations that, in any particular case, could not be articulated so indisputably in one's lifetime but that is now beyond alteration through reciprocal obligation. That such a martyr may, at times, fear he is not demonstrating, or indeed creating, an array of associations that trail him and make him whole may be read into the remark made by a twenty-one-year-old Palestinian student who surprised all who knew him by blowing himself up in Tel Aviv, having left behind a text message on his friend's cell phone that read, in its flowery prose and first-person plural voice: "We lost you. If it was in our hands, in the middle of the dream, we will come to you. We missed you. We don't know if we are going to be missed by you."[14]

Although the recruitment and training process undoubtedly involves significant peer pressure, that factor alone does not account for the particular form of death employed. If the warriors of ancient Greece or medieval Japan would rather be placed among the dead heroes who fall in combat and never grow old, the modern Arab warrior may, by sacrificial death, seek to create an imagined community of the permanently indebted, a network made inviolable and immortal through a form of death that freezes his place in the world of men. Indeed, those who sacrifice their bodies may, at that moment, be seen as the literal embodiment of a kind of group ownership, one whose relational essence they confirm with their personal act of ultimate embeddedness.

By now hundreds of Arabs have killed themselves in attacks on opponents. Nationalistic and religious fervor are undoubtedly crucial for many of these individuals, and the alienation of a lost generation brought up in Europe, to say nothing of the range of local variation across Arab and Muslim cultures, cannot be underestimated. But faith and politics alone do not explain why terrorists engage in self-destruction or account for the social meanings that accompany their deaths. Only by seeing the categories through which Arabs conceptualize personal identity, reciprocity, and the gathering together of an array of relationships can we see how this particular act is reinforced by connections to numerous other aspects of their lives. If what the terrorists accomplish is less the guarantee of Heavenly delights than rendering their earthly associations unassailable, and if their deaths perpetuate not an inchoate claim to ultimate salvation but a concrete set of obligations fixed in the lives and minds of their real and imagined consociates, then those against whom they launch their attacks have all the more reason to address the underlying social strains that nourish this form of the attackers' quest for immemorial identity.

FOUR

On the Meaning of Ownership: The Problematic of Property in Moroccan Culture

Both *meaning* and *ownership* may seem to be terms whose definitions are perfectly self-evident. *Ownership* is one's control over whatever can be objectified as property, while *meaning* means—well, meaning. But like so many issues that seem obvious in one culture or at one moment in history, a slight variation may necessitate a whole new key to understanding. Concepts of ownership in the Arab world may appear deceptively like those in the West—or simply as examples of the universals some philosophers impute to all ideas of property. But such apparent commonality can mask the small divergences from which genuine misunderstanding might ultimately arise.

In this chapter I want to explore the meaning of ownership by looking at the array of features that comprise this construct. Indeed, "meaning" means just that—trying to see how the construction of an idea and its attendant relationships crosscut domains (economic, social, political, moral) such that coherence is derived from the reverberations in multiple areas of one's ordinary experience. We will focus on the meaning of owning land, but by exploring the approach to other "objects" (immovables, intangibles, and even other beings) we may more fully grasp some of the central features of contemporary Arab ideas of ownership. Indeed, if we look beyond formal laws of ownership and the informal mechanisms for securing access to resources, we can see the nature of the relationships and the very assumptions about such relationships that inform the overt patterns of property holding. This may, in turn, allow us to see how the particular case study of Morocco may have analogues in other parts of the Arab world, and why we may need to rethink our assumptions about property as only a thing and consider its relational aspects as well.

As in the interpretations of other domains of Arab culture, my usual prefatory caution must be invoked: I am only too well aware of the range of social and cultural difference within the Arab world. Indeed, that variation is exactly what we would expect at every level of any culture, down to the most fractal differentiation. There is no singular essence of any culture to which all else may be reduced, even though we know perfectly well when we are in the Arab world and when we are among the Hottentots or Inuit. In human culture, as in biology, variation is at the root of the matter. The trick is to be attentive to variation even as one seeks to use the comparisons it affords to ferret out the ways in which, to borrow Stephen Jay Gould's phrasings, "islands of form" and "ranges of irreducible variation" are discernible.[1] Thus, as I examine the meaning of property ownership in the specific context of Morocco, I invite the reader to think about not simply whether the points I raise are true in the given context but, more important, whether my interpretation, applied to other instances, furthers our understanding of the very range of variation to which we must attend.

Let us begin with land. The classic Islamic concept of property holds that all land is *rahmaniya*: it belongs to God, and what mankind has is the right to its use (*ihya*, literally the "bringing back to life"). But once one moves from this general proposition to greater specificity, one readily notes that, as Planhol has written, "[c]ontradictory attitudes may be noted in Islamic legislation on the use of land."[2] Productive use may have generally been required to convert occupation to possession, but since the days of the first caliph land was largely considered a collective object to be controlled by the state. The standard theory of land ownership in Morocco, according to the school of Imam Malik, therefore holds that all areas conquered by Muslim armies are held in trust for the Muslim community, as represented by the constituted authority of the state, and thus ultimate title (i.e., the capacity to alienate the land through sale or gift) lies with the sovereign alone.[3] Individual or collective land-holders, by this conceptualization, may have considerable possessory or usufructory rights, but they do not have full control of the land.[4] In fact, matters have always been rather different than this theory suggests.

In one sense, of course, fact and theory do accord: constituted authority could, and often did, divest individuals of their control over property, and thus the uncertainty surrounding title was greater than if the legal system recognized full title in a single entity. Monarchs and (as we shall see) more often their subalterns could divest individuals or groups of their land through sheer force or by claiming the greater collective interest, thus reinforcing the overall sense of insecurity of title. But such insecurity was only relative, for there were numerous ways, both legal and sociological, by which title might be bolstered.

For example, legal doctrine broadly held that although the underlying title to land vested in the sovereign, one could not only use land but sell the surface elements of it, such as the houses and gardens developed thereon. Custom and law also supported additional attributes of possession. If land was not being used, one could secure the rights over it by working the land for a specified period of time, any improvements having to be compensated for should the original owner return within the requisite period.[5] Other ownership agreements allowed the co-sharer a preemptive right to purchase his partner's (or even his neighbor's) share.[6] Additionally, the idea that a portion of a structure (the second story of a house, for example) is wholly separable from any other portion of the property means that while the structure itself can be sold, the space it occupied, being insubstantial and hence not capable of being owned, cannot itself be the subject of sale. Thus, if a house collapsed, title to the site could be lost if another made adequate use of it.[7] As with other forms of nonmovable property, it was not that Islamic law developed an elaborate set of case-oriented conceptions of individual ownership rights but that, in an atmosphere of broad insecurity of title, Moroccans fashioned their concept of land law mainly around the relationships.[8]

Many of these mechanisms are well known. The *ḥabus* (as the *waqf* is known in Morocco) allowed property to be placed in trust with the religious foundation for purposes of securing it against misuse by one of the beneficiaries or misappropriation by powerful political figures, the state included. Habus in Morocco, as elsewhere, came in two basic forms: an outright grant to the foundation (*ḥabus kobra*) or a family trust (*ḥabus 'a'ila*); the latter allowed income to specified heirs, the corpus reverting to *habus kobra* in the event of the extinction of the line.[9] The usual characterization of a family habus endowment suggests that it was often used as a vehicle to dispossess female relatives of even that half share allowed them under the *shari'a*, whereas many such endowments were actually intended to secure these women against the inequities of the inheritance rules or the depredations of their husbands and their own male kin. Because family endowments could eventually result in highly fractionated shares, however, habus property was vulnerable to being bought or appropriated by the politically or financially powerful notwithstanding the apparent protection of the foundation itself.

Other mechanisms for securing property included the grant or recognition of land by the government to collective entities. In precolonial times the *makhzen* (the central government) commonly granted tribes or tribal segments tracts of land in return for providing security services to the Moroccan state. Taxes could be forgiven or tax farming granted, families could obtain ongoing use of the land by virtue of the role played by their warriors as contract protectors of the state, and the tribe or fraction as a whole could maintain a degree of solidarity based on the common land grant. Similarly, the makhzen could make over to a religious brotherhood or lineage of descendants of the Prophet such lands—and (in effect) the people who, living upon them, would continue to work them—as a form of royal grant. In both instances the makhzen was more concerned with securing access to resources that the state or its local minions might try to appropriate than with creating independent institutions capable of establishing legal rights.

The relative insecurity of title and the accompanying mechanisms aimed at solidifying security are not, however, simply related as cause and effect, and it is insufficient to merely list the devices available and to trace them across time. For running through this varying structure of property law and property distribution lies a set of conceptual constructs that simultaneously renders it comprehensible to those engaged in its use and provides guidance for the actual relationships one finds on the ground. The usual way into such a consideration for students of property law has been the distinction between seeing property as the relation of an individual to a thing versus the view of property as the relationships between and among individuals and groups as they relate to that thing. Extreme examples of the two are not hard to come by. If I create a work of art, I may (at least in Western culture) see it as an extension of myself—a self that I have actually created, in part, through this endeavor. At the other extreme, the land I own may be hedged with all sorts of interests other than my own—zoning regulations, tax implications, environmental rules, and so on—all of which describe my relation to others in terms of that property.[10] But this "thing-relations" distinction is analytically useful only up to a point. As J. W. Harris indicates, elements of both factors are at work in almost every situation, whether we analyze matters according to an elaborated distribution of rights and duties or powers and privileges, or according to the psychology of attachments to things.[11] As in all matters philosophical, different cultures may interpose different emphases, and in the Moroccan situation it is particularly helpful to see how the relational aspects of property have been so thoroughly interwoven with all other relationships that it may be possible to think of the ties people have to things as being variants of their ties to persons. Let me explain.

It is broadly agreed in Islamic thought that "freedom establishes the capacity to possess (*sifat al-malikiyya*) which is the trait distinguishing man from the other animals."[12] Whatever the merits of a general claim that humans are by nature possessive, what matters, of course, is the set of implications this possessiveness entails in any given cultural system.[13] Western philosophy and jurisprudence have variously emphasized the foundation of possessory rights as flowing from the Lockeian input of one's labor, the separation of and control over some object from the general course of unowned things, or the public communication of one's claims.[14] While such theories are in some sense relational, they are concerned at least as much with the identity of person and thing. For Moroccans, by contrast, the emphasis starts and ends with the relational. Thus, for Moroccans ownership implies that in the exercise of one's God-given reasoning powers, one can move about to create ties of dependency with others, thereby securing oneself and one's dependents as much as possible in the universe of flux and human maneuvering. Given this orientation, property becomes less a relation between oneself and a thing and far more the embodiment of one's success in securing oneself through these webs of indebtedness. To look out on one's holdings is to see the people tied to you; to calculate the value of one's assets is to grasp the extent of one's access to the relationships those resources both enable and represent.[15] To own something is thus to assert—indeed to feel most deeply—the peopled environment one has constructed about oneself, in the certain knowledge that such is the defining nature of a person.[16]

Many of the implications of the Moroccan idea of ownership are discernible through the terminology used for its expression. The word *mul* (pl. *mwalin*), which is usually translated as "owner" in English, can be used in various ways. A wife may be called the *mul* of the house, the rich the *mwalin* of their times, an expert the *mul* of his craft, the residents of a territory the *mwalin* of that land, a descendant of the

Prophet "my lord" (mulay). And of course God is mul ana—"my mul." What seems to be generally implied by this semantic range is that a mul is one who is characterized by his or her relationships, that union of person and lived-in place, whether mundane or mystical, through which one's identity is created and affirmed.[17] Indeed, to be without such connections is to be no one. The Quran (42:6) says that "the unjust have no patron [mul] and no helper," and it is precisely this lack of entanglements, so essential to being human, that makes one who is neither a mul nor attached to other mwalin so lacking in personhood. In the absence of any Arabic verb for "to have," possessive forms of the term 'and plus the name of a person or place indicates their mutual attachment, as the object becomes an attribute of that to which it is connected. Indeed, as Pandolfo suggests, it is often the enclosure of a substance, like water in a canal or blood in the body, that transforms it into something that has a distinctive character, a quality of the relational, and consequence in the world.[18]

A number of things follow from this orientation. Legal scholars have spoken of property in the West as tending toward the agglomeration of rights, that is, the accumulation of ever-increasing powers that an individual (as opposed to, say, a feudal lord or monarch) possesses over various items of property.[19] In Morocco, the equivalent would, I think, have to be seen from a slightly different perspective. There the collective interest lies in the preservation of the "game" by which one can fabricate ties of obligation to others.[20] Thus it makes sense that Moroccans would believe, like many other Muslims, that the greatest danger is not of tyranny but of such "political disaffection" that social chaos (fitna) becomes rampant, destroying the whole fabric of predictability of others' behavior fashioned out of such webs of indebtedness.[21] Privacy equates not with a sphere of individualistic self-fashioning but with no adverse act becoming so public as to disrupt social relationships.[22] Adverse possession turns on the notion that "when a person is away his 'right' [haqq] is away," the concept of haqq implying not visible control but the distribution of obligations that define a person and compose a community of believers.[23] In each cultural instance what reverberates through the system is the sense that, as people construct larger or smaller constellations of affiliation, the properties they come to dominate are expressive of the relationships they represent to themselves and to the world at large.

Property as thing is no more "natural" than is property as relationship: both the community of believers (umma) and the person (as the cumulation of various traits and ties) are equally "natural."[24] The "personality theory" of property, in the Moroccan context, views things not as extensions of the self but as nodes in the demonstrated capacity to form bonds of obligation.[25] One can see how it is part of the same taxonomic order, for example, to have as great a possessory interest in a daughter's virginity (and hence marriageability) as in any physical asset, for it is through such a daughter that ties to others will be formed and security increased. Similarly, the ability to maneuver freely in the world—such freedom of movement being crucial to the Arab concept of the mature man—is reflected in such diverse property practices as the capacity to gain "ownership" rights in an area where one has acquired a protector's guardianship or the separation of land from water to allow for irrigation.[26]

Seen from this relational perspective, some of the events in Moroccan social history begin to make greater sense. In his excellent summation of Moroccan property history, Rémy Leveau describes how powerful members of society would frequently divest the less powerful of whatever property rights they possessed. Such divestiture was used for a variety of reasons: by the makhzen it was used to discourage the development of a rural bourgeoisie or to put down competing forces; by one fraction of a tribe it was used to divest other fractions of their lands; and by foreign governments it was used to allow greater opportunities for tax avoidance or joint investments at the expense of small holder interests. Yet, strikingly, even though there was great opposition to colonization, with more than four hundred thousand Moroccans dying in the ensuing struggles, this divestiture itself engendered relatively little persistent bitterness. For centuries rural Moroccans may have expected tribal solidarity to assure them of whatever land-holding security they might possess, but that very tribal solidarity was conditioned on the formation of networks that were commonly recognized as no more stable than the people who momentarily fashioned them. Thus, when the "game" turned against them, it was not as if a vested right had been taken from them. The combination of ultimate title in the Muslim conqueror and the expectation that one's security on the land was only as good as one's own ability to enforce it merged with the belief that land represented relationship, not indissoluble dominion over things. Leveau concludes thus:

It is now clear that the uncertainty and deficiency of property rights in pre-colonial Morocco created situations that encouraged the exploitation of personal connections and a search for complementary forms of protection, with the aims of consolidating wealth and reducing insecurity for those who wanted to accumulate capital and undertake investments.[27]

Although I do not agree with Leveau that the causal direction runs solely from property rights to social structure—if anything I would think it the other way around—I do agree that it is the cultural emphasis on property as relationship that is crucial. Leveau notes, to his surprise, that the peasantry did not hold the state responsible for driving them from the countryside in the postindependence period: "[T]he Moroccan peasant had relatively little attachment to his land, preferring to run the risks of emigration to Europe or the *bidonvilles* [shanty towns] on the outskirts of the coastal cities rather than submit to the decisions of the agrarian bureaucracy."[28] But this is quite comprehensible if we focus on land less as thing than as relationship. For what Moroccans (more than, say, Algerians and Palestinians) were able to do was to transfer their quest for relative security from land holding to other available domains—precisely that emigration to cities or abroad (while sending money home to secure their base and spread their risk), or to other opportunities in the public or private sector where they could continue to do what they had been doing conceptually with land.[29] The introduction, in post-Protectorate times in Morocco, of a land registration system based on the Torrens system has not substantially altered this pattern. While it may reduce the contentiousness of property disputes and even the interconnections that real and potential conflicts entail, the process of having to rely on others to fund the registration process and the utilization of titles to negotiate still more complex relations does not contradict the fundamental focus on ownership as relationship.[30] Since the "meaning" of ownership was the cumulation of social attachments, so long as Moroccans could believe in its transferability to other domains the loss of land was not as devastating as Westerners might expect.

Indeed, the dependency of land titles on relationships is inscribed in the very nature of memory, documentation, and dispute. Thus, a land title commonly referred to the inheritance or purchase through which it was obtained rather than its metes and bounds; until the Protectorate began, maps were all but unknown, but even after they did come into existence, boundaries were defined mainly by the persons who owned adjacent properties rather than by fixed stakes or natural markers.[31] This emphasis then dovetailed with the cultural concentration of bonds of trust and relationship, and memory was based on accounts of these ties. "Certainty" and security lay in the neighbors, and even in urban areas their importance as witnesses to one's domestic affairs or their assistance in daily life and major crises often placed them ahead of one's own kin. "Better your neighbor who is close than your kinsman who is far away," as the common saying goes. But with the formal process of title registration, the ability to assess another's credibility began to suffer. The irony is that, in such circumstances, the certainty of having to negotiate relations that accompanied the uncertainty of property holding was becoming the enemy of that very trust that accompanied the open-ended nature of property as relationship.

We can see the reverberations of this emphasis on property as relationship in numerous other domains of Moroccan culture. Although men are known in part for the things they own, a man begins to obtain a distinct identity not when he acquires goods but rather when he begins to form his own bonds of obligation. There is a defining moment when a man moves out of his father's house and sets up a place where he can ingratiate in his own name. The prospect of leaving the father's house is often fraught with enormous tension. I have watched individuals being subjected to considerable pressure not to move out, when just moving next door is the break for independence so important to being a mature man from the Moroccan point of view.[32] Similarly, the absence of "citizenship" as a distinct status in the Western sense is also consistent with property as relationship. In the past one may have obtained the protection (*mezreg*) of a patron for one's dealings or been allowed to settle in a given territory and partake of its benefits and obligations under such patronage. But, characteristically, this is an entirely personal tie and not a separate status that operates irrespective of persons.

When King Hassan II died, people lined up at post offices throughout Morocco to send requests to the new monarch—and demanded that they be sent "return receipt requested" so that they would be assured of their personal connection to him! The common saying that three days after a man's death he ceases to exist reinforces the idea that a "person" is someone who has an impact on relationships, not simply one who controls various items in the world. Time, too, is categorized in terms of whether sets of relationships have an impact on current attachments. Thus, in trying to determine what is true about a person, chronology is seen as less indicative than networks of affiliation.[33] Unlike in many Western countries, in Morocco property ownership is not a prerequisite to the right to participate as a full member of society, whether in collective councils or, more recently, through the exercise of the franchise. Again, participation has long turned on one's ability to forge associations such that one's "word," by having an impact in the world of relationships, counts for something in the counsels of similarly recognized persons.

In addition, as we have also seen, it is crucial to any Moroccan's idea of himself that he be free to move about to forge relationships wherever they may prove most beneficial. Innumerable images exist of someone not being a real man because he is "bound up" (*rbeṭ, thqef*), immobilized, unable to negotiate his own associations.[34] And the fact that public space is not a zone for which one feels individual responsibility is consistent with the idea that space is the blank sheet on which relationships are inscribed, and that a parcel that is no one's personal expression of relationships is a kind of no-man's land and hence without real meaning.[35]

A delicate balance must often be sought between the properties (and attendant relationships) that one wishes to have publicly known and those one would as soon keep relatively secret. Or, to borrow a distinction used by some classicists, some property is visible and some invisible. In ancient Greece this distinction correlated not only with avoidance of taxes or the entangling claims by relatives and neighbors, but with motivation and the appropriate form in which a dispute might go forward.[36] Moroccans, too, would readily appreciate this distinction. They are often eager to hide assets among different associates in order to limit the expectations of mutual aid of those who are close to them; at the same time they are aware of the limitations such secrecy places on dispute resolution, which requires the parties to make public the nature of their assets. When there were still a large number of Jews in the country, one way to address this problem was to form an economic tie with a Jew, either through loans or actual joint ownership. Not only were such forms of ownership common in Morocco, but the tie usually carried an element of the invisible about it even when it was public inasmuch as the Jew was not going to try to convert an economic tie into some form of marital, political, or religious obligation.[37] Creating a habus trust for family members is also a way of converting the invisible to the public, thus changing the means by which it may be protected. Moreover, at least in theory, the formation of a trust removes it from the free play of association to which it might have been put, thus stopping or preventing (the literal meaning of the term *waqf*) not just attacks on the corpus but freezing certain changes in attachment that might be formed through it. And while women may often have to give up their legal claims to property they inherit, the more significant factor may be that they are thereby reinserting into the realm of the negotiable precisely the asset that is often so vital to a man's relational identity.[38]

What is true of real property is also true of intangibles. For if the claim to a thing needs to be perfected by establishing relationships with reference to it, we would expect that ideas, or "intellectual property," would not constitute protectable property without some form of action bringing people into relationship. To suggest to an honest dealer in the marketplace that selling pirated tapes and CDs is tantamount to theft from the idea's originator thus tends to fall on deaf ears. The usual response is that no chain of relationship has been established whereby the person who had the idea gave it recognizable effect in the world of relationships. This would not, however, be the case if someone used another man's poem or song when it was well identified with him, when people related to one another because of his work, or when there was a direct link between the idea and the relationships formed through it.

That property for Moroccans equates primarily with the demonstrated capacity to form bonds of indebtedness surprises us, then, only if we fail to think of its meaning for the Moroccans themselves rather than in Western terms. The question for Moroccans is not, as Erich Fromm put it for modern Westerners, whether to have or to be. Moroccans have long since recognized, as Roscoe Pound put it, that "wealth is made up largely of promises."[39] Without seeming to accept the proposition that "all property is theft," Moroccans attribute no inviolable security to property, recognizing that one's title is, like all else in life, only as good as one's capacity to forge relationships in terms of it.[40] William James's ideas that "an instinctive impulse drives us to collect property" and that the loss of property yields "a sense of the shrinkage of our personality, a partial conversion of ourselves to nothingness"[41] are readily challenged by the Moroccan emphasis on ownership as relationship. And the idea that even such intangibles as one's songs or poetry can be a sort of property makes perfect sense when one appreciates that for Moroccans the control of words is the key to creating relationships that have an impact in the world.[42] Thus to see ownership predominantly in relational terms is both to challenge some of the universals of property as a philosophical concept and to grasp how, for particular cultures, ownership relates to other features of the larger sociocultural system.[43]

In terms of other parts of the Arab and Muslim world, the implications of the meaning of ownership and property in the Moroccan situation are enormously intriguing. Historically, as Michael Cook points out, with the exception of Syria in the 1950s, agrarian unrest has not been a central part of the unrest leading up to Middle Eastern revolutions, although it has been an issue afterward.[44] There is no basic idea of a just agrarian system in Islam. Peasants were outside the conquering Muslim's conceptual order. In a Syrian tradition the Mahdi is even said to give all the land to Christians, with the Muslims remaining in jihad and collecting taxes paid them by the peasants.

In more contemporary instances the place of land is not altogether dissimilar. It would be worth asking, for example, whether the intense popular anger felt in places like Algeria for the loss of land to the colonizing French—as well as the lack of genuine attachment to attempts at "socializing" land holding in the postindependence years—does not turn on this very question of land less as thing than as proof of relationship. For many Algerians the loss of their land base literally immobilized their efforts to form negotiated relationships: they could find no adequate outlet other than emigration and were cut off from various resources upon which they could—and had in the past been able to—fabricate the ties that define a person. In the Arab east one may encounter related variations on this theme. The sense of nostalgia common among eastern Arabs—a feature quite absent in Morocco—seems to attach less to the loss of particular places than to the loss of social relations, the capacity to seek security through relational identity (with its attendant ideas of respect and honor) that connects not with a utopia of acquisition but with the ability to avert fitna through social embeddedness. For the Palestinians, nothing is worse than being confined to a terrain through which they cannot move to advantage. Such an act deprives them not simply of particular parcels of land within Israel or the West Bank, but of those lands as relational terrains, areas in which they could move to effect among others. Moreover, no adequate substitute is being provided them in the countries of their exile, nor are they able to construct a viable society within territories that are under their partial control.[45] The equivocal meaning of the land of Palestine is captured by its leading poet, Mahmud Darwish, when he says that "there is a love story between an Arab poet and this land" while also noting, "[h]ome is a place where you have a memory. Also it is impossible to return. Return is just a visit to a place of memory, or to the memory of a place."[46] When one focuses on property as relationship, one begins to see that certain de facto arrangements (such as the division of water or the movement of workers across boundaries) come closer to the functional meaning of property in the lives of those affected than does the exclusive focus on national boundaries and recognized sovereignty.

Indeed, property in the Arab world may not be seen primarily in terms of a legal attachment, backed by the power of state, that one can use to assert personal control or, conversely, as a right to be asserted against the sovereign powers of the state. Rather, given its relational focus, property is something that the state, as itself the very embodiment of unreciprocity, ought to show little interest in, protecting instead the multifarious ways in which individuals need to be able to freely negotiate with reference to it, as would be true with any other matter fraught with interpersonal possibilities. Property is not the bulwark against the state it is often seen to be in the West; rather it is one among many vehicles for association, and state action can (and inevitably will) be interpreted and legitimized in those terms alone.[47]

What the people themselves understand by such concepts as ownership and property thus remains a central concern for anthropologists, even though it has received relatively little attention in recent years.[48] Using both the philosophical literature to help sort out the issues and field-based ethnography to sort out the responses given by different Middle East communities, it may be possible to direct attention away from Western ideas of what property must mean and toward what it actually represents in the lives of the people in this critical part of the world. Mutual understanding must precede mutual agreement, and only if we begin to grasp more fully the attributions contending parties apply to one another—natives to colonists, citizens to their governments, members of one culture to those of another—will we be able to comprehend the implications the ideas of ownership and property have for both history and future engagement.

FIVE

Islamic Concepts of Justice

At a recent lecture on Islam and gender, a small group of Muslim women wearing headscarves and long dresses listened intently to the speaker. When the lecturer mentioned "rights," the Muslim women expressed no reaction; when she referred to "power," they expressed no reaction; when she spoke of "equality," they expressed no reaction. But the moment the lecturer used the word *justice,* every woman nodded enthusiastically.

If "rights" is the language of discourse for people in the United States and "liberty" or "freedom" or "solidarity" for other nations and times, "justice" is undoubtedly the watchword for Muslims when their place in the political and moral order is at issue.[1] It is the term that suffuses every element of Islamic thought and culture, from the Quran to the most commonsensical of aphorisms. Many of the usages suggest some quality or application of justice. "Be just," says the Quran (4:134, 6:153), "even if it is to your own kinsmen"—and by that phrasing, drawing on what Bernard Lewis calls the *trajetio ad absurdum* mode of argumentation, it demonstrates that while favoritism may be expected, justice should prove the rule through the exception."[2] Justice should also incorporate the capacity for individuals to move, at least to some degree, across dominant social categories. Justice is not necessarily the natural state of things, however. "If you find a moral man," says the poet al-Mutannabi, "there is a reason he is not unjust"—and by that he indicates that justice is not a natural phenomenon but one that arises only through the advancement of one's reason and placement among a community of righteous believers. Nor is justice to be accounted through single events alone. "If the times are just," says a common proverb, "one day is for me and one day is against me"—and by that people know that the times are a peopled moment, and that one may only expect that on balance justice will outweigh injustice rather than expect that it will triumph at every moment. Even Osama bin Laden, in his 2002 "message to the American people," urged the country to "escape your dry, miserable, materialistic life that is without soul. I invite you to Islam," he concluded, "to follow the path of Allah alone who has no partners, the path which calls for justice and forbids oppression and crimes."[3] Justice, then, is not a simple abstraction: it takes on both the qualities of the particular Muslim cultures in which it is found and calls forth the implications of an entire worldview and universal faith.

Justice as a Cultural Concept

If justice is the keyword to much of Islamic sentiment and discussion, frequent reference to the idea of justice, by believers and commentators alike, may simply tend to replace one unknown with another. The attributes and overtones of justice, much less the concise meaning or sense of its concrete presence or absence, often escape the discussion. A famous sixth-century formulation of "the circle of justice" states, "With justice and moderation the people will produce more, tax revenues will increase, and the state will grow rich and powerful. Justice is the foundation of the powerful state." An eleventh-century Turkish work states, "To control the state requires a large army. To support the troops requires great wealth. To obtain this wealth the people must be prosperous. For the people to be prosperous the laws must be just. If any one of these is neglected, the state will collapse."[4] The present head of the important Haqqania madrasa of Pakistan, Maulana Sami, simply declares, "Only our Islamic system gives justice."[5] And Fuad Khuri, the Lebanese anthropologist, writes, "Given the substantial stress placed on 'justice' in Islam, I reckon that if democracy is to establish roots in Arab countries, it will have to be linked to the concept of justice more than to the confusing ideology of freedom."[6] Suggestive and iconic as these propositions may be, they still leave the felt content of the concept of justice unarticulated.[7]

To say that such emphases on the word *justice* predominate does not, then, get at the common meaning people find in it, the reason why they hold it up as both emblem and instrument, why they can apply it with such immediacy and emotion to situations as diverse as a personal slight and the character of an age. The Arabic term commonly translated into English as *justice* is ʿadel, a term we should expect to be richly textured, open-ended, and yet sufficiently precise that people can know when it applies and when it is inapposite. The usual image associated with ʿadel is that of balance, of two things that offset each other such that equilibrium, though not stasis, is maintained. When justice is invoked in Arab cultures, the idea of balance—indeed of scales—is not infrequently called to mind.[8] But even this notion begs the question, for the issue is as likely to be what balances with what as whether some means of assessment, if not of actual measurement, is appropriate in a given situation. The Quran (99:7, 101:5) suggests that in the weighing of a soul a grain of difference may tip the balance for all time, but in everyday life Muslims would appear to see the elements being balanced as not simply interchangeable but as dependent for their measurement on the purpose and agent of that measurement.[9] After all, if the idea of justice fits into a larger cultural pattern in which context is crucial, in which negotiated associations are in a constant state of flux, and in which the appraiser is more central to credibility than a set of "objective" standards, we must go beyond even the most elaborate of literary and religious connotations to the sociological reality that gives this concept its indisputable force.

I have elsewhere suggested that justice as a cultural concept has three primary components in Arab thought—that it is composed of a kind of regulated reciprocity, that it is discernible through worldly consequence, and that it is dependent for its implications on the relationships described within a broad range of sociological contexts.[10] Reciprocity implies that all relationships have an obligational element and that the course of wisdom, to say nothing of human nature, is to forge associations of indebtedness that can be called up at a later time in any number of possible forms.[11] In this context, accepting interest on a loan (*riba*) constitutes a form of unjust enrichment: the discrepancy between a negotiated price and the added "carrying charge" of interest delays and renders problematic the equalization of the parties' transaction; it therefore threatens a breach in those immediate, face-to-face relations that are so vital to economic exchange. Justice is the running imbalance of these affiliations, such that *injustice* is the failure to recognize one's ties to others and the generalized rules by which such ties may be formed. To know another's range of obligations is vital to appraising him as a reliable partner and hence as a person who knows how to balance his own needs and those of his dependents. It is the effects one has in the world of relationships that is the primary index of one's credibility and grasp of the world. A man who simply contemplates the world as it moves about him—a mystic or a seer—may be responding to another sphere of forces, but he is not engaged in grappling with the world of justice and injustice.[12] Indeed, since justice is an aspect of the person and not a disembodied isolate, only a full knowledge of the contexts of a person's attachments can give one a sense of the qualities of justice that may cohere in that individual.

Justice as regulated reciprocity reveals itself in a host of concrete ways. In commercial relations it incorporates a series of precise types of contracts, none of which, however, protects the foolish or ignorant from the repercussions of their own bad bargains. It shows itself in the domain of compensatory justice, where each person is expected to be responsible for the exercise of his or her reasoning powers to avoid doing harm to others. And it reveals itself in the way that people characterize periods of time as just or unjust depending on the extent to which this free expression of reciprocal advantage and its inherent limitation on the arbitrary acts of others has given the community as a whole a sense of verisimilitude to divine expectation.

Justice, too, must incorporate some possibility of moving beyond the features associated with the predominant social category with which one is identified. This shows up with special force in gender differences. From the perspective of many Muslim men, women have categorical qualities that are distinctive to them—features that range from the generative to the psychological, intellectual, and attitudinal. Thus, women are seen by most men as more prone to passion than to reason, more in need of that guidance by men prescribed for them in the Quran (4:34), and more appropriately restricted to private than public domains. At the same time, however, a countervailing concept also comes into play, namely the idea that people should be able to move beyond predominant categorization. Thus, a poor man should have access to the resources of persuasion, wordplay, negotiated indebtedness, and outright chicanery—whatever bases might form the platform for his rise in the world—rather than be limited by rank, money, descent, or inheritance from playing "the game." It is here that the rhetorical device mentioned earlier (trajetio ad absurdum) emerges, for the argument that *even* someone of a given sort may cross the boundaries of the expected is part of the sense that freedom to move in the world of relationships is necessary for there to be true justice, notwithstanding the threat to social order posed by this freedom.[13] An educated woman, for example, may be given custody of a child rather than her uneducated husband, even though the law is generally to the contrary; or a woman who is adept in the marketplace may grudgingly be regarded as an honorary male for certain public engagements. For many women, as for many men in their own way, it is evidence of injustice that they may be held too rigidly to category. Fatima Gallaire, the Algerian playwright, captures this element in *Les Co-épouses* (*House of Wives*) when one of the wives laments,

We come into this world with a flower between our legs. It is the source of fear for as long as we have it and the source of unhappiness when we lose it. This cannot happen to a man because he comes into the world with a gun between his legs. With that primary weapon, he wins all battles against the flowers. . . . Is that what one calls justice? Is it that? That's justice? Is it my fault that I was born a flower? Is it my fault that I'm not a gun?[14]

It is in ritual that anthropologists often find confirmation of the socially normative, and it is in the ritual roles of women that support may be found for the view of justice as being appropriate to a combination of category and capability. In Islam, women possess very little in the way of collective ritual obligations. They have no special role in public or household prayer, their ritual involvement being largely restricted to birthing practices and customary rites of passage. But an important indicator of the relation of category to capacity as an enactment of justice comes in haj, the pilgrimage to Mecca. For there, not only are all pilgrims dressed in the flowing white sheet that will ultimately form their burial shroud, but men and women, who may normally be kept segregated, are mixed together, and the women appear unveiled.[15] This could be interpreted simply as a ritual of reversal, one of those characteristic moments in which the inversion of the ordinary marks the moment as truly out of the ordinary, only to have the social order reconfirmed at the end by returning to everyday practices. Indeed, one could see such a ritual as reconfirming the ordinary after risking disruption during a transitional ritual state. But one may also see this ritual as a demonstration of justice as equivalence. For even though men and women may appear as equals in the pilgrimage, one can also see this as an instance in which each person comes before God in his or her own true condition (*ḥal*). The haj would seem, therefore, to perform not uniformity but the acceptance by Allah of each in his or her particularity. Gender is not blurred or occulted: it is part of what any individual always is, a feature (among many) that inheres in and creates the social person who now stands before God. It is not that men and women are rendered alike; it is that individual appraisal, as both a member of a category and one who may stand outside it, is conjoined in a demonstration that appearance alone is insufficient to capture spiritual standing and genuine justice.[16]

Women are an important test case for the meaning of justice in other ways. The Quran (4:3) would appear to permit a man multiple wives provided they are treated "equitably": "If you fear that you will not act justly towards the orphans, marry such women as seem good to you, two, three, or four; but if you fear you will not be equitable, then only one, or what your right hands own."[17] This passage, as we will see in the following chapter, might seem logically problematic given the focus on orphans rather than on women generally. One interpretation is that each wife, regardless of her status, must receive the same support as the others or that, since they must be given equal affection (which might be thought impossible), one can never have multiple wives.[18] A more common interpretation is that equal treatment does not mean identical treatment in all respects. This holds true for both a monogamous marriage and a polygamous one. Thus, when a dependent is offered in marriage by her marital guardian, the principle of marital equality (*kafā'a*) does not require that the status of the husband and wife be identical.[19] The notion that being equal does not mean identical but roughly equivalent is consistent with other passages in the Quran. Justice requires that one focus on what is distinctive to the entire social persona of each individual, for it is through such attention to difference that the equitable may be achieved.[20] "Equity," it has been said, "is preferable to equality."

There are, of course, passages in the honored texts of Islam that suggest that individuals are truly equal, a view perhaps best represented in the hadith in which the Prophet says, "People are as equal as the teeth of a comb."[21] But it is also clear that, as in all aspects of the Arab variants of Islamic culture, context matters. Women may be as eligible for salvation as men, but because it is commonly believed, especially by men, that women's passions tend to overcome their reason, one needs to know whether they are sufficiently educated to obviate this "natural" tendency. Similarly, Jewish tribes may be equal to those of the Muslims in the context of warfare against outsiders, but not in other instances. "All men are descended from Adam and Adam was made from clay," says another hadith, but the idea that men are also equal "except in knowledge" demonstrates the highly contextual nature of this proposition.[22] Human qualities exist only in the context of a person's total attributes. "*Taqwa* (piety)," writes Fazlur Rahman, "is an attribute of the individual and not of society," an assertion that applies to other moral qualities as well.[23] Indeed, the very fact of difference is played up in Islam rather than submerged. In one of the most fascinating passages in the Quran (49:13) we read, "O mankind, We have created you male and female, and appointed you races and tribes, that you may know one another."[24] And elsewhere (16:95, 42:6): "If God had willed, He would have made you one nation." Now it may seem that if God had wished us to know one another He might have made us all the same. But it is precisely in having to come to understand one another as separate, in having to appraise a single feature in the context of an entire array of personalized features, that the moral challenge and the commonsense vision of human nature and society come into accord.[25] The king of Morocco, Muhammad VI, was able to further reforms in the Code of Personal Status by asserting that women are equal to men yet sustained a statute that was not entirely gender blind.[26] And if men must not only be responsible for the sustenance of dependent women but have predominant access to such resources as land through which they can affect the well-being of all those who surround them, then the inequality of rights afforded women may be justified in terms of the men's need to have the wherewithal to build their webs of indebtedness to the advantage of all.[27] In such an environment, defining equality as identity can seem both wrongheaded and immoral.[28]

Determining what makes two entities equivalent is not a matter of mechanical application. It involves every aspect of gaining knowledge in the world. In the West, physical measurement came to be used in many domains only when qualitative appraisal came up against shifting populations, uncontrollable demands on others' reciprocity, and the introduction of new philosophical and religious measures such as "moral certainty," "reasonable belief," and "preponderance of the evidence."[29] For Arabs, context is critical, and it is not possible to compare contexts in merely quantitative terms. Until very recently, merchants in many Arab markets commonly used multiple systems of measurement when dealing with a wide range of commodities; they may still give either a level or heaping measure depending on whether they are trying to solidify a patron–client bond or are engaged in a onetime sale. Even the "right" to an allotment of irrigated water may be altered when the expert in charge believes that a party has obtained an amount appropriate to his current circumstances.[30] As in the negotiation of relationships, multiple factors keep multiple possibilities alive; rigid measure would undermine the relativity of the personal and with it the sense of free movement vital to ever-alterable relationships. The unit of perception is the person-context, and entities are envisioned not as utterly discrete but as contextually segmented portions of a chain of connections.[31] Whether in law or religion, judgment must be of the whole person, hence it makes no sense to Muslim jurists I have interviewed to exclude information about prior acts since there is no way to know a person without knowing as much as possible about how he or she has interacted with others in a wide range of contexts. The Quran (6:153) recognizes this individual appraisal: "And fill up the measure and the balance with justice. We charge not any soul save to its capacity." Disruption—indeed injustice (*ẓulm*)—arises from the diminution of the ability to make unquantifiable assessments; justice results from being able to engage in the process of continually groping for the information and criteria by which to appraise another and render that person responsive to one's own identity or context. Like Stuart Hampshire, Arabs might argue that men are not "consistent in their emotions, in their alliances, and enmities" and that justice actually comes through conflict. The opportunity to make one's case (so "that contrary claims are heard"), while maintaining the flexibility of ambivalence and ambiguity, is paramount to Arabs' sense of justice.[32]

Action, when combined with reason, is integral to justice. It is not enough to believe that something should be; one must commit oneself to bringing it about. Knowledge and action are similarly related: the eleventh-century scholar al-Hujwiri said that "knowledge should not be separated from action."[33] Indeed, it could well be an Arab saying, rather than one that comes from Wall Street, that "to know but not to act is not to know."[34] Action here refers to efforts that affect relationships, not mere movement or engagement with things separate from their relational implications.[35] Labor alone does not produce value—it produces relationships with the potential for mutual claims. Human interaction, not unenacted intent or impersonal roles, is what holds a community of believers (umma) together and staves off that most feared of results, social chaos (fitna). Causality, then, is not a matter of straight lines applicable in all situations that appear similar. Because no two persons or contexts are identical, one must—whether in a court of law or in the general quest for information—seek out the chain of relatedness that is peculiar to the situation. Tendencies (sing., *ṭabīʿa*) are distinctive as to type, but they may be multiple and entangled, and understanding such causality, even to some ultimate sentient being, is more an art to be acquired through experience than a capacity to be mechanically applied.

If being a full person means being able to move to effect in the world of relationships, we can also see why anything that interferes with this capacity affects justice itself. Concepts that are often framed in terms of honor might be conceived more appropriately as expressions of legitimate self-concern or integrity.[36] For if the free quest for interpersonal obligations is blocked, the sense of injury can be intense, and in a cultural system in which one must constantly service one's obligations and be free to create them, a hindrance may be taken as a threat. This sensitivity to anything that may adversely affect one's ability to maneuver in the world of human relationships manifests itself in everything from the chafing dependence of a son on his father or an apprentice on his master—each needing eventually to break free to forge alliances in his own name—to the assertion of one's "right" among drivers on the road or concern that a potential ally's remark is actually an oblique insult.[37] Coercion alone is not necessarily an assault on justice, provided there is an opportunity for renegotiating one's situation. But when another turns his back, when the running imbalance of reciprocity is cut off from further reconfiguration, when one's ability to enter the process of building attachments is itself limited to just one means (e.g., monetary), then the idea of justice will commonly be felt to have been violated. Small wonder, then, that Arabs will say that even an unjust government is better than a corrupt one, since corruption itself means the failure to share your largesse, whatever its source, with those with whom you have formed ties of interdependence. Almost nothing could be worse than blocking that maneuverability.[38]

Understanding what is taken as injustice becomes another way of grasping the meaning of justice itself. Ibn Khaldun said that "injustice can be committed only by persons who cannot be touched, only by persons who have power and authority."[39] He was suggesting that where there is little interactive relationship, none of the features to which we have been pointing—emphasis on negotiation, reciprocity, maneuverability, and access to multiple bases for building indebtedness—are likely to be available. Injustice lies in being barred from "the game." Injustice, of course, is often felt rather than articulated, and most Muslims tend to believe, like Montaigne, that institutions, far from eradicating injustice, often reinforce it. Face-to-face relations are required for justice. The state, as unreciprocity incarnate, is often regarded as injustice incarnate. For most Muslims, justice is not, as Adam Smith said, the least of virtues because it is the one that simply entails the avoidance of harm. Rather, justice is the most essential, if indeterminate, of virtues for Arabs because it keeps open the quest for equivalence, a quest that is seen as central to both human nature and revealed orderliness in a world of reason and passion.

When the Quran (42:6) says that "the unjust have no patron or helper," it underscores the role of the intermediary, not because Islam requires an indirect approach to God but because the establishment of interpersonal bonds is essential to fostering the interdependence that alone yields justice within the community of believers. Purpose—here the furtherance of the community of believers—is thus essential to justice. In this regard, Islam echoes Amartya Sen's idea that differences are vital to egalitarianism and that bare assertions of equality without regard to broader social goals are of no real meaning or effect.[40]

Cultural Postulates and the Concept of Justice

One might, therefore, compare a set of ideal-type postulates about Islamic justice and culture as a way of teasing out some of their common assumptions. In doing so one must remember that, like many classificatory systems, this is not meant as a direct representation of extant concepts but as suggestive of some of the principles through which many Muslims may grasp the world as ordered and meaningful. Variation is key here. These propositions are not meant to be directly mapped onto specific Muslim groups; rather, the variant suggested below is a generalized one for Arabs. Such an outline may help us to see some of the conceptual apparatus that informs the sense of justice as an active element of everyday life, however varied the local version may be.

Postulates of Arabo-Islamic Justice	Postulates of Arabo-Islamic Culture
Justice requires reason plus action; justice is not an abstraction but a form of action in the world	All things possess a natural disposition (tabiʿa); the nature of humans is to actively contract relationships with one another
Justice is a personal attribute; by the impress of just persons on their times, justice may become an attribute of an entire community in a given age	Persons stand at the center of negotiated webs of indebtedness that must be constantly serviced; communities have no independent, superorganic existence

Postulates of Arabo-Islamic Justice	Postulates of Arabo-Islamic Culture
Justice requires reciprocity: corruption is unjust because it interferes with reciprocity, and it is only just to share with dependents	All bonds are obligational; corruption means failure to share largesse with one's obligational network
Justice is the entitlement of a person of given attributes; it requires a process of assessing persons and contexts in which contrary appraisals may be heard	One must constantly seek knowledge about others' attributes and contexts of relationship, not relying on status alone to define another
Chaos (fitna) is the greatest threat to man; if there is chaos there is no justice, hence tyranny is preferable to chaos because ordered relationships always imply a degree of control over the other's acts	Conflict is natural but attachment to wise leaders may develop reason and limit undesirable passion; entanglement in webs of reciprocity holds chaos at bay even though it may constrain maneuverability
Justice arises through the middle course, not by applying inflexible rights	Only those "rights" (*ḥūquq*) exist that are enforceable; rights exist by their effects in the world
Ambivalence and ambiguity are not antithetical to justice but are constitutive of it; only divine justice constitutes a unity; justice must remain open-ended in order not to foreclose new relationships	Ambiguity and ambivalence are vital to fashioning mutual indebtedness; connections can be made only among entities with something in common, hence the quest for bases of attachment
Justice means equivalence, not equal in the sense of treating entities identically regardless of their nature and individuality; justice must allow for category shifts	Persons and contexts are not static categories; even a person of a given disposition (tabiʿa) may take on qualities usually associated with another category
Justice trumps freedom; freedom means the ability to contract interdependencies, which requires that others attend to one's identity and thereby show respect	So long as one is able to move to effect in the world, one is free; so long as one can maneuver within one's dependencies, one's place and apt treatment may be created and sustained

This outline is not meant to be exhaustive or indisputable. Quite aside from centuries of dispute among theologians and the differences among different divisions of Islam, both sectarian and regional, the idea of justice is never a matter of simple agreement. We see at present a counterdiscourse by a number of Muslim women, arguing, for example, that the true meaning of the Quran and hadith is that of full equality by gender and that justice calls for the trumping of local custom by Prophetic example.[41] Nor is it to suggest that justice as process means that only one mode of proceeding is agreed upon by all. But in addition to the broadly shared orientation toward human nature and culture that this paradigm represents, and the multiple domains that it suffuses, we can, perhaps, see that for Arabs justice always implies a combination of ordered modes by which one can discern and engage others in legitimate relationships. Justice requires a high degree of maneuverability consonant with unfixed circumstance. And it requires that the actions of any ordinary person or government official be considered as a totality, and that, taken as a whole, such individuals demonstrate a commitment to the social conventions and modes of reasoning that alone can protect society from chaos. Aristotle's ideas may have been all the more congenial to Arabs for his having argued that the corrective aspect of justice is as important as the normative, and that while the judge must apply law one also needs umpires who apply equity rather than unalterable rules.

Unlike John Rawls's idea of justice as a relationship among institutions, and somewhat closer to Paul Ricoeur's idea of justice as maintaining the good life by establishing "the right distance" on all matters, the Arab variant of Islamic justice keeps its eye firmly on human relationships.[42] For Arabs, the real world of relationships *is* the expression of the ideal. The purpose, the intent, and the meaning of justice all cohere around that sense of the equitable, rather than the identical, through which the characteristics associated with gender and background, modified by the accomplishments of reason, yield an extraordinary range of persons and settings. Paying attention to difference is a matter of common sense and a moral obligation. Such attention to the differences among persons may seem to imply what in other contexts has been called "the sin of equivalence," the assumption that similar acts have the same moral standing despite their historical grounding and the ongoing disadvantage to one of the parties. But if, for the Arabs, "a difference is not a distinction," if variation is not indissolubly linked to gradations of moral superiority, then we can again appreciate the formulation of one Arab scholar who remarked that equity is preferable to equality. What remains to be determined is how such equations will play out in a world in which the positions of all parties may be undergoing considerable change, and in which the world at large affects the Arabs' sense of justice in ways that neither can fully control.

PART TWO

Readings and Re-readings

SIX

Reading the Quran through Western Eyes

One of my unsubstantiated images of post-9/11 America is of numerous coffee tables around the country with a copy of the Quran sitting on them for months.[1] Eager to show both the lack of any prejudice against Islam and a sincere willingness to separate the terrorists from other Muslims, the buyer had purchased a translation of the Quran, fully intending to read it. But after struggling through the first few pages, the reader set aside the book, albeit with every intention of getting back to it soon. In time, like that promise to finally read Proust this summer, the coffee table needed to be cleaned up, the book migrated to the shelves, and the reader never quite got back to it.

Why? After all, even those who do not study the Hebrew Bible or New Testament, or who do not find them of enormous spiritual centrality, commonly regard at least certain sections of the scriptures as interesting and even uplifting. What is it about the structure or narrative style of the Quran that makes it difficult for Western readers to sustain interest? And if one does work through substantial parts of the Quran, what is it that Westerners often find incomprehensible or unappealing about this text?

Understandably, nonbelievers will not approach the Quran with the same assumptions as a believing Muslim— that it is the exact and unaltered word of God handed down through His last Prophet, that much of the Hebrew Bible and Gospels was altered and now only the Quran contains God's unchanged truth, and that (at least for a vast majority of the faithful) the Quran contains all knowledge—from the most obvious elements of everyday experience to the most arcane aspects of scientific knowledge—within the compass of its verses.[2] Western readers may reject the characterization offered by Thomas Carlyle, who called the Quran "a wearisome confused jumble, crude, . . . insupportable stupidity, in short!" adding, "Nothing but a sense of duty could carry any European through the Koran."[3] But they may find that reading the Quran is, for them, surprisingly boring. They may appreciate, even if they do not agree, that orthodox Muslims believe "Prophets must be regarded as immune from serious errors [and that] Muhammad was such a person, in fact the only such person really known to history."[4] And they may even understand that it is as true for Muslims as James Barr noted for Christians that "what fundamentalists insist on is not that the Bible must be taken literally but that it must be so interpreted as to avoid any admission that it contains any kind of error . . . of historical, geographical or scientific fact."[5] But all of this good will may still render the Quran rather impenetrable to Western eyes and, given its perceived tone, not as consonant with their "Abrahamic values" as they might wish.

Two hurdles in particular present themselves to such readers: the style in which the Quran is presented and the cultural assumptions that underlie much of its meaning. What Carlyle, like many others, had seen as "endless iteration, long-windedness, entanglement" is actually a form of organization and prosodic revelation quite different from the Jewish and Christian sources. When the chapters (*suras*) of the Quran were compiled in the years following the Prophet's death, they were organized from longest to shortest rather than presented as a simple chronological tale or collection of parables.[6] The Quran tells relatively few stories, the thrust being more akin to seeing God's utterances and humankind's actions as facets of a gem rather than as a revelation unfolding through time. Indeed, in Arab culture, as we have suggested, time does not reveal the truth of persons, as it does in the West. Rather, time forms a continuum that, in the case of the sacred, may be interrupted by Prophetic insight and ritual engagement. The result is that what is true about people cannot come from chronological stories; it must come from seeing issues and persons in multiple contexts regardless of their arrangement in time.[7] Thus, the truth that a Western reader finds authenticated by the trajectory of a story is here rendered in chapters that could, like a postmodern novel, be arranged in any order yet still reveal their truth as it is refracted through numerous contexts. Since this is not a style Westerners associate either with revelation or with gripping narrative, the text of the Quran often fails to capture these readers' interest.

To various Western commentators this "narrative disruption" is either evidence of the inherent incomprehensibility of the Quran—its free-floating, etherealized, or impenetrably mystical quality—or proof that the Quran was not the reduction to writing of what was directly revealed through the Prophet but the collation of numerous bits and pieces, many drawn from or through non-Muslim sources as the expression of a new religion or as a form of preexisting messianism, during the years following Muhammad's death.[8] To others, most interestingly the social critic Norman O. Brown (himself not a student of Islam), the Quranic suras are apocalyptic statements, bursts of nonlinear epiphanies, each containing the overall divine revelation.[9] Like James Joyce's *Finnegans Wake*, which Brown says was also boring to those first reading it, each passage is "not beautiful but sublime," not a refinement on prior civilizations but a rhetorical act of full-blown revelation, an attempt "to change the imagination of the masses."[10] Brown may be emphasizing an interpretation that is more fitting for some Muslim mystics (*sufis*) than for ordinary believers in his account, and he certainly is propelled, in this and other aspects of his interpretation, by his own Freudian orientation.[11] But there are two elements that bear on any assessment of his argument. First, orthodox Muslims believe that the Quran itself is proof of Muhammad's prophetic claims, indeed of its own veracity: it is not miracles that prove its truths but the fact that the Quran is literally inimitable, that no human being could create sentences like those in the Quran.[12] That Westerners could ever have spoken of Islam as "Muhammadanism" was wildly off the mark, but it would not have been altogether incorrect to have coined a term like "Quranism" to describe Islam. And second, the Quran employs what literary scholars have in other contexts called a cornucopian style, in which the sheer profusion of instances, unlinked by direct connections of time or causality, pour forth in such abundance as to overwhelm criticism based on ordinary reason or logic.[13] Whatever the history of its revelation or construction, the Quran may have to be read by Westerners more as an example of instantaneous assertion than as the kind of gradual, cumulative revelation of truth through which the sacred texts of the West have deployed and shaped our attention and belief.

This is not to suggest that the Quran has been regarded by believers as precluding interpretation. To the contrary, the history of Quranic interpretation is rich and varied, notwithstanding great differences from the course of Western biblical interpretation. While early Muslims may have interpreted the Quran rather freely, by the second century after the Prophet's death, when the schools of Islamic law had jelled and the collections of Prophetic Traditions were largely settled, interpretation subsided.[14] Studies of grammar and the context of revelations were employed in commentaries on the Quran, but even reports of the Prophet's own days could not initiate a valid form of interpreting the sacred text directly. Interpretation (*tafsīr*) may or may not have been punished by the first caliph, and there were certainly scholars who tried to address some of the issues the Quran posed as questions, as if they were not rhetorical inquiries but invitations to the application of reason. But the predominant thrust of these interpretations—whether through "tradition" or "opinion"—was that the basic text was self-elucidating; guidance to the actions it prompts, rather than its "real" but obscured meaning, could come not from direct interpretation but through customs and practices that in no way endanger the integrity of the text or risk dividing the community of believers.[15]

In short, Islamic thinkers early on sought to limit speculation and innovation, particularly as it related to any ideas or practices that might challenge the uniqueness, the very unity, of God by mixing the human or idolatrous with Him. For dominant orthodox Islam, God's creative power "is not 'renewed' at every moment, but rather at every moment is 'created' from A to Z."[16] Where the Protestant Reformation challenged Church authority by making individual interpretation of Holy Writ possible, Islamic thinkers tended to regard any serious questioning of the Quran's meaning as potential admixture and hence evidence of foolishness or disbelief.[17] Later revelations that appear to contradict earlier ones have been regarded either as evidence of God's gradually acclimatizing believers to the new message or simply as proof that humankind cannot treat God's word by rationalism alone: "And for whatever verse We abrogate or cast into oblivion," says the Quran, "We bring a better or the like of it; knowest thou not that God is powerful over everything?" (2:100; also 16:101).[18]

To the extent that one may generalize, then, one can suggest that Western and Arab styles of interpreting sacred text differ in several significant ways.[19] Sura 3:5 says, "It is He who sent down upon thee the Book, wherein are verses clear that are the Essence of the Book, and others ambiguous." But it goes on to characterize those ambiguities by saying, "As for those in whose hearts is swerving, they follow the ambiguous part, desiring dissension, and desiring its interpretation; and none knows its interpretation, save only God" (3:7). Thus, direct interpretation starts with a limitation, one that manifests itself in an avoid-ance of historical and hermeneutic studies of the text.

Islam, like many other faiths, claims universal applicability. A com-mon belief is that the Quran was actually transmitted to all peoples after its revelation but most individuals then forgot it—as implied in the Arabic term for humankind (al-insan), "the forgetful ones." At the same time, the spread of Islam has been, and continues to be, phenom-enal, notwithstanding the vast range of cultures into which it has pen-etrated. For many, this insertion has seemed less unfamiliar than for others. In more patriarchal societies, or those in which references in the Quran seem like direct representations of what people experience in their everyday lives, the terms and contexts of the Quranic ideas are already close to home. For many others a very important principle makes Islam compatible with their existing ways of life. For in virtually every Muslim society one encounters two key propositions: (1) that un-less a local practice is directly contrary to one of the few clear prohibi-tions in the Quran, people believe the practice *is* Islamic and not merely some custom that needs to be set alongside Islam; and (2) that almost everywhere and at every time one finds a local saying and practice to the effect that local custom can take precedence even over Islamic law (shariʿa).[20] These features have contributed significantly to the spread of Islam since it means that one does not have to give up one's pre-existing ways to become a Muslim. But for many modern Westerners, who are less prone to find the culturally and socially familiar in the text of the Quran, or who do not come from systems in which, say, matters of family law have been left to religious authority rather than uniform state laws, the Quran can seem to be linked to a world quite remote from their own.[21] And since much of Quranic interpretation "serves to align it with established social custom, legal positions, and doctrinal assertions" that are distant from those of most Westerners, the text may not readily speak to their background.[22] Coupled with a tendency, based on the tradition of Biblical interpretation, to read such texts for their broader moral principles, the fact that the Quran does not mainly present these ideas either as parables or stories that seem to touch many Westerners' own situations may contribute to an impres-sion of the text as quite foreign indeed.

Some of the differences in textual interpretation between Westerners and Arabs relate to problems of translation. The standard Muslim the-ory is that the Quran is untranslatable. Since it was delivered in Arabic and must never be subject to change, translation poses a threat to the integrity of the text. For those who have sought to translate the Quran into Western languages, the range of variation can appear quite great. To choose just two examples: Fazlur Rahman translates Sura 70:19–21 to read, "[M]an is by nature unstable. When evil touches him he panics." A. J. Arberry, by contrast, renders the passage thus: "Surely man was created fretful, when evil visits him, impatient." Where Rahman renders a line in Sura 33:72 concerning man as "he is, indeed, unjust [to himself] and fool-hardy"—the bracketed phrase being in Rahman's original—Arberry translates it as, "Surely he is sinful, very foolish," the difference between "unjust to oneself" (*zulm an-nafs*) and "sinful" being potentially enormous.[23] Indeed, it has been suggested by one Western scholar that the promise to martyrs of forty (or seventy) virgins awaiting them in heaven is based on a mistaken translation: The word *virgins*, he argues, actually means "white raisins," a delicacy of great rarity—a translation error that could come as quite a shock to any martyr arriving to claim his eternal reward![24] Differences of meaning are exaggerated, perhaps, by translation, but if there were a tradition of seriously determining the meaning of the Quran through detailed philological investigation of the original Arabic terms, the risk of changing the clear meaning may have been too great to be acceptable.

Even when the Quran is not rendered in a different language, issues of "translation" arise. Early written Quran manuscripts had neither vowel markings nor punctuation. Like the Torah, the knowledgeable reader can usually insert the vowels without great difficulty. But problems can arise. To take an English example, it makes a big difference, there being no other indication as to word breaks, if one reads "godisnowhere" to mean "god is now here" or "god is nowhere."[25] Even if there were a tradition of valid textual interpretation, however, Muslim scholars have rarely questioned which word was actually meant given the possibilities of using different vowel combinations. Scrutinizing punctuation, too, is frowned upon as a vehicle for raising questions about the meaning of a passage, even though the difference a comma makes could carry enormous philosophical and theological implications. Look back, for example, at Sura 3:5–6, quoted above. After suggesting that only God knows the right interpretation of His message, many translators begin a new sentence that reads, "And those firmly rooted in knowledge say, 'We believe in it, all is from our Lord.'" But since there is no punctuation, that sentence could be combined with the preceding one to read, "But no one knows its interpretation except God *and* those firm in knowledge: Say 'We believe in it, all is from the Lord.'" This latter reading is enormously different, for it would suggest that interpretation is left not solely to God but also to those who are knowledgeable. Such a reading might be seen as license for scholars or others to authoritatively interpret the Quran, versus precluding any such human involvement.[26] Instead of employing it for the exploration of Quranic meaning, grammar was, for the most part, made subservient to i'jāz the proof of the inimitability of the Quran's composition, the impossibility of its being the product of any human hand.[27] Moreover, avoidance of any interpretation of meanings integral to the text precluded any study of the historical nature of the Quran as a literary or theological document. Again, if the Quran is unchanging, how could one study its meanings by looking at the history of terminological change, much less base one's interpretations on pre-Islamic meanings?

A modern Westerner, coming from a different interpretive history of his own sacred texts, might then be tempted to read a Quranic passage through a close parsing of the verses. Take, for example, the passage that is usually cited as the mainstay for permitting a man to have more than one wife, Sura 4:3. It reads, "If you fear that you will not act justly towards orphans, marry such women as seem good to you, two, three, or four; but if you fear you will not be equitable, then only one, or what your right hands own; so it is likelier you will not be partial." Leaving aside the treatment of slave women, which seems to be what is at issue in the reference to one's "right hands," the passage (at least in this punctuational form) could certainly appear to apply only to orphans. Just as the Hebrew Bible limits polygyny to the levirate (marriage to a deceased brother's widow so that her child would be the heir of the deceased), one could read this Quranic verse to limit multiple marriage to orphans, as a way of including them within the genealogical community.[28] Yet for whatever additional reasons such passages never seem to be read in this fashion since there is no legitimate tradition of treating the Quran as if it were anything but "clear."

Although one cannot supplement the Quran from the outside or parse it grammatically or historically from the inside, one can permissibly elaborate on its provisions indirectly in two ways: by referring to the practices and utterances of the Prophet himself, and by expanding on what the sacred law (shari'a) counsels. Again, since the Quran is always seen as "clear" (mubin), citing the hadith, or Prophetic Traditions, is not regarded as an actual interpretation of the Quran but as guidance to practice through prophetic example.[29] Moreover, since the Quran cannot be subject to direct interpretation, there can be no hierarchy of authorities who are acknowledged experts in such readings.

Rather, those who are regarded as better or worse guides for knowing what the Prophet actually said or did, as well as for the elucidation of the law, build up followers who accept (or at least employ) their advice, whether in life or in law. Authoritative collections of the hadith exist, then, along with a vast array of published or privately commissioned opinions about the requirements of the law. As has often been noted, what is within the domain of theology in many other religions is, for Muslims, largely worked out in the domain of law. Authoritative readings of the law themselves turn on the ability of scholar-jurists to garner respect from others rather than on a strict hierarchy of established scholars, so the personalism that suffuses all other domains of Arab culture is carried over into this realm as well.[30]

The Quran is, of course, a written text, but a vital aspect of its fixity, as well as its socioreligious role, is connected to its oral transmission. The word *qur'an* means "recitation," and if one thinks of scripture as something that must be recited—in a sense, orally returned to God, as recognition of His great gift—one probably comes closest to the meaning of the concept.[31] The written Quran is said to have been compiled into its final form in the 650s during the reign of Caliph Uthman ibn Affan, who reputedly had all other versions destroyed.[32] Since, as we have already indicated, the Arabic used did not contain diacritical marks, certain consonantal clusters could be read in quite different ways. For example, the same characters can mean "he said," "he was killed," "to kiss," "before," "front of body," or "elephant."[33] Recitation could increase this uncertainty because different groups used different pronunciations and hence might generate divergent meanings, but by the tenth century, written versions had succeeded in regularizing the text. However, oral recitation remains critical. In theory, the Quran should be fully memorized—carried in one's heart, as people say—and certification as a teacher of the Quran commonly has required proof of full memorization. Committing the Quran to memory has several effects: it perpetuates the personalism of knowledge transmission and the validation of utterances through reliable persons; it helps to keep the written text from being corrupted (in the way the Bible is said by Muslims to have been) by requiring public recitation before those who have also memorized the Quran; and it draws together a community, most of whose members might be illiterate, through a recitation that, though distinct from prayer, has similar unifying functions. Nowadays, Quranic recitation is a very popular form of performance, with the art of listening, as much as the styles of recital, being the subject of much discussion.[34]

To many Westerners, the recitation of the Quran may appear end-lessly repetitive, and the text itself may seem boring because of the frequent recurrence of the same issues or phrasings. But there may be a significant difference in the cultural meaning of repetition. To many Muslims, repetition is not the simple iteration of identical entities but a demonstration that at each point a choice can be made. Like that most characteristic artistic form, the arabesque, each joining of enti-ties is a possible branching, each represents a decision about direction, indeed each connection memorializes a choice made. Apart from its emotional evocation, its communal unification, and its personal act of commitment—all of them key elements in the entire religious pattern—repetition is understood by many as an expression of reason rather than its submersion. In a culture in which the full play of individual wills is raised to enormous intensity only to be countered by total submission to God, dissolution of the personal through communal prayer, and rit-ual reversals of social roles in various ceremonial acts, recitation of the Quran is yet another way of articulating and containing the propensity for intense individual maneuvering with the still greater force of collec-tive and religious immersion. If the Hebrew Bible and the New Testa-ment, to a great extent, point through time to the truth of a timeless message, the Quran and its enactment point to its timelessness through the demonstration of each reciter's personal choice and commitment. The recitation of the Quran and the authorization granted a new reciter by a prior one reinforces the view of humankind as at once embedded in interpersonal relationships of their own making and inescapably oc-culted by their own mortality and divine will. Obviously, if a Westerner is reading the Quran only for its ideas or its poetry, many of these fea-tures of enactment and communal involvement will not be evident.

None of this means, however, that the Quran will seem utterly for-eign to the Western reader. To the contrary, it refers to persons and events that are central to the Hebrew Bible and the New Testament, so much of it may, at first glance, seem quite familiar.[35] Bearing in mind, though, that the Islamic theory of those earlier texts is that they were corrupted and that the only correct version is that found in the Quran, Western readers may find that the nature and moral of a Quranic story is quite different from that found in their own sacred texts. Several ex-amples may be worth noting.

The story of Adam and Eve is readily familiar to Westerners, but they may be struck by the different version that appears in the Quran. The Quran never refers to Eve by name, only as Adam's spouse (2:33). It speaks of Adam and Eve in the plural, as having been created from a single soul, and does not refer to Eve as having been formed from a part of Adam's body (4:1, 39:6). The Quran also never mentions the snake. Nor does it blame Eve for humanity's fall. Indeed, it is Adam who is twice cited as responsible for the loss of Eden (20:115, 20:1321). God's admonition to Adam and Eve is clear (20:120): "Said He: 'Get down, both of you together, out of it [Eden], each of you an enemy to each; but if there comes to you from Me guidance, then whosoever follows My guidance shall not go astray." It was only in the second century after the Prophet's death, perhaps (as some Western scholars speculate) when Islam felt strong enough to overwhelm surrounding religions by incorporating aspects of them, that commentators, as part of the process of tracing Prophetic wisdom through chains of reliable witnesses leading back to Muhammad's companions, adopted the view that a woman named Eve was created from a crooked rib of Adam that can never be straightened, and that menstruation and painful childbirth are punishments for her innate foolishness.[36] To those who believe that men are more capable of reason than women and must therefore serve as women's overseer, the Quranic version of the Fall may be read as an indication that Adam failed in his greater duty of oversight and thus deserves the primary blame. For modern Muslim women who believe the Quran posits men and women as equals, the Quranic version of the story may be taken as evidence that men and women, forged from a single soul, are identical in susceptibility and basic humanity. By whatever light one interprets it, the Quran's account of the first humans may strike many Western readers as more open-ended—especially as it relates to the vision of women—than they might have expected.

The nature of men and women arises, too, in the story of Joseph and Potiphar's wife. Readers of the Hebrew Bible will recall that the wife of Pharaoh's aide, Potiphar, tries to seduce Joseph; when he resists her overtures, she accuses him of attacking her, after which Joseph is thrown in prison, where he begins interpreting dreams. In the Quran's account, Potiphar's wife similarly seeks to seduce Joseph; when she cries out after he rebuffs her, a group of men related to her rush into the room. One of them, however, notices that Joseph's garment is torn from behind, rather than in front, thus substantiating Joseph's claim that he was trying to get away rather than trying to attack her (12:25). The conclusion drawn in the Quran is that one should beware of even one's own kinswomen because of the tendency of women generally to lie. Unlike the Adam and Eve story this may support the stereotype Western readers have of the Quran's representation of women. But this story is now used by many judges as a basis for paying attention to circumstantial evidence, a procedural element that in legal settings may work to the benefit of women.[37] As a modern Muslim scholar has noted, Islamic law often consists of shifting from one text that is exhausted to one whose time has come.

A final set of examples concerns the representation of Jesus in the Quran. Jesus is, of course, regarded as a prophet by Muslims, and there are many indications that Muhammad had very great respect for him.[38] Unlike the Gospels, however, Jesus is not represented in the Quran as having died and been resurrected. Instead, in the Quran Jesus is said not to have perished at all but to have simply ascended to Heaven. Jesus is thus rendered a special case, but not an example of miraculous resurrection. The Quranic version of the end of Jesus' life on earth is consonant with the Quran's emphasis that the proof of its truth is not the working of miracles by the Prophet, and it may be viewed as a means of placing Jesus in a line of prophets that comes to an end with Muhammad. The Western reader will, therefore, find a number of passages in which Jesus is honored—in the view of some, singled out as an instrument for the denial of polytheism and as a sign of God's omnipotence— even though Christians themselves are regarded as occasional enemies of the new faith.[39]

If some of the stories in the Quran are familiar to Westerners but are told from a very different angle, some of the themes Westerners may see as dominant in the text may strike them as no less curious. Over the years a number of students and friends have read through the Quran and told me what themes leap out at them. It may be worth addressing briefly three such themes: the idea of fear, the place of doubt, and the relationship to non-Muslims.

The ordinary Western reader may be forgiven for sensing that the concern with fear is pervasive in the Quran. After innumerable passages in which humankind is cautioned to believe and do as the text prescribes, there follows the strict admonition that if one fails in this regard severe punishment will ensue. The Hebrew Bible also refers frequently to fear, but while the tone certainly communicates God's omnipotence, the sense is more of awe than of premonitory fright. Indeed, men in the Old Testament frequently struggle with God or his agents and even disobey God—think of Moses or Samuel or Saul. But the Quran allows of no such direct confrontation with God. Notwithstanding the many references to the "rights of man" as being the domain within which he must make rational and responsible use of his God-given capabilities, the "rights of God" are never to be overstepped, and hence the idea of direct struggle for, or even any overlap among, the powers of each is unthinkable. To cross God is not to risk utter destruction; it is to be assured of it. God is, of course, consistently characterized as merciful and compassionate, and on Judgment Day anyone may turn to the Prophet to act as an intermediary for God's mercy. But the Western reader may more readily feel the element of fear than that of mercy in the constant references in the Quran to the fate that awaits those who are found wanting. Compassion appears conditional, and the New Testament idea of a loving God seems to be missing from the Quran's representation of the Almighty. God is never referred to as a father or by any other term of kinship. Humans are portrayed as naturally ungrateful of God's gifts (1:244), and since the Quran now informs humans of their duties it also indicates that failure to comply yields automatic punishment (e.g., 1:232).

But this may be a mistaken reading, just as interpreting fear as awe rather than fright may be the truer sense of fear in the Hebrew Bible. For while fear of God may imply a reminder of man's inferior status, it may, as some commentators suggest, go more toward the fear one should have if one fails to exercise one's God-given reason to control one's passions and their socially harmful potential.[40] Moreover, to the frequent characterization of the Quran solely as a charter for correct action, it is crucial to add that the idea of intention (*niya*) is quite central. "There is no fault in you if you make mistakes, but only in what your hearts premeditate" (33:5). Indeed, if one struggles with one's possessions and oneself (4:97), if one realizes that no more is being asked of any person than he or she is capable of doing (2:286; 6:153), and if one grasps that "no soul bears the burden of another" (96:164), then the mercy God promises may overpower any sense of fear.

Among the unforgivable acts are many that bear on the community of believers and others that concern the individual's own relation to God. Backbiting and false accusation (Sura 104), failure to keep one's contracts, and unwillingness to mediate a dispute are threats to the community, threats that are particularly serious because many duties can be enacted only within a collective context and because the chaos that accompanies disruption to social ties could even lead to the dissolution of the faith. Toward God one of the most serious infractions is the registration of any doubt whatsoever about the Quran's message. "This is the book, wherein is no doubt," begins the first sura (2:1) after the invocation, and, as we have seen, doubt was early on equated with unbelief in Islam.[41] What earns unbelievers a "painful chastisement" from which they can expect "no helpers" (3:85) is precisely the rejection of

God's unitary existence coupled with rejection of the community of faith through which one could have gained the intercession of both the Prophet and His people. On the Day of Judgment, when society no longer exists, when each soul will have to stand for itself (82:16), when "men shall be like scattered moths" (101:3), it is precisely that individual commitment to the message brought by Muhammad that will be tested.

Western readers may also be struck, quite understandably, by the representation of non-Muslims in the Quran. Much of the language can seem exceptionally harsh. "O believers, take not Jews and Christians as friends; they are friends of each other" (5:56). "The Jews have said, 'God's hand is fettered.' Fettered are their hands and they are cursed for what they have said" (5:68). And there are the passages extremists have used to castigate Jews generally, passages that refer to those who have gone astray as "apes and pigs" (56:65, 5:60).[42] These, however, are balanced with other statements: "Surely they that believe, and those of Jewry, and the Christians and those Sabeans, whoso believe in God and the Last Day, and works righteousness—their wage awaits them with the Lord, and no fear shall be on them, neither shall they sorrow" (2:59).

We have already seen that the image of Jesus and Mary is a positive one.[43] Abraham is called a *hanif-muslim* (3:59), one who has believed and submitted, and by not engaging in sectarian divisiveness he has demonstrated his conformity with the ideal of human nature. As with the treatment of Jews, when the Quran is particularly negative in its image of Christians, it tends to focus on two features: whether the religion (or some of its members at a given time) are opposing the Muslims, and which individuals or groups within each confessional community are disfavored. "If they fight you, slay them—such is the recompense of unbelievers—but if they give over, surely God is All-forgiving, All-compassionate" (2:187). This proposition, which is elaborated in the works of al-Wahhab, the central figure in current Saudi orthodox Islam, thus sets as a condition that people of the book will be allowed to practice their religion provided they do not oppose Islam.[44] Thus, particular Jewish tribes were to be slain or accepted as allies or subalterns depending on whether they fought against Islam. The treatment of such minorities, especially Jews, incorporated discriminatory taxation and the wearing of badges of distinction by various Muslim regimes, and nowadays the equation of Jews with monkeys and pigs has become a staple of the extremists' rhetoric. But the Quran itself sets a standard that is both less categorical and more contextual than citation to the harshest of statements alone might seem to suggest. The Quran frequently refers not to the condemnation of Jews or Christians as a whole but to monks and rabbis, tribes and individuals who either pervert the written word God once gave their followers or who undermine relationships and faith through their own corrupt practices. Here as elsewhere, the focus on the individual initially emphasizes the relationships and origins that describe him, features that are, however, capable of being quickly superseded by individual qualities and actual relationships. While later Muslims have indisputably distorted certain passages of the Quran for their own purposes, it is difficult to see in the Quran a pervasive tone of hostility to other religions. Rather, the tone is largely one of insisting on the primacy of the community of Islam and the treatment of members of other faiths on an individual rather than collective basis.

Yet even if a Westerner is prepared to accept that Muslims must take the Quran literally, how, one may ask, can certain propositions contained in that text be accepted when they seem insupportable in the modern age? How, for example, does one handle the issue of slavery, which the Quran permits but no reasonable Muslim, however devoted to the literal meaning of the Quran, would openly advocate nowadays?[45] Does this not imply some challenge to the idea of the Quran's inerrancy? And how can anyone believe in some of the things the Quran takes as given, such as the existence of a parallel world of unseen genies? Of course, one might argue that every religion shares this problem. At some point, for at least some believers, it becomes difficult, or at least irrelevant, to continue believing something that is supposed to be regarded as literally true. One may doubt whether the burning bush ever existed or whether water was really turned into wine; one may feel ardent attachment to the faith but exclude from one's thoughts the distinct impression that Jonah was swallowed by a fish, that the Buddha remained still in a turning world, or that Shiva actually held the entire universe in his mouth. For Muslims, the question whether there is something in the Quran that even a literalist may find difficult to accept is thus posed by what might be called "the problem of the genies."

The Quran, as the unaltered word of God no believer is comfortable doubting, could not be more explicit on the subject. Not only do genies exist, but their qualities and actions are given concrete explication. The genies (Arabic: male, *jinn;* female, *jinnia;* plural, *jnun*) are mentioned thirty-two times in the Quran.[46] Composed of smokeless fire and invisible to all but the greatest of men, they may be good or evil, Muslim or non-Muslim, prone to be found in places that are wet or polluted, or likely to hover over treasures to frustrate humans who try to get at buried riches. In the Traditions, the Prophet himself is said to have met and overcome the genies, while in popular tales (most famously in the West, *The Arabian Nights*) they may be called upon for curative powers or aid in a special need. Classical scholars have written at length about genies' interactions with men, from their control by King Solomon to the ability of men to transact business with them. Some commentators, such as al-Farabi, tried to avoid discussion of them by playing on ambiguous definitions; others, such as Ibn Khaldun, relegated them to the realm of knowledge that God has reserved to himself. Only a few, such as Ibn Sina, have been bold enough to question their very existence.[47] Whatever their origins in Islamic thought—whether many are pre-Islamic Arabian spirits now relegated to the role of ephemeral genies or are best understood as the textual inclusion of folkloric elements now rendered Islamic—the genies occupy an important place in popular thought and Quranic literalism.[48]

Two places where genies still have currency are in the question of marriage with a genie and criminal responsibility where a genie is involved. Historically, many scholars argued that one could indeed marry a genie, and recent newspaper advice columns have cited instances of the practice as well.[49] Some have argued that it is not possible if the jinn does not appear in human form, others that the result of the union will be no children, while still others account for the pregnancy of a woman not otherwise likely to have been sired by the woman's husband as an act attributable to a jinn. Similarly, criminal cases have been brought in which the defendant claims to have been infested by a jinn who made him commit the crime or that it was not he who caused an injury but the jinn who inhabited the victim. Egyptian courts that have dealt with such matters tend to conclude that while genies certainly exist, they cannot attack a person's soul and hence cannot replace human responsibility for the taking of a life.[50]

From the perspective of modern social science, the attribution of acts to genies and their treatment by local healers or officials suggests that the genies serve an important function in Arab societies. A common denominator in many instances is the sense of being trapped in an uncomfortable social situation. A woman who is feeling pressure from her relatives or her husband may find in the genie a vehicle through which she can escape blame or discomfort. Arab psychiatrists thus commonly find that a patient will respond more to treatment by a native healer for spirit infestation than to modern medication.[51] Jinns are also said to account for the behavior of a person imprisoned by Israeli authorities on the West Bank, the jinnia who has come to entice a man in such circumstances being herself Jewish.[52] In each instance, the relative powerlessness of the individual, in a society in which freedom of movement is so vital to personal identity, is undoubtedly related to explanatory reliance on the actions of the genies.

For some Muslims the problem of the genies is treated much like other issues where the explanation is given in terms of the Quran's insight into something confirmed by modern science. The genies may, for example, be identified as microbes, all but invisible life forms whose capacity to cause illness is confirmed by science.[53] Many other Muslims are bemused by the problem of the genies, and it is a common subject for jokes of all sorts. But amusement may be preferable to doubt, which (as we have seen) is far more dangerously absolute compared with the ambivalent nature of humor. Analogies for proper life actions can still be drawn from stories about the genies, but amusement has not resulted in the development of explicit modes of interpretation or specific mechanisms for setting aside one provision in the Quran while retaining others. Indeed, the retention of the genies, as an outlet for explanations that skirt individual responsibility or direct confrontation at the socially most sensitive points of relationship, continues to serve both a belief in the literal truth of the Quran and proof of its effectiveness in the world of human endeavors. Belief in the genies may be no less rational than many beliefs in the West—where religious exorcism and belief in personal angels is not uncommon—but it has not, or at least not yet, risen to the point of being an opening for questioning certain things mentioned in the Quran without such questioning appearing as a challenge to the inerrant and unchanging word of God the Quran embodies.[54]

Modern Islamic thinkers are faced with an exceptionally difficult problem as they set about creating modes of Quranic interpretation that do not alienate their coreligionists by appearing to attack the text itself. Scholars such as 'Aishah Abd al-Rahman seek the original meaning of Arabic terms within the text of the Quran, while others such as Mohamed Arkoun attempt an openly structuralist account.[55] There are still others who assert that the customs of the Prophet's day (especially the very patriarchal customs) need to be extracted from the Quran so that the immutability of the Quran can be founded entirely on the timeless, context-independent propositions present in the text. At the same time, however, it is important to remember that when the Sudanese modernist Mahmoud Muhammad Taha argued in the 1950s

that the inconsistency of the early Meccan and later Medinan messages calls for human interpretation and that he believed himself authorized to speak for the meaning of this "second message of Islam,"
his views were deemed heretical and he was put to death in 1985.[56]
Similarly, when Nasr Hamid Abu Zayd published a book in Egypt proposing the study of the Quran in its historical and social context—thus
implying, to critics, that he was treating the Quran as a man-made
product—he was condemned as an apostate and, in 1995, his marriage was annulled.[57] It may be highly significant that a number of
those now attempting interpretive approaches to the Quran should be
women—a fact that may, however, itself undermine their arguments
in the eyes of Muslim men.[58] One Western commentator concludes,
"After all that has been accomplished, one threshold of Qur'anically
legitimate exegesis remains to be crossed—a systematically comparative approach to scriptural analysis."[59] But the issues that may exercise
Western students of the Quran are not those that concern many believing Muslims. As Richard Martin has said, "Quranic studies in the
West have often aimed at solving problems Muslims have not recognized as such."[60] Yet even those who find the interpretive approaches of
Western scholars antithetical to Islam admit, as S. Parvez Mansoor has
said, that "sooner or later [we Muslims] will have to approach the Koran
from methodological assumptions and parameters that are radically
at odds with the ones consecrated by tradition."[61] Whether Muslims
worldwide will find a way of addressing the Quran critically without
appearing to challenge its literal veracity will undoubtedly remain as
vexed a problem for the foreseeable future as it has posed for believers
in the past.

———

The Quran is sitting on the shelf. It may even have been placed alongside the other sacred texts. But there it remains—nicely bound, iconic,
unread. Perhaps the next time a passage is quoted in a television show
or commentary one's gaze will settle on it for a moment and a tremor
of guilt will be felt for never having quite gotten around to it. It would
be nice to quote a phrase or two to friends, to have found in it some
greater sense of familiarity—of stories or characters or miraculous
events—some feeling that what Muslims mean by inner struggle or
compassion or mercy really does accord with one's own understanding
of those terms. And then one recalls how many people—well over a
billion—from every segment of the globe (including over six million in

the United States itself) have found the Quran the centerpiece of their religious life. Perhaps it is that ever-resonant expression "If God had willed, he would have made you one nation" that ultimately reminds us of the wisdom that comes from understanding difference. Perhaps, one wistfully concludes, when I have a bit more time, I might try again to read it.

SEVEN

Why Portraits Hold No Meaning for Arabs

I have a confession to make: I just don't believe portraits. What I mean is that when I look at a portrait or photograph or bust of an individual, I do not think I am learning anything that is "true" about that person. I may make up a story about the person's inner state or qualities, his likely reactions or how his personal history is writ on his face or demeanor. I may, of course, learn a great deal about a style of art, the artist's own idea of the person, the way an entire age may have imagined others, or something about my own background and feelings. But there is very little, if anything, I draw from a bare portrait that I would be prepared to call the truth about the individual portrayed. Perhaps I have been put off by that famous experiment in which people describe a series of photographs as depicting ordinary men—all of whom turn out to be Nazi war criminals. Or perhaps just looking at a portrait reminds me of a remark a friend once made about biographies: "I have never read a biography I thought was true," she said, "and I have never read a work of fiction I thought was not." Truth, of course, does not have to be some ultimate, positivistic, laboratory-demonstrable thing. It can reside, in whole or in part, in the eye of the beholder, it can be partial and still insightful, it can be biased and yet revelatory, it can be captured by those with power yet betray countervailing claims. But a portrait, at least to my Western eyes, is supposed to go beyond mere identification, to have *some* truth-bearing quality, some relation to "what is so" about its subject. And yet, despite all the cultural conventions that conduce me to do so, I can never quite bring myself to trust that implicit claim. Like my friend's view of biography, I believe more in our own artifacts than in what they purport to show.

All of which brings me to the Arabs. Westerners are used to hearing that Islam does not permit the representation of human beings and that that is the reason why portraiture did not develop in the Muslim world. It is true that in most places and times, detailed portraits are not common in Islamic (particularly Arabic-speaking) cultures, but in other moments and portions of the Arab world—especially in the medieval period in Iraq, to say nothing of Persia and South Asia—figurative art was extremely common.[1] Indeed, the assumed bar to such portraits is either misleading or simply untrue, notwithstanding the common aversion to representational art in Arab cultures. Text and history must, however, be considered before we can offer an alternative explanation to the general aversion to portraiture in Islam.

The usual claim is that human representation is forbidden by the Quran itself. But that is not strictly accurate, as there is no such straightforward prohibition in sacred text. While the Quran is clear on the issue of idolatry, it is not explicit on the subject of portraits.[2] In the most frequently cited passage supporting a ban on portraiture, it is actually Jesus who says, "I have come to you with a sign from your Lord. I will create for you out of clay as the likeness of a bird; then I will breathe life into it, and it will be a bird, by the leave of God" (3:49). Thus, it was not given to ordinary mortals but only to Jesus, as one of God's chosen prophets, to fashion life—and then only with the permission of God.[3] In the eyes at least of later commentators, the fabrication of any statue or picture of a human being is thus tantamount to a God-like claim to the power of creation itself, the term for a painter (*musawwir*, or "fashioner") being one of the terms in the Quran that refers specifically to God (59:24). Nor is there any unequivocal prohibition attributable to the Prophet himself.[4] There are, of course, varied interpretations of the hadith, the Prophet's acts and utterances as traced through credible witnesses, which, along with the Quran and the *sunna* (the more explicit injunctions of the Prophet), constitute the foundational sources of Islam. Thus, according to one Tradition, when the Prophet triumphantly entered the Ka'ba, the most sacred site in Mecca, he ordered the destruction of all pictures except one of Mary holding the infant Jesus on her lap.[5] In a number of hadith the Prophet is reported to have said that angels will not enter a place where there are pictures; in some he forbids representations on certain items but not others; in another he notes with favor the picture of his future wife Aisha.[6] Indeed, representations of the Prophet himself are to be found from the first two centuries following his death, and though there appears to have been some discouragement of human pictorial representation, even at this early date there were no rules specifically barring portraiture.[7] The existence of so few comments on the question of representation in the years immediately following the Prophet's death is taken by many scholars to suggest that, the question of idols aside, pictures were simply not a major concern of the young religion.[8]

It was not until some years later that commentators on the Quran and hadith began to assert their antipathy to portraiture. The thirteenth-century Shafi'i scholar al-Nawawi, for example, summarized the position of many of his predecessors when he observed, "The great authorities of our school and of the others hold that the painting of an image of any and all animate beings is strictly forbidden and constitutes one of the capital sins."[9] Notwithstanding scholarly opinion, artists found ways around some aspects of this broadly accepted interdiction. Since to many it was the representation of animate life that was forbidden, artists would add embellishments such as wings to human figures to render them "untrue."[10] In one hadith a painter asks the redactor, "But, once and for all, am I not to practice my trade, am I to give up representing animate beings?" To which the reply is given, "Yes, but you can always chop off the animals' heads so they won't look alive, and you can do your best to make them look like flowers."[11] In many instances and periods, stylized faces, when shown, were quite without individuation, while representations of the Prophet either had the face scratched out or veiled.[12] When faces were painted, the representation of emotion was all but absent.[13] Instead, conventional gestures were usually employed to suggest emotions,[14] each period having its idealized forms.[15] In some instances, particularly in the Mughul and Persian miniatures, human figures, including portrayals of the Prophet, appear quite commonly.[16] In some periods and parts of the Arab world, iconic human figures can be seen in either crudely animate postures or very highly developed iconic and allegorical representations that underpin kingly or spiritual status.[17] Thus, as Barry has shown, even Sufi mystics, who must have known they were being portrayed, allowed themselves to be represented in figurative art of the medieval period.[18] The formal aversion to representation, however, has remained strong in some quarters of the Muslim world until very recent times. On a visit to New York in 1955, for example, King Ibn Saud of Saudi Arabia, following on earlier complaints by Islamic nations, persuaded local officials to remove a statue of the Prophet Muhammad from the balustrade of the New York Court of Appeals, where it was among a group of statues of great law-givers of the past.[19] For the most part, contemporary Arabs are willing to accept individual pictures, though not of the Prophet or God.

A distinction thus needs to be made between what may be referred to as figurative art and, for our purposes, portraiture. By the former I mean those iconic representations of humans that are rich in the de-tails of office or spiritual standing and that serve to present the indi-vidual portrayed as a legitimate claimant to the qualities and powers of a given position. These representations do not portray the individual in highly personalistic terms; people of the time would, I strongly sus-pect, be very hard put to identify the individual portrayed from the stylized facial representation alone. Indeed, such identification would appear to be submerged in the context of the symbols of power and piety. By comparison, what I mean by portraiture is the representation of an individual in such a way that physical identity would be immedi-ate and central, whatever else is being presented about status, and that the portrayal is susceptible to being read by those of the culture and period as a vehicle for determining features of personhood, character, and connection that are accessible through that portrayal. So if there is no Quranic or Prophetic prohibition on portraiture, and (the proscrip-tion on statues and pictures of sacred figures aside) if representation of the human figure was frequently honored in the breach, we may have to look elsewhere to explain the relative dearth of individual portrai-ture in Islamic cultures. To do so we may benefit from reading between the lines of the past with the help of the present, and going beyond the realm of art itself to entertain a broader cultural account.

The explanation I would like to offer is quite simple, yet its implica-tions reach into every domain of Muslim life. My argument is that for Arabs the portrait of an individual is all but meaningless. This may sound very strange indeed, since obviously the individual could be rendered in such a way as to be quite recognizable, and even many features of an unknown person—clothing, posture, facial expression, gesture—might be readily understood. But "meaning" is, by definition, about connections. It is about conveying and creating the information that makes a portrayal comprehensible. It is about stitching experience together in a way that has, at least for the moment and for a given set of viewers, the capacity to articulate a sense of the orderliness of their shared world.[20] To a given set of viewers the meaning of a portrait may, therefore, be absent or trivial if it does not convey essential knowledge about the person portrayed—if it does not convey what such viewers take to be "true" about the subject of the picture. Because such pictorial knowledge is not an absolute but is deeply suffused by the distinctive meaning it possesses in different cultures, we cannot understand why a Western-style portrait of an individual might be meaningless to an Arab without also understanding what it is that would make any such person come alive in their minds.

Throughout this book it is suggested that Arab cultures place enormous emphasis on relationships. Endowed with reason by their creator, human beings are expected to maneuver to their own and their dependents' advantage in order to secure themselves in an uncertain world. Indeed, dependencies must themselves be created through ingratiation and reciprocity, personal networking and a constant quest for information and alternative resources. To know a person, then, is to know his or her ties to others. One sees this emphasis in everything from the centrality of the poet as the true fabricator of the terms of relationship to the idea of property, in which an object is seen primarily as the focal point of relationships rather than the demonstration of an individual's connection to a thing.

This emphasis informs the visual arts as well. Two brief anecdotes may help here. Some years ago a group of young men in the Moroccan city where I was working asked me if I would join them at the showing of an American film so that I could explain anything they did not understand. When I asked the name of the film, they told me that it was *West Side Story.* I decided to go along. At first the young men were captivated by the film. Two gangs approached each other. Then one man pulled a knife. Then someone from the other group pulled a knife. And then they both began singing. The Moroccans turned to me in astonishment: What kind of men do you have in America, they asked, who start singing when they should start fighting? My attempt to explain musicals was a complete failure. Films, they insisted, are lifelike, and therefore they must be "true"—they must show things as they are; otherwise they are just "lies." The response of these young men may, to a certain extent, sound in the approach taken toward human representations in the theater by Arab commentators who distinguish between representation and imitation, the former being as forbidden as portraiture while the latter is at least tolerated because it is not "real."[21]

The second anecdote refers to my occasional use of a set of photographs of an individual Arab, unknown to the viewer, that were taken at different moments in the subject's life. After spreading out the pictures on the table, I ask the viewer to tell me about this man. Most Westerners looking over my shoulder would probably begin to arrange the pictures chronologically. But the Arabs do not do that. Instead they begin talking about the different sets of relationships the man in the pictures has, relationships that are described regardless of their order in time. If one asks about chronology, viewers will, of course, account for it. But for these Arabs time does not (as for Westerners) reveal the truth of persons; for them it is contexts of relationship that reveal what a man is really like. Even the acceptance or rejection of modern technology can only be understood against such a background of relational meaning. Cell phones, for example, are immensely popular in the Arab world, in part because they are perfectly adaptable to the omnipresent process of forging and servicing relationships. However, the Saudi ban on cell phones with built-in cameras makes a good deal of cultural sense when one appreciates that it is not simply a matter of banning all images; rather, it is precisely the relationships that can be formed through these images—of young men and women seeing one another and establishing potentially uncontrolled ties—that is so threatening to social order.[22]

From this perspective, no portrait can represent a person in a way that is meaningful for Arabs. But unlike a portrait, stories can paint such a picture, because as individuals are described in a number of contexts the multifarious aspects of their interrelationships become known. Poetry, too, can paint such a picture, because the poet captures the terms of relationship and thus identifies and creates the connections among people that make each of them distinct.[23] Telling about the actions of other sentient beings—animals, Jews, women, genies, saints—can paint such a picture, because the calculus of reason and passion that each category of person uses as a baseline for creating webs of indebtedness reveals their overall character. But a bare portrait—one that is devoid of the relational—conveys no such reality. Humanity is animate, Arabs seem to be saying, and without our gregarious connectedness one is left with little more than a superficial likeness. Early theologians could approve the use of shadow puppets, notwithstanding the prohibition on representations that were animate or cast a shadow, because one could see the holes through which the strings passed and thus not mistake the puppets for living creatures.[24] The Quran itself emphasizes that the animus of a creature, the infusion of breath or life—the operative word *nafs* also implying "soul"—is separate from mere corporeality, and the body is often referred to as a lifeless portrait or figure, as in the words of one Quranic passage: "Then he brought out before them [the people] the portrait [body] of a feeble calf" (Sura 20:88). But as important as animation may be, it is arguable that the crucial factor is whether the representation is true to the relational capability of humankind. Even in pictures of the medieval period where faces are portrayed, the ways in which we see people interacting with others—groups in Paradise, scholars arguing, kings directing, even the Prophet admonishing—exhibit a relation of status rather than of personal interaction. Perhaps what is really irreligious about a portrait or a statue, then, is not that it claims God-like powers to animate, but precisely the opposite—that it dissolves this God-given animation and renders His creation both untrue and an insult to the reality of one's maker. In a religion that stresses the unity of God, one of the gravest sins is that of "associationism" (_shirk_)—confuting the purity of God with any other entity, as, for example, through idolatry. The emphasis on avoiding association thus confirms the centrality of the relational through its opposite, for it is precisely the inapposite relationship, the eradication of mutual obligation, that could so easily threaten to bring about social chaos (fitna).[25]

One might point out that pictures are now very common in the Arab world—pictures of leaders hang in many shops and homes, huge portraits and statues of Saddam Hussein were everywhere in Iraq, and even less egomaniacal heads of state in the Arab world have their pictures on every coin and piece of paper money in the realm. Yet each of these instances is, I would argue, the exception that proves the rule. For these representations are not portraits in the Western sense, nor are they approached in the same way as in the West. Such pictures are entirely iconic. They are not "read" in terms of what they reveal about the character, associations, interior state, or interpersonal possibilities the image might, in other cultural traditions, appear to invite or suggest. Like the profile of a British monarch on a coin or the bas-relief of a Roman emperor on a medallion, these representations convey no sense of interpersonal involvement or assessment.[26] Indeed, when there is disagreement with a leader, the common practice is to (iconically) remove the picture for a time rather than reinterpret it. In all the interviews I have conducted in North Africa about the portraits that hang on the wall of a shop or in the guest room of a home, I have never heard anyone engage in an analysis of the character of the person as stimulated by such a picture.

Except once. And here, the style of discussion was revealing. For a brief moment in the 1980s, the Moroccan currency departed from the usual representation of King Hassan II as an ageless monarch, seen in profile, as if gazing, like all his royal kind, into a future of which he was the supreme architect. In the paper money that appeared in this short interval, something quite unusual for the currency of any country occurred. The King was now portrayed looking the viewer straight in the eye. No longer the young man of earlier representations, his face was now a mass of lines and furrows, a forger's nightmare, his look the one of direct engagement Western travelers have often noted among the Arabs—an intense stare that is usually interpreted as a capacity to see if you are telling them the truth. People commented on the look, the wrinkles, the aging. What they did not do was employ the portrait as a vehicle for commenting on the king's character or inner thoughts— something they were not reluctant to do in other contexts. Indeed, the only comment I heard about the king's look was extremely negative and salacious, for if (as many people showed me) you folded the bill a certain way some of the writing, instead of indicating the bill's value, could be made to read, "he shits on you." Just as pictures of the king would disappear from shops when people were not particularly pleased with his policies—as, for example, when he made everyone "voluntarily" support the construction of the world's third largest mosque in Casablanca—and just as some public rallies were not really what they appeared to be about but were displaced protests—as when the march against U.S. involvement in the first Gulf war was as much a lightly veiled protest against the king's domestic policies—so the representations of leaders are interpreted not as symbols of relationship but as signs of power.

Art thus becomes a different kind of cultural form than it is commonly imagined to be in the West. Art in the Arab world is not an immediate point of entry to the truth of a person, a surface manifestation of an essential inner truth. Nor is it a vehicle for self-reflection, a mirror into an inner morality that can be separated from actions, roles, and utterances. Rather, art fulfills its capability when it provides a framework within which the choices of the individual can become manifest. Thus, calligraphy and the arabesque are the classic instruments of artistic revelation. Hedged by divine admonition, they are at once convoluted and organized, both a template for the creation of interconnections and proof that such juxtapositions are not without deeper order.[27] A portrait cannot physically create the possibilities the inscribed word or arabesque can offer; it cannot become something to model oneself after, lacking as it does the very essence of any such model, namely the ways in which the individual's animated choices are configured. Nor, from the Arabs' perspective, could an abstract representation of one's relationship capture the process through which associations are formed over time. But the arabesque can. Like prayer it incorporates repetition, where repetition is itself seen not as mere iteration but as a demonstration of the God-given ability to choose at every juncture. The recent discovery by Western scientists that Arab mathematicians grasped the nonrepeating nature of seemingly repetitious Islamic decorations and fashioned their patterns according to this highly sophisticated formula should, therefore, come as no surprise if one considers the cultural meanings attributed to these forms. It may have been the cultural idea that prompted the quest for a geometric rule capable of rendering this process visible, or it may have been that once they came upon a design that "felt right" the artists and mathematicians sought to grasp the underlying rule. Either way, we may, in this instance, have one more example of how a cultural style was rendered compatible with a highly complex demonstration of the quasi-crystalline structure through which it could be artistically represented. Like architecture, mathematics, or prosody, the arabesque demonstrates the overall framework of processes that make possible, but do not predetermine, the ways one may add on to existing structures without the constraint of prior design.[28] And like the conventions of etiquette, conversation, and storytelling, the arabesque (unlike the portrait) creates the world of relationships through speech-like forms arrayed, for the most part, on the interior of a public space, monuments to the ability of an individual to realize, if only for a moment, the figures of our speech as constitutive of our very humanity. No static picture, Arabs believe, can ever achieve this goal.

Many of these points are brought home with great force in Orhan Pamuk's novel *My Name Is Red*.[29] In the story, an Ottoman sultan, captivated by the art of the West, commissions several of his artists to prepare an illuminated manuscript celebrating his glories through the use of portraits drawn in the Western style. Believing that such portraits are both an affront to Islam and the miniaturists' art, one of the illuminators begins killing those who are cooperating in the enterprise. Western art, he believes, wrongly assumes that every man or beast should be "an imitation of one another," when in fact all representations should be similar, without individual style, and that "imperfection is the mother of style." To pursue such individualistic representations means that "everyone will consider it a special talent to tell other men's stories as if they were one's own." To the contrary, the novel's murderer, like other preservers of the Islamic artistic tradition, believes that it is only right for the true masters of Islamic art "to depict the world the way God saw it, and [that is why] to conceal their individuality they never signed their names." In European portraits, by contrast, "men are worshipping themselves, placing themselves at the center of the world." The "Frankish infidel," notes one of the miniaturists as he experiments with having his own portrait painted by a Western artist, "was committing the error of looking at the world with his naked eye and rendering what he saw," thus painting the sultan the same size as a dog or Satan, instead of depicting objects "according to their importance in Allah's mind." Even Satan is heard wondering aloud at the Westerners' hubris:

Is man important enough to warrant being drawn in every detail, including his shadow? If the houses on a street were rendered according to man's false perception that they gradually diminish in size as they recede into the distance, wouldn't man then effectively be usurping Allah's place at the center of the world?

Urging that such portraits are not of his doing, Satan concludes that the European artists "are not satisfied. Don't laugh. It's not the content, but the form of thought that counts. It's not what a miniaturist paints, but his style." Indeed, the contrast in styles calls the order of the world into question. "Let's say we were to turn down a street: In a Frankish painting, this would result in our stepping outside both the frame and the painting; in a painting made following the example of the great masters of Herat, it brings us to a place from which Allah looks upon us; in a Chinese painting, we'd be trapped, because Chinese illustrations are infinite."

Although its context is the Turkish Islam of the Ottoman period, Pamuk's book captures a number of Muslim, particularly Arab, ideas about the extent to which one can interpret from external appearance the character or intent of another. It is a common feature of Islamic morality, for example, that one should not speculate on the unseen, especially since it might affect another's reputation. Thus, among some schools of Islamic law, if a man is thought to have a bottle of liquor under his cloak, but it cannot be seen, one must not, upon pain of prosecution for slander, claim he is harboring the forbidden substance. Fiction, too, cannot reveal some deeper truth about how a person relates to others. As one writer suggests, fiction may be dangerous, as it was in medieval Europe, not for its lack of correlation with reality but because it is not an accurate account of how relationships are actually formed when men speak and interact with one another.[30] Nor should the wise person indulge in speculation that cannot be validated by reliable persons. Only people who have built interpersonal networks themselves can be relied upon to assess another's worldly consequent acts. Even poetry, like religious argument and political leadership, depends on the poet's ability to marshal supporters who, by the relationships they form with reference to his terms, substantiate his assertions. But portraits lack all these elements of independent corroboration. They cannot be self-authenticating precisely because the process of forming interpersonal ties is incapable of static representation; no one reads into such pictures the background assumptions of dynamic relationship that are conceived as integral to the more consequential act of storytelling, poetry, or cinematic representation.

Portraiture contradicts the culturally emphasized modes of telling the story of another in several key respects. Franz Rosenthal has said that for the Arabs history is biography, yet the form and content of these biographies is obviously not identical to those of the contemporary West.[31] As we have seen, since time does not reveal the truth of persons, it is not chronological unfolding that is key to understanding another. Instead, it is the range of their relationships. Thus, physiognomy was used in some Muslim courts not to assess character or motivation but to determine the place a man actually came from and hence the associations and modes of relationship that identify him.[32] Commonly, rather little was said about a person's physical appearance. Some writers have suggested that the reader was expected to imagine how someone looked; others employed standard metaphors (e.g., likeness to a rose or gazelle) to convey a generalized image.[33] To this day, it is rare for an Arab to concentrate on a physical description of a person since people are not revealed through a pictorial narrative.[34] Speaking of the early Islamic period, Allen says that "an aniconic [i.e., antirepresentational] religion left no central cultural story to be told by visual narrative."[35] Without showing how people build relationships, even a caption could not convey the information an Arab viewer might seek in such a representation.[36]

It was Erich Gombrich who argued that the viewer does not so much read *out* of a picture as read *into* it. The viewer brings, often as an entire gestalt, an understanding of what sense may be found in a picture, and may then confirm, revise, or reject that view accordingly.[37] If there was a time when Westerners believed that we could gain insight into another's soul through that person's face, and if that sensibility has been undercut by modern psychology and postmodern contextualism alike, then we may have grown more skeptical about what we can judge about another's character from a portrait alone. We may now think that the small gestures captured by fast film or the body language conveyed by a moving picture still reveal the inner person to us. Or we may have become so uncertain about representations (cannot even a bad man appear beautiful? cannot an evil man appear beneficent?) that we no longer bring much in the way of common evaluation to a picture. Or have we, for all our emphasis on reality as appearance, come to think of people more as the Arabs do, in terms of their acts rather than their faces?[38] However we interpret the course of Western portraiture as a vehicle for accessing another's fundamental being, only through an understanding of how technology, religion, social movements, and personal identity interact can we grasp the meanings that are brought to the portraits of our own or another age.

What is true for the West is no less true for the Arabs, hence one must start from their perspective to grasp what they expect to see in a portrait. Sacred text and its subsequent interpretations are only part of the story. For even the word of God, like the pictures fashioned by men, is comprehensible only against a backdrop of assumptions about human nature and human society. The human image is as much a text as any written account, a screen upon which one can work a vision of one's world. If it is accurate to suggest that, speaking always in terms of themes and variations, for Arabs the preeminent focus that unites both religious precept and social insight is the unavoidably relational quality of the world of sentient beings, then it is reasonable to suggest that this is precisely the orientation brought to the visual arts. A portrait that is, from their perspective, unable to engage the viewer in this most central of processes is, by definition, without serious import, and one does not need a formal prohibition to bar that which carries very little meaning in the world as Arabs may understand it.

EIGHT

Protecting the Prophet: Understanding Muslim Reactions to the Danish Cartoon Controversy

In 2005, a Danish newspaper's publication of twelve cartoons, most of them explicitly portraying the Prophet Muhammad, sparked very strong, often violent reactions by Muslims around the world. Much has been written, in the light of this controversy, about the conflict between freedom of the press and deference to religious sensibilities, Muslim grievances and Western inconsistencies. But the broader meaning that Muslims have brought to these portrayals has often remained poorly understood. Like the controversy over Salman Rushdie's book *The Satanic Verses*, the pictures did not merely trigger a response of cultural pride or defense of a revered figure. They also highlighted the meaning of the Prophet Muhammad himself—indeed the role of prophets in Islam more generally—and the unspoken assumptions about the relation of individual believers to this central religious figure. Moreover, these events underscore the ways in which intention is ascribed to those who make potentially blasphemous utterances or otherwise portray others, particularly sacred figures, in what are perceived to be socially harmful ways. Without grasping this larger context, much of the reaction may itself be reduced to cartoon-like proportions, an example of seemingly unreflective violence conducted by cardboard automata and Western stick figures acknowledging some forms of humor or irony while bridling at others.

Several points will be central to our analysis. First, I want to suggest that, given the place of prophets in the early development of Islam, Muhammad was transformed from the role of a prophet *simpliciter* to that of a master, a role that to this day resonates very deeply in Islamic, especially Arab, cultures, and that this has an important effect when it is he who is the subject of the questionable representation. Second, given their emphasis on developing bonds of association to stave off social chaos, many Muslims depend on the evaluations of others for their own sense of identity and worth. These evaluations have a profound effect on the ways in which the Prophet is conceived and defended. And finally, the attribution of motives and intentions to those who purvey such graven images or slanderous statements reflects the ways in which such attributions are made in Arabic-speaking cultures generally. Before exploring these themes, however, it may be useful to review the Islamic approach to the portrayal of the Prophet, the approach to potentially slanderous or blasphemous utterances, and how these factors relate to the idea of the prophets and those who speak ill of them.

Although the Quran clearly bars idols, it does not explicitly bar other forms of figurative representation.[1] As we have seen, the passage usually cited as forbidding pictures is actually one in which Jesus creates the figure of a bird that could be infused with life only if God were to permit it (Sura 3:49). On Judgment Day, say the Traditions (hadith), the artist will be found powerless when called upon to bring his representation to life and will be condemned accordingly. It would be tantamount to blasphemy in Islam to claim for an artist, as Oscar Wilde did for Holbein, that "he created life, he did not copy it."[2] The prohibition on drawing humans derives from later scholastic opinion, including the interpretation of the above passage as limiting representations altogether. But the Prophet's own practices were much more ambiguous. After his death Muslims collected reports of what the Prophet said and did during his lifetime, reports that eventually numbered more than seven hundred thousand. These were reduced and redacted into authoritative collections that are somewhat contradictory on the subject of human representation. In some accounts the Prophet says that angels will not enter a dwelling where pictures are present. In others he forbids images on curtains (perhaps because their movement might suggest the artist was trying to make them seem alive) while permitting them on pillows. In another tradition the Prophet is shown a picture of Aisha (his future wife, then only nine years old) and expresses approval of her appearance. In perhaps the most famous tradition the Prophet, upon entering the sacred Ka'ba in Mecca for the first time, is said to have placed his hand over the portrayal of Jesus and Mary and forbade its destruction while permitting the eradication of all the other, pantheistic representations. Chronicles indicate that pictures of the Prophet were not unknown in the early years of Islam, even on prayer rugs. But in the first centuries after his death rulers and scholars began to forbid all pictures. Nevertheless, over the centuries, monarchs not infrequently had illuminated books prepared in which the Prophet was clearly portrayed.[3] In other instances, the Prophet's face was obscured by a veil or the facial features of an earlier painting were scratched out. In some pictures stylized animals or plants stand in for various human beings, while in others "[s]ome of the humans have a distinct line drawn over their necks, symbolically defying them to come to life and thereby demonstrating the artist's denial of his intent to compete with God in creating life."[4] Among the Shiites of contemporary Iran, an alluring picture of the Prophet as a teenage boy, a flower behind his ear and his garment dropping off one shoulder, is readily available in the marketplace.[5] Thus, the history of representations of the Prophet and other human figures is by no means one of undeviating prohibition.

Notwithstanding the absence of unambiguous grounding in sacred text, the prohibition on representations of Muhammad has long been the standard in Muslim countries.[6] For the vast majority of believing Muslims, the prohibition is nearly as certain as if it were clearly set forth in the Quran. However, to understand the sense of injury experienced by Muslims, one must also briefly recall the specific nature of both the Danish cartoons and the Rushdie affair, against which Muslims have reacted with equal vigor.[7]

The Danish Controversy

The trouble began when Danish writer Kåre Bluitgen, unable to find anyone willing to illustrate a children's book about the Prophet, challenged artists to "draw the Prophet as they saw him." The cartoons were published in the widely circulated newspaper *Jyllands-Posten* on September 30, 2005, but controversy did not ensue until several months later, when the Copenhagen imam Ahmad Abu Laban distributed the cartoons in the Muslim world—along with several that were not among those published by the Danish newspaper. These latter cartoons portrayed the Prophet in bestial and sexual ways the newspaper cartoons never did.[8] The original twelve cartoons were later reproduced in a number of publications in various parts of the world. Protests then began in several Muslim countries, ultimately resulting in the deaths of more than a hundred people.[9] Very few American publications carried any of the cartoons.[10] Citing other instances in which various European writers and cultural institutions had rescinded representations of Islam in the face of Muslim protest, Flemming Rose, the culture editor of the Danish newspaper who commissioned the cartoons, wrote, "Of course, we didn't expect this kind of reaction, but I am sorry if some Muslims feel insulted. This was not directed at Muslims. I wanted to put this issue of self-censorship on the agenda and have a debate about it."[11] The Muslim writer Ziauddin Sardar analogized the cartoons to those portraying Jews in Europe in the interwar years. Few, however, noted the many Muslim cartoons representing Jews as Satanic.[12] In response to the Danish cartoons the Iranians staged an anti-Jewish cartoon contest largely inspired by the comments of Iranian President Mahmoud Ahmadinejad's denial of the Holocaust.[13] When the exhibit of 204 such cartoons went on display in Tehran in late August 2006, the cosponsor of the display, the Iranian newspaper *Hamshahri*, said it wanted to test the West's tolerance for drawings about the Nazi murder of six million Jews. One cartoon, for example, showed the Statue of Liberty holding a book about the Holocaust in one hand and making a Nazi salute with the other.[14] The Danish situation, of course, was not without its local political context, which has been described by one reporter thusly:

Denmark's November 2001 election was a watershed moment. A Willie Horton–style advertising campaign criticizing the lenient sentence handed to second-generation Palestinians convicted of rape galvanized right-wing support for the center-right Liberal Party's anti-immigration platform. When the Liberals' Anders Fogh Rasmussen became prime minister, his minority governing coalition's greatest ally became the nationalist Danish People's Party, whose leader Pia Kjaersgaard has at various times called asylum seekers untrained illiterates and posited that the accumulation of Muslims leads to mass rapes. Together, Rasmussen's minority government and the Danish People's Party possess an absolute majority in Parliament. Soon after the election, they passed Europe's most restrictive anti-immigration laws to date. Four years of this governing coalition had a dampening effect on integrating Muslims in Denmark, and went a long way toward increasing racial tensions there.[15]

The cartoon most frequently described is one in which the Prophet's turban is in the shape of a bomb with a lit fuse. What almost no one has noted, however, is that emblazoned on this turban-bomb is the Arabic profession of faith, the statement that there is only one God and Muhammad is his messenger. Whether one sees this as the cartoonist's attempt to suggest that it is the faith itself that is being blown up or that Islam is an inherently violent religion, the fact that hardly any Western reporters recognized what every Muslim would most immediately notice is remarkable. Indeed, like all the cartoons, the artist placed a label "Muhammad" on the image; otherwise there would be no way to know that this was offered as an image of the Prophet rather than some generic Muslim. Another cartoon presents the Prophet as a dopey character with a toothy grin in a police-like lineup while another individual, perhaps the cartoonist, is trying to figure out which one of the half-dozen figures is actually the Prophet. Among others in the lineup, as perhaps only Danes would have been quick to recognize, are the head of the right-wing nationalist party, Pia Kjaersgaard; a sixties peacenik; and a figure of Christ. In this image the Prophet is also holding a tablet or slate on which are written words that appear to be from a Scandinavian language but are very garbled, itself either a takeoff on the claimed legitimacy of the Quran as having been transmitted through an illiterate Prophet who could not have altered the word of God if he had wanted to or as a further suggestion that the Prophet is like an ignorant immigrant who does not even understand the local language.

A second cartoon would appear to portray the cartoonist (but possibly the Prophet, the placement of the name being rather ambiguous) wearing a turban with an orange in it and holding a drawing of a stick figure who has a turban and a beard. Written on the orange lodged in the main figure's turban are the words "PR stunt." Local readers of the paper, including Muslim immigrants, would no doubt have associated the image with the Danish idiom "orange in the turban," which implies a stroke of good luck. Another cartoon shows recent suicide bombers, still emitting smoke, being told on their arrival that heaven is all out of virgins. Once again, the cartoon drives home the unobvious point by placing the Prophet's name in the corner lest the heavenly greeter be mistaken for someone else. A third cartoon does not show the Prophet but includes a crescent and six-pointed star with an overarching hood-like shape and the words "Prophet! Daft and dumb, keeping woman under thumb."[16] Several more cartoons show the Prophet either with a scowl on his face as he wanders the desert with a donkey, or with something over his head that could be horns, a halo, or a crescent moon. In a fourth cartoon the artist is hunched over his drawing board, fearfully hiding his portrayal of the Prophet. But the only observer of this act is a picture on the wall that my Danish colleagues say resembles the country's prime minister, thus perhaps suggesting that it is really only the Danish government, with its overly accommodationist policy, that is discouraging such portrayals.

Many Muslims, of course, were greatly offended by these cartoons. It took several months following their initial publication in Denmark before reactions set in—reactions that were, in part, manipulated by autocratic governments that were less than eager for the process of democratization to spread to their countries and who, for more duplicitous reasons than many of their own citizens possessed, were willing to allow democracy to be equated with licentiousness. Throughout, the expressed core of Muslim anger was directed toward the insult the cartoons were said to constitute to the Prophet Muhammad himself. The most common explanation for this sense of outrage was that such representations are simply prohibited or that the particular portrayals were defamatory. Each of these assertions, in turn, had its rationale. Textual authority aside, two explanations are commonly given for the ban on picturing the Prophet: that such pictures could lead to the treatment of the Prophet as an idol, in direct contravention of Quranic proscriptions against idolatry; and that since there are no accurate pictures of him, any depiction of the Prophet would necessarily be a lie. Moreover, for such pictures to deliberately ridicule the Prophet is to engage in the most blatant form of expressing disbelief in the revelations of the Quran and could therefore undermine the cohesion of the community of believers who have accepted his message. These are the same claims made against other representations of the Prophet that have caused great outrage.

The publication of Salman Rushdie's *The Satanic Verses* had earlier created a similar reaction. Drawing on the texts that indicate the Prophet was, for a short time, willing to allow several pagan gods to be part of an Islamic order, only to recant and designate those verses as temptations of the devil, Rushdie's book was also initially ignored until the Iranians and disaffected Muslims living in Britain used it as a basis for attacking anti-Muslim hypocrisy. As in other instances, Muslims rushed to the defense of the Prophet because Rushdie not only suggested that the Quran was not the exact and unaltered word of God but something that had been created or changed by the hand of man. Moreover, Muslims were deeply upset by the author's reference to a group of prostitutes who bore the names of the Prophet's wives. Muslims based their defense on several grounds: that the Prophet, though human, is a sacrosanct figure; that Britain's law protecting only slurs to Christianity was a highly discriminatory statute; and that unless Muslims stand up for the faith—even to the extent of issuing a fatwa calling for the author's death—Islam will not be true to its messenger or to the needs of the community of believers.

Yet as strongly as each of the defenses raised in the Danish cartoon and Rushdie affairs may be asserted, none quite gets at the question why the Prophet needs such vigorous and absolute defense; indeed, none quite gets at the deeper question of the meaning of the Prophet to the believer, such that any depiction, demeaning or not, should precipitate such concern. To understand the reaction, therefore, we must first consider what role prophets play in Islamic thought and what role Muhammad in particular plays in the cultural imagination of contemporary Muslim communities.

Defending the Prophet

We commonly think of Muhammad as a prophet without further asking what that means in the Muslim context. Approached from the perspective of the Old and New Testaments, Westerners may assume the issue of prophecy is not terribly problematic. Prophets, sent by God, appear from time to time to correct the believers who, individually and collectively, have strayed from the true path. Thus, a long line of prophets can be noted—from Amos and Hosea to Isaiah and Micah—each of whom arrived at a moment when the faithful needed a reminder of correct moral action. But if there was a long tradition of prophets in Judaism—though none had appeared for many centuries prior to the Prophet's time—and a partial continuation of that line into Christianity (at least among Jewish, though not pagan, converts), there was little such tradition within the pre-Islamic community of Arabia. There, the prevailing religious sensibility was both eclectic and pantheistic. Abraham and many other gods were selectively and often multiply worshipped, the Ka'ba in Mecca itself having become a central shrine for many such deities, one of whom, Allah, was widely regarded as the *primus inter pares*. What was poorly developed was any independent line of Arab prophets or elaborate tradition of their role. The Quran, it is true, does mention five "Arab" prophets (Hud, Salih, Shu'ayb, Ibrahim, Muhammad) and indicates that when the message brought by the first three was rejected, the groups addressed were destroyed by God. And while a pilgrimage site exists in the Hadramaut for Hud, knowledge of the first three of these Arab prophets and how they were recognized is all but forgotten.[17] When Muhammad announced himself as a prophet and eventually converted those who fled with him to Medina and those who returned with him to Mecca, he became in a very real sense the first, as well as the last, in the line of distinctively Arab prophets. This made Muhammad's status at once unique and somewhat problematic.

The problem lay in knowing how to regard one as a prophet when, within the new faith, there was, for all intents and purposes, but a singular example. Of course, in one sense the "problem" was readily resolved: Muhammad had come with a message from God—a message that summarized and replaced the Bible and the Gospels, which, Muslims have always maintained, had been distorted by their original recipients. In that sense he was a clearly recognizable and unproblematic prophet.[18] Unlike earlier prophets and Christ himself, Muhammad did not prove his legitimacy by miracles. Rather, as the Quran repeatedly states, it is the message itself—which no human being could have created—that is the sign and proof of its own veracity. But since there was no tradition of distinctively Arab prophets, it was less clear what role a prophet should play in the context of Arab tribal society. Hebrew prophets were not themselves rulers; they were the scolds of rulers. They were not generally the alternatives to rulers; they were the figures who recentered rulers and ruled alike. But Muhammad did not have a preexisting tradition of distinctively Arab prophets into which he could simply be amalgamated. Instead, he began to cumulate a number of more familiar roles. Indeed, much of his legitimacy came from this process of combining roles that had previously been kept distinct in Arab society. Thus, he took on three roles in addition to that of a prophet: the role of a tribal head (*sheikh*), the role of a war chief (*qāʾid*), and the role of an arbiter (*ḥakem*).

The sheikh was the head of a group of variable size and constitution, but one that had a core of kinsmen and their dependents who could claim some real or asserted basis of common descent. War chiefs were usually chosen by a congeries of tribes and their clients as the temporary commanders of a united force facing an outside threat. The arbiter, by comparison, could intervene among contending factions to bring his personal and/or spiritual powers to bear on the (at least temporary) resolution of disputes that might threaten the ability of tribal groups to affiliate with one another in the face of needed unity.[19] That Muhammad was able to combine within himself these diverse positions not only multiplied the power of each exponentially; it also constituted proof, in the context of Arab culture, that he was a unique and legitimate prophetic figure, just as the distancing or incomplete leadership of Hebrew prophets was part of that culture's way of demonstrating divine direction.

Despite the cumulation of these multiple roles during his lifetime, simply categorizing Muhammad as a prophet after his death may not have accorded sufficiently with existing Arab sociopolitical categories and thus may not have rendered him in a way that people could readily comprehend. For Muhammad was, whatever else was true of him, regarded as decidedly human: flawed and forgetful, occasionally weak and susceptible to deception (think, for example, of his initial acceptance of the Quranic passages, usually referred to as the Satanic Verses, and his brief inclusion of several idols as part of a Muslim pantheon), he had to retain his humanity in the memory of his followers every bit as much as his message had to remain indubitable. Hebrew prophets were often deeply flawed men, and the Prophet, as we have noted, was not without failings. But he was not regarded as fundamentally flawed. Indeed, most Muslims believe that God created Muhammad before He created mankind and that God held him up from the outset as the archetypal human being. But exactly what role could Muhammad occupy that would, along with his more distancing prophethood and three-pronged political role, render him truly familiar to the Arabs after his death? One thing they could (and did) try was to increase his moral and religious guidance through the elaborate collection and eventual redaction of his reported sayings and actions (the hadith and sunna). Another was to institutionalize his qualifications in the position of caliph even though Muhammad had designated no successor. But neither of these proved independently effective. Where personalism was of the essence of leadership and the routinization of personal ties was all but impossible, where the tribal ethos was one that spread power out and away from permanent incorporation in a given line of descent and even a paramount chief could not expect to pass his network along to his successor, some way of conceptualizing this no-longer-present presence had to be found that made cultural sense. Fortunately, there was one other category available to which the successor community could turn: the category of the master.

The second most frequently used word in the Quran—after the name of God—is the word that translates as "knowledge" ('ilm). To Arabs, knowledge in any form is highly prized. Knowledge of sacred text is, of course, enormously respected, but any individual who possesses knowledge—whether of a craft or of custom—may be called by a term that means "master" (mu'allim). A master can be emulated and loved as a man, not revered as a god, and the wise individual will attach himself to such a master to increase his own knowledge and contacts. Muhammad fit this category perfectly for the Arabs. They could see in his acts and utterances how they should conduct themselves, and they could seek to emulate and protect him as a means of articulating their own adherence to his guidance. No less important, they could strive to become masters in their own right without several factors that would otherwise apply to the master–disciple relation, namely the need to separate from the master in order to become one independently and the deep ambivalence that accompanies all power relations in Arab society.[20] By virtue of his status as a prophet, Muhammad, seen as a master, becomes immunized from these two features of the master–disciple relation: he becomes the ritual reversal of the pattern and thus a confirmation of the process of emerging as a master in one's own right in all other domains. To see how this might operate, we should consider the master–disciple pattern more fully.

The relationship to a master presently shows itself in a number of different but clearly related domains. For example, when a man seeks to move out of his father's house, there is often great tension. It is vital that he do so if he is to ingratiate and form alliances in his own right, but the very fact of separation may weaken the father and raises potential concerns about family solidarity. Since the relationship to one's father, which moves from enormous indulgence in childhood to greater formality in adolescence, is often fraught with ambivalent emotions, the successful separation is both a challenge to the father and a necessary test of the son's ability to replicate society by forging alliances as any adult man should. In the context of religion, particularly where Sufi orders are involved, the master–disciple pattern is central to the replication of the religious system. In Arab society generally, one must take on the qualities of knowledge in order to be recognized as knowledgeable, but as opposed to, say, straightforward inheritance, that process can occur only at some cost to the certainty of the outcome. In both the father–son and religious master–disciple contexts, as well as others (e.g., where the apprentice interacts with the master craftsman, where the client interacts with the patron), the ambivalence to power present in all relationships constitutes part of the freedom necessary for social maneuvering and part of the countervailing threat to social stability. What is to be preserved, however, is the testing of the ability to forge such links. Thus, it is the process of alliance formation that is crucial, and all the countervailing forces that are at work when this applies to other persons are, as we shall see, ritually reversed and thus reinforced when it is the Prophet who is the master.

The disciple is in an ambiguous position: he must preserve the pattern even as he may have to challenge a master. Since Arab societies are not constituted at all points by a limited array of master positions, what is at work is not necessarily a zero-sum game. Indeed, there are incentives to protect the master and not simply challenge him, incentives that include the continuing utility of his support and asserting one's status as his former dependent. Therefore, there may be as much defense of the master as striving for recognition in one's own right. The master may be the archetype of model behavior, but his own career line will seldom have embodied the only possible way to advance. Where one man might build on the basis of kinship, another might effect social debts through action as a go-between; where one man might rise through strategic economic transactions, another might secure himself by choosing the right people to depend on. What matters in all these situations is that the process of building dependencies remain intact and the ambivalence toward the master be structurally contained.

A second factor of overall importance to Arab social structure and the place of the Prophet within it concerns the importance of others' opinions. In a system that prizes personally fabricated and maintained social linkages rather than inherited position or a strict hierarchy of power, where the self cannot be fractionated into a series of contradictory roles and contexts are more decisive than innate tendencies, one's identity and self-regard are deeply dependent on the opinion of others. In many legal proceedings, in order to be considered a reliable witness one must present others who regard one as such; to be a tribal leader one commonly had not only to win the approval of one's fellow tribesmen but to be regarded by one's enemies as a person of consequence, as one who "has word." The power of weakness even plays a role here, for the client can choose among possible patrons, and women, the archetypically "weak," can exert power through their sexuality, their magical potential, their influence over their sons and daughters-in-law, and their role as the holders of men's good opinions of themselves.[21] To cast up the Prophet as one you love and who will be your go-between in the advancement to Paradise is to reinforce a needed acknowledgment not unlike those cast up in the world of everyday social relations. The regard for and of the Prophet is the heightened version of the ordinary and thus both a confirmation and an exceptional instance of it.

Historically, the Prophet was also an intensely practical, this-worldly figure. He legitimized the need and methods for building a community of believers by constructing a nested set of individually negotiated associations, thereby reinforcing that model for others. In the hadith, as in the spirit of the Quran, Muhammad commends to his followers a set of expectations that could be thought of as an Islamic equivalent of the Ten Commandments.[22] The list, however, might look rather strange to those starting from the perspective of the version(s) found in the Hebrew Bible. Certain commandments are absent altogether. There is no prohibition on killing and stealing, for example, but not because Arabs did not take such actions seriously. Tribal life was constructed such that killing and raiding were not unexpected. The emphasis, however, was on the ways of limiting their adverse effects on the social order.[23] Thus, if one were to extract a somewhat sociological version of Islamic commandments, they might go something like this: (1) retribution must be limited, violence being measured and proportionate; (2) men should be evaluated equally in computing blood money; and (3) disparity among men (especially as it relates to wealth) should be tempered (e.g., through a regular charity tax; Sura 2:177). The Muslim commandments would add these propositions: (4) do not engage in backbiting, and (5) do not become one of the hypocrites. These last two practices, which are frequently mentioned in the Quran, are so vital because each can cause inordinate disunity within the community. When Dante, who may well have borrowed his vision of the circles of heaven and hell from Islamic sources, places the hypocrites in the next to lowest circle of hell, he is, like the Muslims who fear such false supporters of the faith, acknowledging the enormous dissension such people can cause. Backbiters, too, divide people, undermine trust, and clear the way for social disorder.[24] In addition, the Quran instructs believers to (6) honor their contracts, (7) refrain from unjust enrichment (riba; Sura 2:275), (8) keep their oaths, (9) stay within the "bounds of God" (while remaining free to arrange relationships within those bounds), and (10) refrain from expressing any doubt whatsoever of the fundamental tenets of the faith. Indeed, the common denominator in this hypothetical set of Islamic ten commandments would be the fear of fitna, the social discord that could rend the community. Limited killing and stealing do not do this—conflict may even, as social scientists have often argued, hold a society together. It is the practices that are seen as potentially undermining the *process* of alliance building, and hence the building of social order, that deserve the highest sanction.

The Prophet led the way in this social and moral scheme. And one follows him not just because he appears as a prophet but because he proves the validity of his vision by his earthly, human endeavors—

whether as a three-pronged sheikh/qaid/hakem or as a master. Yet, as we have seen, this particular master cannot be subject to the same ambivalence that role normally entails. Hence he above all others must be treated as a master toward whom no ambivalence is felt—a difficult task given the very nature of the category itself. To divert this ambivalence without raising the Prophet to god-like status thus calls for the strongest possible protectiveness: one must constantly demonstrate that no ambiguity is felt toward him. This can be done in several ways. Arabs frequently say of the Prophet, "I absolutely love this man." This is not the love that Christians express toward Christ, for there is no question of any divinity where Muhammad is concerned. Nor is it the love of God that Judaism sometimes expresses, a combination of awe and filial attachment; the Quran never uses fictive kin-terms for the relation of men to God. Rather what is being expressed is an intense emotionalism combined with an equally significant ambivalence—an ambivalence one can tolerate toward other masters, even toward a father, but that could endanger the community as a whole if allowed to be felt, much less become overt, in the case of attachment to the Prophet. So Muslims must demonstrate their lack of ambivalence by protecting Muhammad from representations that would necessarily involve multiple interpretations, and hence the potential for disagreement over his true qualities; they must express his uniqueness by not expressing any doubt or uncertainty. It is a relationship that touches deep psychological and emotional chords for Muslims, for what makes the Prophet a man and a master must be denied at the same time that the master–disciple relationship, with all its ambivalence, is being reconfirmed by his amalgamation into this status.

The ardor of some men to protect the Prophet is further intensified by the increased restrictions on their own abilities to escape the role of disciple in their ordinary social lives. With unemployment high in Arab countries, with a college degree more likely to result in status inconsistency than socioeconomic advancement, with men's age of marriage climbing well into the late twenties, and with young men bridling at the dependency on their families, the entire pattern of availing oneself of multiple ways to build up a network of attachments and hence an adult identity has been seriously strained. Islam is not a religion with numerous rituals that mark transition from one stage of life to another, nor is the Arab variant of the social structures connected to it one in which a young man can assert himself except by his own accomplishments as a social actor. For Arabs the social environment is one in which "an impulse to self-protection" and the claim that people need to be protected "from the rudderless world" are exacerbated by restrictions on the freedom of social movement. The quest for a figure toward whom one can demonstrate the engagement and protectiveness of a patron–client relationship thus becomes a vital means of showing involvement in the world of affairs that the Prophet validated.[25] Attachment to a fundamentalist leader often becomes the only remaining way to demonstrate incorporation in some sort of network, one that can be displayed in public protest, one that can be reinforced by protection of the ultimate master, Muhammad.

None of this is inconsistent with the display of pictures of other religious leaders. In many of the demonstrations protesting the Danish cartoons, as in most political rallies, it is common to see marchers carrying pictures of the ayatollahs Sistani or Khomeini, or of such secular figures as the late Yasser Arafat or a national politician. Marchers will even kiss the pictures and handle them with extraordinary care. If there was a simple prohibition on human representations, one would hardly expect such pictures at all, much less the emotional displays that surround them.[26] And, of course, the pictures and even statues of political leaders, to say nothing of the use of images on coinage, television, and films, are widespread in Muslim countries. But, again, the prohibition is both uneven and, more important, quite rigid where the Prophet is concerned: his humanity and his exceptionalism are simultaneously emphasized by the prohibition on his portrayal.

Tying many of these cultural features together is the role of intention in representations or statements that are seen as blasphemous or slanderous. One of the Prophet's most famous statements is that "all acts are in their intention." The Quran (33:6) itself states that "[t]here is no fault in you if you make mistakes, but only in what your hearts premeditate." In the Rushdie affair, a number of Muslims couched their criticism of the author precisely in these terms: "he knew what he was doing," they said, by writing this book; he knew how offensive he was being.[27] Rushdie responded to this criticism by writing, "He did it on purpose is one of the strangest accusations ever leveled at a writer. Of course I did it on purpose. The question is, and it is what I have tried to answer: what is the 'it' that I did?"[28] Elsewhere I have argued that the "it" is the introduction of doubt into a system that equates all doubt about religious fundamentals with unbelief.[29] But the point here is that the Muslim emphasis on intent cuts both ways.[30] In the West, particularly in the novel, the intent of the author has largely been displaced, while for Muslims it remains a central feature of assessing believability. Thus, an explanation of another's behavior is incomplete without an attribution of the inner state giving rise to the behavior. In a great many everyday social and legal matters, this intent is, I believe, read out directly by Arabs from their categorization of the overt act itself; in other instances, especially for the more philosophically inclined, it may be regarded as so interior as to be irrelevant to the appraisal of observable acts.

In either event, the attribution of an interior state is indispensable to commonsense views of the meaning of another's acts. In the context of blasphemy, this has several implications. First, it is not appropriate to accuse someone of blasphemy, or other automatically punishable deeds, unless that person intended a sacrilegious insult. The hadith that says "God loves those who hide their sins" is thus not an assertion of hypocrisy but of the strong belief that unless an act threatens social order it is not correct or necessary for men to probe into the interior states of their fellows. But since an insult to the Prophet challenges not only his veracity as God's messenger but, as I have suggested, his place as the legitimizer of the master–disciple relation, a threat to his credibility is indeed seen as a threat to the social order. And second, the concept of intent, though not elaborately developed in ordinary parlance or the language of Islamic law, is vital to the process of reciprocity that holds society together. For it is by concentrating on the actions one takes toward oneself and others, and the link made between those acts and one's God-given capacity to form meaning and associations, that the very freedom to construct ties wherever they may prove most advantageous unites a vision of society as formed by reasoning men with the attribution of intersubjectivity that makes their actions comprehensible. It is like those other instances in which a kind of strict liability applies, cases in which, for example, one cannot say one did not intend to marry or that one did not intend to plow up another man's field. For just as those practices, if easily excused, could lead to resentment and social chaos, an insult to the Prophet may admit the possibility for ambivalence and doubt, a possibility that society cannot abide.[31]

The Danish cartoon controversy and the Salman Rushdie affair were, of course, vastly overdetermined. Any number of concerns and grievances—from Western treatment of Muslim countries and the impact of a global economy, to the depredations of local governments and the desire of local leaders to solidify their religious base—could have been sufficient to cause a significant reaction. Indeed, it is particularly common in many Muslim countries for public protests to be about something utterly different from the ostensible issue—say, a veiled attack on some policy of the local government. Provocations can be found wherever sensibilities can be found. When Pope Benedict XVI, on September 12, 2006, cited a medieval text saying that Muhammad had brought only "evil and inhuman" things, the Muslim world was outraged; when a German opera house that same month canceled a performance of Mozart's *Idomeneo*, in which the severed head of the Prophet is represented, proponents of free expression were outraged; and when Danish television showed a right-wing group displaying further cartoons depicting the Prophet, the government had to warn Danes to avoid traveling to Muslim countries. It may be true, as the American cartoonist Jules Feiffer once said, that "outside of basic intelligence, there is nothing more important to a good political cartoonist than ill will." Many Muslims saw the Danish cartoons as part of a long-running attitude of antipathy to Islam and its adherents. To suggest, however, that the cultural meaning of the Prophet is central to an understanding of Muslim reactions to the cartoons is not to downplay any of the other sentiments that are present in this reaction. To the contrary, it is to add context to the emotional valences that crosscut and reinforce whatever other factors may be at work. The Prophet is the ultimate condensation of Muslim attributions. It should now come as no surprise to those in the West that to touch him is to tease up many issues, felt and inexpressible, on which an entire sense of identity and social order turn.

NINE

Theorizing from Within: Ibn Khaldun and the Understanding of Arab Political Culture

Projecting onto the Past

Suppose you were to describe a historical event—or even a long train of occurrences—relying mainly on your deepest assumptions about human nature and human relationships. If, for example, you grew up assuming that we are all conceived in sin and must rely on the strict instruction of those who understand the sacred texts to guide us away from our natural dispositions, how would your historical account be shaped? Or suppose your views about the fundamental differences in the nature of men and women seem to you perfectly obvious; would you—could you, should you—set them aside when engaged in explanations of history? Imagine that your culture supplies you with a narrative format for presenting the course of events, one that is compatible with other domains (religious, economic, familial) but one that still remains quite distinct from those found in other places and times. Would taking explanations that appear appropriate in one domain and applying them as causative in another—explaining, say, a president's decisions in terms of his relation to his mother (as you might explain the actions of a sibling or a lover), or explaining market forces in terms of the human lust for gain (as you might argue in some religious contexts)—make it seem to you that you had offered an explanation that was too simplistic or reductionist?

Some of the most famous historians have made their mark by explicitly trying to form a theory of history based on a view of fundamental human nature. Others have not been completely open about their views of human nature, and readers have ever since debated the implicit assumptions in their accounts. And then there are those who lie somewhere in between, historians who have a view of humanity and tell us how it bears on the course of events but who also seem to work with assumptions that for them are so obvious as to go unmentioned. If such writers seem "modern" to us in some ways we may err in thinking that they must also share our background assumptions since their historical accounts are so recognizable and appealing. It is in instances of this latter sort, perhaps, that we must be especially cautious.

The noted Arab historian Ibn Khaldun (1332–1406) may be such a case. It is precisely because many commentators have found his thought to be so "modern"— because he appears to cast his explanations in a form we can all too easily assimilate into our own historiographic tradition—that his kind of theorizing requires closer attention. Although one is always mindful of reading too much from the present into the past, perhaps an understanding of Arab culture in the present may nonetheless inform our understanding of Ibn Khaldun's way of theorizing more than six hundred years ago.

Ibn Khaldun in the Western Imagination

From the eighteenth century onward, Western scholars have characterized Ibn Khaldun as one of the truly great social theorists—a systematizer of deep historical trends, one of the first "social scientists." It is possible, however, that this characterization has a touch of the ethnocentric about it. We in the West have been so keen to make Ibn Khaldun "one of us"—that is to say, a theoretician in our sense of an analyst who seeks and formulates answers to social questions at a particular level of abstraction—that we may not have fully appreciated that his was a somewhat different kind of theorizing, one that, for all its appearance of modernity, was totally bound up in a world of concrete actions so conceived as to make abstractions of the sort we imagine ourselves to be practicing quite foreign to his own sensibilities. If this interpretation has merit, several important issues may turn on that misjudgment. First, Western scholars may not have always stated with clarity the distinctive kind of theorizing in which Ibn Khaldun was engaged; second, those who refer to his well-known historical ideas may not have adequately considered how much his type of theory building is embedded in the cultural orientations that informed his world view; and third, that world view, grounded as it was in commonsense assumptions about human nature and society, may still be so much a part of contemporary Arab/Islamic thought that to misconstrue Ibn Khaldun's kind of theorizing is to misunderstand much of social thinking throughout the world up to the present day.

A number of contemporary commentators on the Arab world have argued that there is no distinctively Arabo-Muslim anthropology—no intellectual basis for formulating a distanced and general view of the structure and operation of human societies. Like the members of most communities, it is argued, people within the region know full well the rules that operate in daily life but do not see those rules as abstract "social facts" forming systems that account for the working of different societies. The result, say some of these analysts, supports a kind of neo-fundamentalism, a view of society so naturalized from the standpoint of living within its tenets that one cannot see how society—one's own, much less any other's—is actually put together.[1] Of course, such a stance would not be distinctive to Islamic cultures alone—indeed it may be particularly characteristic of any ardently religious group—nor does it mean that self-reflection or doubt are utterly absent. But it may imply that different ways of thinking about history, even though they produce roughly similar results, can still rest on very different assumptions.

In his own life—as in the lives of his cultural successors—Ibn Khaldun placed great emphasis on knowing the customs and practices of other groups one might encounter. But for him and contemporary Arabs there was and is a clear emphasis as well on understanding human behavior through the specific contexts and circumstances in which such actions are embedded. Context is not a mere setting or stage for the enactment of universal human nature but an integral part of any act a historian might seek to understand. Indeed, this emphasis on how context modifies human disposition is deeply entwined with Arab social orientations; to treat Ibn Khaldun's statements about history as if they existed in a social and political vacuum is thus to distort his form of historical understanding. It is only by attending to Ibn Khaldun's distinctive placement in the world of Arab culture, no less than of his own time, that we can appraise his insights for the present.

Ibn Khaldun in His World

Ibn Khaldun must have been an extraordinary individual: scholar and diplomat, wide-ranging theoretician and clear-eyed political operative, a man who literally climbed down a citadel wall in the middle of the night to confer with the "barbarian" Tamerlane and figuratively scaled a wall of incomprehension and tribal isolation to understand his fellow men. He had watched the reconquest of Spain by the Christians and had himself emigrated to Tunisia in its wake; he had seen the destruction wrought by plague, the decline of the Mamluk Empire in Egypt, and the invasion of Mongols from the east. Mid-fourteenth century North Africa was, in his youth, rent by internal strife, as one Muslim regime after another attempted to solidify control. After his parents died of plague, Ibn Khaldun followed the departing Marinid rulers to Fez, where, like most of those serving the powerful in such times, he veered from one attachment to another, sometimes part of a sultan's literary circle, sometimes the ruler's prisoner as plots and counterplots, jealousies and intrigue roiled the court. He moved from positions in Spain, back to North Africa, and eventually to Egypt, where he served as a judge, lecturer in law, and head of a Sufi convent. The years spent in partial retirement had allowed him to write his most noteworthy work, the *Muqaddimah*. Never fully able to resist involvement in political affairs, never fully allied to any one political leader, Ibn Khaldun embraced a combination of thought and action that, in his philosophy and in his culture at large, marked him as a true man of his times.[2] From the intense fluctuations that he both witnessed and chronicled, Ibn Khaldun sought common patterns and the eternal truths to which they bore witness.

But his kind of analysis is not as similar to contemporary theories of history and society as modern analysts have made out. In the process of rendering Ibn Khaldun so like thinkers in the West, and by melding his form of historical analysis into Western ideas of the universal, we risk losing his insights into the distinctiveness of political cultures and the greater lessons he may still teach us about the need to understand the specificities of one's own time and place. Commentators such as Akbar Ahmed have rightly emphasized that Ibn Khaldun is very much an *Islamic* thinker.[3] I would add that Ibn Khaldun is also very much an *Arab* thinker whose views about Arab political culture have special currency in our times, and that the distinctiveness of the social and political forms he analyzes may be lost if seen only as a contribution to grand historical theory. More particularly, I want to consider three points: (1) that Ibn Khaldun's theory of history is deeply embedded in an appreciation of the contexts of human actions and their highly pragmatic consequences, rather than constituting some highly generalized vision of cyclical social movements; (2) that both his way of considering and finessing the role of individual leaders is consonant with the orientation of one coming from an *Arab* (perhaps especially North African) background; and (3) that for these and other reasons, the Western tendency to emphasize the similarities between the historiography of Ibn Khaldun and that of many Western analysts obscures the distinctive style of his own form of theorizing.

Human Nature and the Course of History

Ibn Khaldun is best known for his grand theory of state formation—that tribes well up out of arid regions to take over cities, where in turn they grow self-indulgent and lose both their edge and their collective solidarity.[4] But Ibn Khaldun alternately assumes and asserts that in his new science human nature manifests itself not as an automatic response to forces of climate and necessity but in relation to highly contingent circumstances. His concern for larger social forces in no way effaces his intensely pragmatic feel for the ways in which social solidarity, economic advancement, and the flourishing of arts and crafts take place. They are not, he repeatedly indicates, dependent on inevitable forces but emerge as local circumstances permit.[5] This viewpoint was and still is characteristic of much of Arab/Islamic thought; to borrow a common Arab saying, "men resemble their times more than they do their fathers." The course of events depends on the degree to which particular social groupings employ their God-given reason to place themselves in contexts where the forces of history *may* assert themselves. The achievement of what Ibn Khaldun called a "rational regime aimed at the common good" versus one aimed at the selfish interests of a single ruler comes about only through the actions of men operating in a world of highly pragmatic and connected associations.[6]

In such a world the role of the leader becomes essential. It is sometimes forgotten that when Ibn Khaldun posits a form of solidarity that may propel a group to great acts—what he called *ʿaṣabīya*—this occurs not through some obscure Durkheimian effervescence but has at its heart, as Franz Rosenthal includes in his definition of the term itself, "man's innate psychological need to belong and give political support to a group *dominated by one or more leading personalities*."[7] " ʿAsabiya," says Yves Lacoste, "refers to the influence of leaders of men in a very specific historical context."[8] Writing at a time when, as Abdesselam Cheddadi notes, Islam was sufficiently confident of itself to see the world in Islamic terms, Ibn Khaldun could join his understanding of human nature to that of the state in a distinctly Islamic way.[9] He believed that injustice is natural to mankind, that the sense of humiliation or injured pride (na'ara) that comes through ordinary engagement in the world gives rise to the rectifying need for solidarity through supporters. He distinguished between governments based on reason and those based on religion, and saw the latter as more likely to last if well implemented. Drawing on solidarity as a source of legitimate constraint, ruling groups are nevertheless doomed to last little more than three generations as their breadth and intensity inevitably decline—even in states informed by religious fervor. Strong personalities, backed by money and the offer of status and power, may unify a group for a time, but not nearly so well as during the first impulse of felt offense that rallies a group from the margins to grasp their place at the center.

The problem of the leader is one that Ibn Khaldun at once addresses and evades. His personal history of disappointment with the numerous political leaders he served may well have been critical in leading him to a form of explanation that seemed to erase their importance. Yet he never fully frees himself from their role in history. An example can be seen in his analysis of the relation between leaders and followers. As Muhsin Mahdi indicates, for Ibn Khaldun superordinate groups "cannot form a harmonious whole except when arranged hierarchically with an undisputed leader at the top."[10] Indeed, since it is the qualities of a person—not the limitations of institutionalized offices—that are crucial, it is not surprising to see Ibn Khaldun assert that even the Messiah will need to possess the qualities of a leader.[11] But Ibn Khaldun never quite addresses the role of these individual leaders directly, and it is in this avoidance, as in his explicit comments on the subject, that he is being characteristically Arab. Let me explain.

Ibn Khaldun does recognize the critical importance of the leader as the embodiment of certain qualities that, for better or worse, will propel his group to greater heights or, in that most natural of tendencies, lead him, once successful, to undercut the solidarity of his own supporters as he seeks to assert his royal dominance. But Ibn Khaldun may also be characteristically Arab when he finds it difficult to relate the question of personality to historical trends. The Islamic conception of history is not one of proof in this world of that which Allah has foreordained so much as it is the story of individuals creating a community of believers as an expression of humanity's God-given capabilities. Ibn Khaldun is unusual in that he feels the need to go beyond the question of personality in order to discern the forces that propel an individual and a community to the next stage of development. But the intermediate idea of an institution—in the sense used by Western social scientists to refer to the performance of a role that is not a function of personal attributes—forms no part of his theory. The reason, I believe, is twofold: he does not (1) view the individual as acting separately from his personal attributes because (2) the self, in Arab culture, is not envisioned as fractionated—through religious, cultural, or political history—into a set of roles, reinforced as extant and natural by drama, theology, or conceptions of time and space. Seeing the person as unitary rather than fractionable, Ibn Khaldun does not see limitations on power through the segregation of multiple roles played by a single person or that the fractionation of the self might contribute to the development of impersonal institutions.[12] Instead, Ibn Khaldun leaps over this problem and proceeds directly to the question of the ebb and flow of larger historical trends. Yet it is his commonsense orientation as an exemplar of Arab culture that may account for his emphasis on each person as an indivisible entity rather than as a congeries of separable roles, an approach that is central to his overall theory.

Indeed, this emphasis on the unity of the person may have been influenced by Ibn Khaldun's own attachment to Sufism.[13] This mystical, even ecstatic, branch of Islam was a vital part of Ibn Khaldun's experience of the world. Five years before he wrote the *Muqaddimah* he wrote a book on Sufism. The story is even told of him dancing on the rooftop when the ouija board he was consulting gave the correct response to the question he posed it. Yet even here Ibn Khaldun mollified his Sufism with his reason. For not only did he think one only gets from the mystical the confirmation of what one has apprehended with one's reason, but he invited Sufis to hide their mysticism, to focus on the social benefits of even magical acts, to oppose the claims of Ibn Arabi that purification alone could lead to knowledge, and to realize that, notwithstanding the importance of the Sufi sheikh for direction within the spiritual order, in its final stages guidance should come not from the illiterate mystic but from a leader guided through orthodoxy to enlightenment—and all of this set against the fear that popular Sufism could become an undesirable vehicle of political domination. So long as there is no adverse impact on social relations, he said, even fools can do what they want. Reason, he says, is like a balance meant for appraising gold, even though some misuse it for weighing mountains.[14] Thus, Ibn Khaldun's vision of human nature and history is deeply suffused by an integrated set of beliefs: that there are divinely inspired acts, that there are ideal Platonic forms that unify quotidian manifestations, and that it is actual relationships formed rather than abstract or utopian ideals that are instrumental in the creation of social and political realities.[15] It is when these features that are inextricably linked for Ibn Khaldun are approached by Westerners, who find in their parts, though not in the whole, a theorist to whom they can make themselves akin, that the misunderstanding of Ibn Khaldun, the Arab and the Muslim, finds its opening.

It may be that Westerners have often misconstrued the very nature of Ibn Khaldun's theory of history because they have claimed to see in it some of the same elements that are present in theories that have gained currency at various times in the West itself. Eighteenth-century writers, like Arnold Toynbee in the twentieth, may have found in Ibn Khaldun a congenial theorist because his apparent vision of historical cycles mirrored the level of abstraction, if not always the specifics, of their own theories.[16] Some Westerners also may have found resonance with their own views of revolutionary change in his assertion that "[w]hen general conditions change it is as though creation changes from its very foundation and the whole world is turned around. It is like a new creation, a renewed birth, a novel beginning, a newly made world."[17] Even President Reagan got into the act when he credited Ibn Khaldun with an appreciation of supply-side economics.[18] Since Ibn Khaldun wanted his "science of culture" to be a guide for future action, he was giving voice to the important role the historian should play in the practical affairs of the day.

But the Western assumption that Ibn Khaldun's theories map directly onto our own may be misleading. The level of abstraction at which Ibn Khaldun was operating and that at which many Western commentators operate are only partly similar. To Ibn Khaldun, theory is not separable from action, for contemplation without involvement would not yield insight into operative patterns. Moreover, he has such a fine feel for the pragmatic effects of any act that what might seem like an inability to reconcile necessity and chance is actually harmonized by the implicit cultural assumptions to which he, as an Arab, subscribes—the vision of the unfractionated self, the centrality of personal leadership, the larger forces of history having no meaning as abstractions about the nature of society without also serving as statements about the concrete course of circumstantial events.[19] Thus, we may lose the sense of Ibn Khaldun as a distinctive kind of *Arab* theoretician if we try to make him over in a Western image—and we may subject him to unfair judgment if we find in him a proponent of the kind of cyclical historicizing no longer favored in the West, particularly since his use of cycles as descriptions of processes was based on quite different assumptions about human nature and human action than seem familiar from his discussions of biosocial types.[20]

As indicated earlier, one must be careful not to project onto the past the circumstances one claims to see in the present, much less to suggest that any culture, least of all that of the Arabs, has somehow remained unchanged over the course of six hundred years. But there are perduring, if variant, themes in Arab culture that go beyond those of religious precept or artistic style alone. Understanding the assumptions about the nature of human beings and society is vital if we are to see the distinctively Arab aspects of Ibn Khaldun's approach and how much it can still speak to our own times. For if we see Ibn Khaldun as a prescient student of his own culture rather than as a Western-style theorist, we can appreciate several elements of his insight that have great currency. If, in a view that still has force in Arab culture, politics is of necessity bound up in personalism, then we in the West must make a concerted effort to understand how this view affects the interpretation of events—and how it differs fundamentally from the way we look at the same circumstances. If the components of a person's identity are not comprehensible when analytically fragmented and shorn of context, then we in the West need to understand more carefully what an institution means in the political cultures of the Arab world. If a theory is a statement of the common threads of events and not an abstract version of them, we may be able to understand that a different kind of social science sensibility is consistent with Arab/Islamic thought than we had imagined and that it is, therefore, all the more unfair, as some commentators have maintained, to assert that Arab culture lacks a view of social forces that are not implicit in religious doctrine. In sum, if we simply measure Ibn Khaldun and other thinkers who partake of his cultural traditions against theorists from the West, we will miss the enormous vitality of their distinctive contributions to social thought.

Indeed, reading between the lines of Ibn Khaldun—for his culture, his type of theorizing, his view of humanity—can enrich our view of history and the social ideas of our Arab contemporaries as well as remind us that we do neither scholarship nor cross-cultural understanding a favor if we simply merge all of culture and history into a common theme. While his language, and many of his specific beliefs, resound with claims to the universal, those universals are themselves deeply rooted in his own Arab culture.[21] The tendency, particularly prevalent among Americans, to presume that all cultures are basically the same should have been brought up sharp by current events. Globalism has by no means eliminated the local; on the contrary, it may have exacerbated it. Between making everyone like "us" and making any one culture better than another there lies a wiser and truer proposition, one that is cogently expressed in the Prophetic Tradition that says, "there is no distinction except as to knowledge," and in that common Arab saying, "a difference is not a distinction." Ibn Khaldun was indeed a theorist—in the original sense of one who both looks at things and has a view of them.[22] It would, however, be unfortunate to lose Ibn Khaldun's appreciation of the distinctive nature of each society—and his own distinctively Arab way of viewing society—in an attempt to render him the founding father of a Western-style grand theory of history and society.

PART THREE

Representatives and Representations

TEN

Knowledge Forms: Muslim Scientists as Fundamentalists

How can a scientist be a religious fundamentalist? To some Westerners the question would seem to call for a simple answer: it is *not possible*. After all, they might argue, science is about questioning, about accepting nothing on the basis of faith alone, about using all of one's powers of reason to challenge assumptions none of which is immune to investigation. From this perspective religious faith and science are not necessarily antithetical—many scientists are themselves deeply religious. But matters of faith and matters of science occupy separable domains, and the criteria for acceptance of an idea in the one ought not to intrude on the criteria for belief in the other.

Posed against this general position is the argument that science and fundamentalism (of whatever sort and degree) are *not incompatible*: it is possible to believe that the rules of the physical universe meld into those of the spiritual, that the material and the religious either share or mutually mask their common principles, or that the realms of belief and reason are indeed so separated that the simultaneous acceptance of both is not a contradiction in terms. The *locus classicus* of this position may be Albert Einstein's famous assertion that "religion without science is lame, but science without religion is blind."[1]

Both positions, and their many variants, are quite comprehensible. Yet many Westerners, looking at Islam in particular, must find themselves intrigued when they learn that a significant number of Muslims who have been trained in the sciences do indeed attach themselves to fundamentalist ideas and movements, ranging from the intellectual and benign to the mind-numbing and violent. Moreover, the knowledge that Arab science was once far ahead of its Western counterpart—and that many classical sources of Western learning have come down to us thanks only to the efforts of Arab scholars—seems to many Westerners only to heighten the mystery. How, after all, could scholars who once thought that science was neutral with respect to religion and culture so substantially relinquish their curiosity about the world and its physical workings?

In this chapter I want to review some aspects of the history of Arab science and the reasons why a number of contemporary Muslims trained in the sciences may be attracted to fundamentalist Islam. In doing so I will explore in the domain of science one of the themes that has figured prominently throughout this book, namely that the meaning of science in the context of Arab cultural history has to be understood, at least in part, in terms of its effect on human relationships. I want to suggest that where the focus on the relational cannot be maintained, the meaning of many cultural products—portraiture, ownership, science—cannot be readily sustained. Put somewhat differently, I want to challenge the idea that the Arab pursuit of scientific inquiry was an exception to other aspects of Islamic culture and to consider that one component of the attraction and rejection of science by Muslims at different times is connected to the way they have seen science as supporting or undermining the relationships among people. It is through this relational logic, as seen from the perspective of Western skepticism, that we may be able to supplement our understanding of why, at the present time, a number of Muslims trained in the sciences also find themselves attracted to literalist faith.

Fundamentalists Who Have Studied Science

That a number of Muslim scientists (or at least individuals with some degree of formal training in the sciences) are indeed fundamentalists is founded on anecdote and impression rather than firm data: I know of no survey that pinpoints this issue with statistical precision. Moreover, it should go without saying that few Muslims trained in the sciences have turned to terrorism and that it is certainly not my contention that there is a direct correlation between science training and fundamentalism, much less terrorism. The concern here is only with the reasons why those who do find themselves drawn to literalist religion and/ or violent action based on religion may have created a rationale that connects their science education with their religious attachments. Although we have very little data to work with and thus can only speculate, we do have some tantalizing clues.

The most commonly cited statement about Muslim scientists and fundamentalism is that of Gilles Kepel, who has said that a disproportionate number of Christian and Jewish fundamentalists are trained in the applied sciences "just like the Islamist militants."[2] Marc Sageman, a former CIA case officer in Afghanistan and a forensic psychiatrist at the Foreign Policy Research Institute, has surveyed the biographies of four hundred terrorists and concludes that 63 percent had gone to college. Of these, three-quarters were professionals or semiprofessionals: "They are engineers, architects, and civil engineers, mostly scientists. Very few humanities are represented, and quite surprisingly very few had any background in religion."[3] It is necessary to distinguish between training in the "pure" sciences and training in engineering, especially since many engineering programs outside the United States are either technical schools or effectively business schools. Indeed, in a number of instances a person is actually assigned to a given faculty, rather than having chosen it, as a condition of admission. It is not, therefore, always possible to tell how much actual science training particular individuals received. With that caveat in mind, we can say that some of the engineers/scientists/fundamentalists who have attacked their own governments or those of the West do have genuine science backgrounds and are world famous. The list could be quite long, but here are some examples:

Osama bin Laden's right-hand man and the founder of Egyptian Islamic Jihad, Ayman al-Zawahiri, is a medical doctor; Abdul Qadir Khan and his team of Pakistani nuclear scientists—who transferred technology to Libya and others—are devout fundamentalists;[4] Ali al-Timimi, the charismatic Islamic scholar and trained cancer researcher, was sentenced to life imprisonment in Virginia for various crimes relating to the support of terrorism;[5] Kemal Daoudi, the son of Algerian immigrants and a brilliant engineering student, was caught in Paris in a plot to destroy the American embassy;[6] several of the terrorists involved in the attacks on 9/11 had training in the sciences (e.g., Mohamed el-Amir Atta, whose lawyer father wanted him to gain the title of "doctor," whose brother is a cardiologist and sister a professor of zoology, studied engineering and architecture in Egypt and then graduated with high honors from the Technical University in Hamburg);[7] Ziad Jarrah, one of the founders of the Hamburg cell, studied dentistry and later aeronautical engineering; Abd al-Salam Farrag, who planned the assassination of Egyptian president Anwar Sadat, was an engineer; Azahari Husin, the Malaysian bomb builder responsible for attacks in 2002 in Bali and against the Marriott Hotel and Australian Embassy in 2003–4, was described as a gifted mathematician who held a Ph.D. from the University of Reading and was a professor of statistics before he became a terrorist leader of Jemaah Islamiah and was killed in 2005; and a number of the Islamist fighters in Bosnia and southeast Asia are reputed to have had training in the sciences and engineering. One even reads of two young Turkish chemists living in Germany and worshiping at the mosque of the Caliphate State, Germany's most radical Islamicist organization, whose attachment to fundamentalism leads them to argue that "Islam and democracy are incompatible."[8]

Science training, it should be noted, is less widespread in the Muslim world than elsewhere. According to the Pakistani physics professor Pervez Hoodbhoy, in the late 1980s Muslims made up nearly 20 percent of the world's population but accounted for less than 1 percent of the world's scientists.[9] Whether it is the poverty and lack of proximity to schools, the quality of teacher training, or (as a USAID desk study suggests) "an authoritarian teaching style that promotes passive learning," those who do obtain a science education, often at foreign institutions, risk a degree of separation from their cohort even as they gain greater opportunities for their own advancement.[10] The Muslim emphasis on the value of knowledge notwithstanding, those trained in the sciences and technology feel the strain of being situated between worlds by virtue of their expertise, and many try to reconcile their interstitial position by attaching themselves to a literalist version of the faith, or at least to the community of believers bound together by such a belief. In a sense they are the modern carriers of a set of concerns that have very deep roots in the meaning of science throughout Islamic history.

Science and Islam

In the West the scientific enterprise of the Muslim world is famous for its rise and for its decline. The former is clear and unambiguous, the latter murky and conflicted. What we know is that from roughly the ninth until as late as the fifteenth century many Arab scholars participated in the translation and study of Greek texts on science, medicine, and philosophy, texts they were responsible for preserving until Europeans reacquired an interest in them and translated them back into European languages in the Middle Ages. Arab and Persian scholars built on these texts, particularly in the fields of medicine, astronomy, mathematics, and cartography.[11] Significantly, the Muslim scholars who concerned themselves with the sciences commonly regarded them as linked to no particular religion. The religious neutrality of science was underscored by Ibn Khaldun in the fifteenth century:

> The intellectual sciences are natural to man, inasmuch as he is a thinking being. They are not restricted to any particular religious group. They are studied by the people of all religious groups who are equally qualified to learn them and to do research in them. They have existed (and been known) to the human species since civilization has its beginnings in the world.[12]

The discoveries of Muslim scholars came in almost all domains. Many of the advances were no doubt connected to the practical implications of science for the faith itself: the need to know the proper direction for the prayers influenced astronomy and cartography, and the emphasis on a unity of spiritual and physical well-being encouraged medical science. But the practical import of their discoveries seems inadequate to account for the florescence of science in the medieval Muslim world. On occasion, theorizing and observation went hand-in-hand, as when astronomers such as Abu Ali al-Hasan ibn al-Haytham in the tenth century combined philosophical and experimental investigations. For others, such as the twelfth-century physician and philosopher Averroes (Abu al-Walid Ibn Rushd, 1126–98), knowledge of the physical world revealed the truth of God's unity and creativity. But combining theory and experimentation was not the usual case, and the exceptions are particularly interesting. The near absence of experimentation for purposes of developing theory is noted by Abdelhamad I. Sabra:

> The general theory of astronomy in medieval Islam exhibits a curious lack of inter-action between theory and observation, though both of these were actively pursued. Observations, on the whole, had little impact on theoretical developments; and theoretical innovations were neither inspired by nor did they lead to novel observations. It is as if each of these two activities revolved within a limited sphere of its own.[13]

Indeed, the only area in which a significant degree of experimentation without clear connections to practicality is said to have existed was in some parts of the field of optics.[14]

Our understanding of medieval Islamic science is, regrettably, very limited. Numerous surviving manuscripts remain unstudied. As Sabra himself has said, the history of the field "has not yet begun," a remark that would apply even more to the sociology of Islam and science.[15] Science, of course, is never divorced from its social and cultural contexts. There were, for example, three systems of numerical calculation used simultaneously in the medieval Muslim world. One, known as finger reckoning, or the "arithmetic of the scribes (or secretaries)," involved writing out numbers in words. Its persistence in the face of better forms was undoubtedly connected to the self-interest of those employing it. As Sabra notes, "The system in fact continued to be used by members of the secretarial class despite the existence of the much superior type of reckoning which had come from India in the II/8th century or earlier, and on which many handbooks were available."[16] Other advances, such as those in mathematics and architecture, were frequently associated with the retention of royal favor. But the factors affecting the meaning of scientific inquiry go well beyond personal advantage: such inquiry is inextricably linked with the ways in which, for a given time and people, the world as a whole seems to make sense.[17]

It is not uncommon to frame the history of Arab science in terms of the relation of science to *Islam*, indeed as *Islamic* science. But it is easy to lose sight of the fact that Islam does not exist in some pure form: it is what a very broad range of Muslims think and do. Thus, analyzing the history of science in the Arab world in terms of Islamic science in the abstract is not of great utility.[18] Rather, one must look for the resonances among multiple domains—including the religious—for any given period or place and grapple with the intricacies of the local even as one seeks common themes.

The second most frequently used word in the Quran, after the name of God, is *knowledge* (*'ilm*).[19] Building on the image, constantly reinforced by sacred text and "common sense" alike, that human beings are endowed by their creator with reason to further the well-being of themselves and their dependents, knowledge is enormously valued. While knowledge of sacred text is the highest form, that of the mundane is admired as well, whether it be of a craft, the ways of others with whom attachments may be formed, or the nature of the world that exists around us. "Travel in search of knowledge," said the Prophet, "even if it takes you to China." Knowledge, however, is not for its own sake, any more than it is valued solely for its practical consequences. The quest for knowledge gains meaning by virtue of the good or ill intention of the person who seeks it and by the actions people take in the formation of their relationships as a result of its acquisition. Thus, what has been included as knowledge, and how the forms it takes are classified, has varied across time and space. In the classical period various philosophers contrasted "religious" sciences with those that are "foreign," the "traditional" with the "philosophical," the "speculative" with the "practical," and the "praiseworthy" with the "blameworthy."[20] What we would categorize as "science" crossed into the speculative and the theological in many of the Muslim classificatory systems. Of particular importance to the value of knowledge for early scholars—and for those who continue in their footsteps—was how it affected the life of the community.[21] Thus, at each point in virtually any variant of Arab society, the focus comes back to the relational—here, how knowledge links people to one another and how it transforms individuals into a community, especially a community of believers. The aphorism "May God protect us from useless knowledge" is aimed not at promoting technological utility but at discouraging undesirable relational implications.[22] Scientific knowledge, as of all other cultural forms, must be valued not primarily for its abstract approximation of some imagined essence but for its involvement as part of the linkage among sentient beings if it is to be considered a meaningful enterprise.

Tempering the pursuit of knowledge, however, are several powerful concepts, in particular the ideas of speculation and admixture. From the earliest days of Islam, Muslims were concerned that speculation would lead to doubt, which would lead to unbelief, which would lead to the dissolution of the community of believers and the punishment by God of all such unbelievers.[23] Again, however, the test of unacceptable speculation was commonly its effect on society, not its production of abstract ideas. Like the Prophetic Tradition that says that God loves those who hide their sins, this admonition was not a product of dogmatic intolerance but was intended to reflect the broader proposition that if a matter began to overflow its bounds and adversely affect social relations, then the thing most to be feared, social chaos (fitna), might readily follow. Similarly, innovation (bid'a), especially through the mixing of elements (shirk) that should remain separate, was also a danger to the social order. In the hands of different philosophers, theologians, and rulers, each of these concepts was given different emphasis and application, but the common theme of the relational effects of an act bound them together.

Support for this interpretation comes from many sources. We have already seen that the intensely personalistic element in Arab culture pervades virtually all domains. It is still true in many places that genuine authority to interpret Islamic law comes after the acquisition of an authorization by one or more scholars who personally grant the candidate an acknowledgment of competency; advisory legal opinions, gleaned from such authorities, are inherently of equal validity, their acceptance by an actual court of law being a matter of highly individual discretion; and the formal tenets of Islamic law are, notwithstanding modern codes and centralized oversight by a ministry of justice, commonly centered at the trial level more on the procedures for assessing the situated identity of the persons before the court than on the development of impersonal roles from which uniform doctrine might emerge. An analogous emphasis characterized the course of science in the Arab world, its formative aspects in the medieval period still having cultural resonance in the present. Toby E. Huff, summarizing the views of numerous scholars, argues that Islamic theologians stressed the inherent limitations of human reason and the belief that moral concepts cannot be generated from individual conscience. Coupled with the idea that causality never implies necessity (since such an idea would entail limitations on God's power of intervention)[24] and the absence in Islamic law of corporate persons and depersonalized standards, science had to operate in a context of personalized (rather than institutionally shared) knowledge. The result was that knowledge, as Marshall Hodgson argues, became the sum of all true statements rather than a quest for the unknown, a proposition that might be supplemented by suggesting that reason was cast as an instrument for gaining one's place in the world rather than creating a sense of how that world is ultimately composed.[25] If science requires the establishment of "impersonal criteria," and if impersonal institutions have not played a dominant role in Arab social relations, then one might readily expect that the role that science would play in the West may be very different from its place in Arab culture and history.[26]

The repercussions for the course of science in the modern Arab Muslim world are suggestive. First, the distinction often drawn in the West between "pure" science and practical applications was not drawn as sharply among the Arabs. There was no simple hierarchy of those possessing knowledge, even including the Quranically informed, a fact that was consonant with the absence of a church structure, the general ethos of individual-centered networks of alliance, and the opportunities for building crosscutting alliances on many different foundations— all of which rendered an enduring hierarchy of persons or groups very difficult to maintain. Second, given the focus on the relational meaning of any act, scientific investigation may have held meaning only so long as it could be imagined as part of the relational order, that is, so long as it seemed to connect people to one another. If ever that should cease to be apparent, then, in this cultural order, science itself might cease to have meaning.

And that is exactly what may have occurred. For when, in the later Middle Ages, science began to turn toward experimentation—experimentation divorced from any clear relational import—it may have been rendered quite literally meaningless. Many factors no doubt contributed to the decline of Arab science: the destruction of major centers of learning (like those of Spain and Baghdad), the initial acceptance of Greek philosophy's emphasis on deduction from first principles and its eventual defeat by those favoring uncritical acceptance of sacred sources, and the rather sharp boundary drawn between what Sayyed Hossein Nasr has called operational and nonoperational knowledge.[27] But what has often been taken as an instance of exceptionalism—that Arab science was far advanced whereas political institution building, for example, was not—becomes, in the present interpretation, no exception at all. Just as the architecture of a building was less dependent on a single overarching plan than on a general theme that could be added to as circumstance varied, so, too, science (like music, art, and social ties themselves) held meaning in terms of the relationships it made possible or visible.[28] When science could only go forward untethered to evident social effect, it may not have been able to retain the popular or royal support the relational imaginary had previously made possible.[29] Nasr's assertion that modern science constituted a radical epistemological break insofar as it rendered the sacred irrelevant may, in no small part, be the exact opposite of the case: science, for the Muslims, was not secular enough, inasmuch as it no longer seemed to be speaking to human relationships and became divorced from social life through abstract and experimental concerns.[30] Moreover, just as in Islamic religious "science," it is the tracing through believable persons—people who themselves have effects in the world of relationships—rather than through some "independent" proof that a proposition gains credibility.[31] This is the same pattern seen in the determination of legitimate versions of the Prophet's acts and utterances, the assessment of a person as a reliable witness in an Islamic law court, or reliance on the authority of an "expert" on any subject of everyday importance. It is the relation of one person to the next, the believability of each being based on his formation of adherents and dependents, that one's claim to authority may be grounded and knowledge itself rendered meaningful. To the extent that believability in a scientific claim rested on its purveyor's ability to marshal believers, credibility in science would have mirrored the means by which it is acquired in many other domains of Arab social life.[32]

If science lost its meaning when it could only become experimental, such a turn was similar to what had been happening in other spheres of Islamic thought, where debates in philosophy, law, and the nature of the state had a roughly parallel development. The rationalists stressed the addition of human reason to divine ordinance, while the legalists argued that human reason could neither discover nor supplement the primary sources of knowledge. For the one, experimentation may have implied discovering the bases of connections; for the other, it could only undermine an acceptance of the ineluctable nature of relationships. To the one, the practical furthered the range of reason; to the other, it limited the scope of submission to the divine. The triumph of the literalists after the florescence of the rationalists during the ninth through fifteenth centuries was, in the present interpretation, not a triumph of literalist ignorance but a decline in the belief that rationalism alone could aid human relations rather than undermine them through systemic doubt. And for all their difference both were, to a degree, asking the same question: what has this to do with the way God has established the ties among men?

We can see a similar emphasis in much more recent times. Take, for example, the teaching of science in Arab schools. Two features of the educational style of most Arab countries are worth noting in this regard: the emphasis on memorization and the compartmentalization of certain areas of knowledge. As in the study of the Quran that many students will have encountered before they enter public school, education consists largely of rote memorizing of materials supplied to the student. The Quran should ideally be committed entirely to memory, and examinations at religious academies continue to follow this ancient tradition to the present. Children are believed to be governed mainly by their passions (*nafs*) rather than their reason ('*aqel*), and only the proximity to mature authority can build up their reason to the point where they can exercise it with greater independence. Males think they are more capable of succeeding in this process than females. Whether it is for boys or girls, the habits formed by memorization are thought most effective for shaping the young. Even science studies are conducted through rote learning, a process that has led one Pakistani physicist to characterize education in most Muslim countries as a system "wherein knowledge is something to be acquired rather than discovered, and in which the attitude of mind is passive and receptive rather than creative and inquisitive."[33]

Substantive fields of knowledge also possess their sociological correlates. Elsewhere I have suggested that only within the past generation have certain concepts of probability begun to take effect in parts of the Muslim world.[34] As the internal movement of people makes prediction and constraint on others' behavior difficult, and as reciprocity and obligation are rendered less powerful, the assumption that only a sentient being causes things to happen may be giving way to an emphasis on how *things* may cause other things to happen. When, therefore, one reads that the educational guidelines for the Pakistani Institute for Policy Studies recommends against linking physical effects to causes—for example, by asserting that hydrogen and oxygen do not themselves yield water but that water results only because of the will of God—one sees how the very idea of dissociating causation from sentience may imply a whole shift in worldview.[35] The assertion of divine causation is not, therefore, a question of religious literalism alone, but of a commonsense vision of how the universe, a place of essentially relational ties, is itself constructed.

In addition, the compartmentalization of knowledge means that one need not follow through the implications that might be thought to accompany a given approach or body of information. For example, it is very common for evolution to be taught at the high school and even the college level only as it concerns lower orders of animals; the question whether evolutionary theory applies to human beings is simply not addressed.[36] One may express doubt about a technological application, but expressing doubts about the fundamentals of the faith is severely admonished.[37] Just as context is crucial to the way in which social relationships, concepts of time, the assessment of persons, and the discernment of truth are addressed, so, too, in the quest for socially useful knowledge knowing how one's own actions affect the networks of others is central, whereas in other cultural and religious traditions quite different ways of sorting experience may prevail.

Why Might a Muslim Scientist Also Be a Muslim Fundamentalist?

The real issue, of course, concerns the attraction of fundamentalist Islam to any of those trained in the sciences. Here, a number of caveats are necessary at the outset. It should go without saying that there are numerous, and often highly contradictory, views of Islam espoused by

Muslims. Moreover, the appeal of these various forms of fundamental-ism is equally diverse. But there is some virtue in generalizing. The attraction of fundamentalism, being so overdetermined, has two im-portant features. First, the fact that people may come to the same con-clusion from any of a number of starting points suggests that funda-mentalism has a certain organic quality to it, that people for whom it holds quite different meanings can find a place under the same tent. And second, if there is indeed a common denominator to their attrac-tion—namely the emphasis on the relational—then it is an attraction with deep connections throughout Arabo-Muslim culture, a set of con-nections that adds a systemic quality to the appeal and durability of fundamentalism. In suggesting how the logic that connects science and religiosity may work for many of these Muslims we can, therefore, see that its very generality, multiple causes, and varied implications are part of its strength. While it may have to be left to others to investi-gate how specific educational programs have affected the connections between Islam and science, it greatly enhances our understanding of the attraction of some Muslim scientists to fundamentalism to see the deeply relational emphasis that informs their views.

It is also possible, of course, that in many cases an individual's train-ing in one of the sciences is irrelevant to his or her attachment to lit-eralist faith. People may be attracted to fundamentalism for reasons having nothing to do with their background in science. They may ex-perience an overwhelming sense of alienation from Western culture or the politics of their home country, they may wish to be more fully involved in Western society yet feel a deep sense of injustice when they find their path blocked, or they may experience some personal crisis such that the need for community support takes precedence over all other concerns.[38] Obviously, attachment to literalist belief or organiza-tions is not the same as attachment to a terrorist group. Sageman argues of those he surveyed who engaged in terrorist acts: "At the time they joined jihad, the terrorists were not very religious. They only became religious once they joined the jihad. . . . When they became homesick, they did what anyone would and tried to congregate with people like themselves, whom they would find at mosques. So they drifted towards the mosque, not because they were religious, but because they were seeking friends."[39] But we cannot assume that one's education or work experience as a scientist is necessarily irrelevant to one's attraction to fundamentalist ideologies. Even if some individuals compartmentalize their science backgrounds or rationalize religion in its terms *how* the various components are configured is not simply a matter of peer support: it may also be a matter of finding a way to create a sense of an orderly world by uniting the social and physical within a single vision of thought and action.

With these caveats in mind we can consider some of the reasons why certain Muslims trained in science may find fundamentalist ideas attractive. Some are drawn to the very precision of Islamic precepts, especially those of Islamic law. Jafar Umar Thalib, the founder of the Indonesian Laskar Jihad, which is linked to al-Qaeda and other terrorist organizations, has said that this is why he starts his recruiting predominantly among university science students.[40] The director of an Arab science institute, himself the holder of a doctorate in mathematics from a major American university, pointed out to me that most of his students for some years now have been Islamists and that the link between their science studies and their religious attachments comes through their seeing the world through axioms that have natural consequences. For example, there is the idea that God is with us at all times supervising our actions; if this axiom leads to desired conclusions (e.g., that given God's omnipresence people will need to be honest at every moment), the students feel they can accept the axiom uncritically, reserving the right to question it at some later date if necessary. In the meantime, one can act as if the axiom is true in order to achieve the desired results associated with it.[41] These students, the director notes, even say that one of the al-Qaeda terrorists could behave in a way that is "normal" before carrying out a suicide mission— i.e., go out drinking the night before—because the relational goal so outweighed the means they were employing that any countervailing precepts could be held in abeyance pending accomplishment of the goal.

This apparent "double-mindedness," the simultaneous holding of two seemingly contradictory propositions, is actually characteristic of many domains of Arab thought, but not in the sense of being a failure of reasoning. To the contrary, it indicates that propositions that do not necessarily go together in Western cultures may not seem contradictory in the cultural scheme of Arab life. The idea that one can put off for a time the complexities of a foundational principle while enacting what is actually most crucial about it—namely affecting the relationships that flow from it—is at one with many other aspects of the emphasis on the relational in Arab culture.[42] Such an approach may also seem to many—and not only Muslims—to be consistent with getting at what really matters. It is interesting to note that the mathematical background of the American Unabomber, Theodore J. Kaczynski, may not have been irrelevant to his actions. As one professor of mathematics pointed out, "The subject and its subdisciplines are axiomatic—that is, they are based on a few fundamental assumptions from which all else follows logically. Thus mathematicians often view themselves as 'radical' thinkers in the literal sense of the word: They get to the root of the matter."[43] Unlike those trained in disciplines that emphasize ambiguity and reflection on the narrative itself, many of those who come from the sciences may find a link between the Muslim equation of doubt with unbelief and their own attraction to essential truths. Malise Ruthven, among others, argues that this stance may be particularly compatible with both Judaism and Islam "since for them behaviour, rather than belief, defines religious allegiance. Orthopraxy—in dress, food, ritual, or family relationships—need not impinge on ideas about the ordering of the universe. The supernatural can be pushed aside without loss of faith or identity."[44]

For those who need to have rules set down for them—rules that make life seem orderly, predictable, and beyond human manipulation—the precepts of Islam and those found in science may have a similarly satisfying edge. Moreover, the opposite of this proposition may, in the case of certain fundamentalists, actually constitute a corollary. That is, they may discover in their science studies not that there are graspable certainties but precisely that the more one knows the less one can be certain of the ultimate truth of one's studies. This discovery may take one of several forms. To a well-trained but not world-class scientist, the realization may come that he will never grasp ultimate truths through his investigations, so he attributes the unknowable to religion;[45] to others it may be that the limitations of their own scientific knowledge demonstrate that there are things they will never know. Both positions have solid foundations in various Islamic philosophies.[46]

There is a long tradition among many Muslim theologians, perpetuated by some of the most well-known Islamist ideologues, that it is precisely the confusion of spiritual values and worldly concerns that leads believers astray. To some this confusion is proof that science has fatal limitations; to others it stems from a failure to demonstrate the compatibility of science and religion; to still others it indicates that a choice must be made between the two. Maulana Sami-ul-Haq, the teacher of many former Taliban cabinet members, for example, says that "it is a failure of cultured secularists in modern day education that Pakistan is a backward society"; renowned Pakistani poet Said Aftikhar Arif remarks that the madrasa, or Quranic school education system, "makes students a guard of Islamic values; we are not trying to make them experts of modern science and technology."[47] While Abdus Salam, the Nobel Prize laureate in physics and a practicing Ahmadiyya Muslim, asserts that "[t]here is no question, but today, of all civilizations on this planet, science is weakest in the lands of Islam,"[48] the more common voice is that of the Turkish scholar and popular preacher Fethullah Gülen, who urges Muslims to know enough science "to fight back against materialism and atheism" but cautions that "[t]ruth is not something that the human mind produces. Truth exists independently of man and man's task is to seek it."[49] While numerous Islamic scholars, ancient and modern, have sought scientific propositions within the verses of the Quran[50] or, like Muhammad ʿAbduh and Jamal al-Din al-Afghani in the late nineteenth century, think that science and religion must progress together,[51] others call for avoidance of science: in the words of Egyptian scholar Sayyid Qutb—the primary theorist of the modern fundamentalist movement who was executed by Nasser—science "is not final or absolute because it is tied to man's environment, mind, and tools, all of which, by their nature, are not capable of giving one final and absolute truth."[52] Thus, even to the extent that scientific knowledge is worth obtaining, it must remain subservient to the spiritual—a stance that enables some science-trained Muslims to retain their scientific knowledge while rendering it in the service of fundamentalist ends.

One might expect that science and fundamentalism would have in common an attraction to certainty, a way of counteracting doubt, even if the particular certainties to which adherents of each might subscribe differ quite markedly. Indeed science and religion may have much in common; what Akbar Ahmed has said of religious extremism could as well be said of science: "fundamentalism is the attempt to resolve how to live in a world of radical doubt."[53] And it may well be, as Anthony Giddens says, that "modernity effectively involves the institutionalization of doubt."[54] But it is also possible that neither science nor fundamentalism is seen primarily in terms of its ability to address certainty. Instead, both may be understood predominantly in terms of the effects they have on human relationships. From this perspective science has often been viewed in Arab cultures as potentially divisive, precisely because adherents to different views become contentious, deeply committed to their respective viewpoints, and so attached to their certainty as to disrupt the possibility of relationship. To borrow a phrasing from an analogous context, one may see "the practice of science as a practice of strife and disharmony over against 'trade in the market,' which does 'lead to agreement.' "[55] Far from leading to some fixed points in a universe of uncertainty, then, the socially dysfunctional correlates of science render it antithetical to a world in which give-and-take can allow one to move freely as a person, precisely the kind of flexibility that terrorists may feel lacking in their lives generally.

This discussion brings us back to the assumptions that inform Arab views of causality and worldly experience. Classical Arab thought has frequently equated imagining that which is not real with dangerous speculation, and regarded such thinking as equally dangerous for the development of sensible social relations and personal morality. Human beings are not thought of as creating relationships out of whole cloth, any more than one adds new pieces to the chessboard to be an effective player. Instead, one assembles what has been made naturally available, knitting together things whose potential compatibility one must learn to appreciate. Connections are not created by the observer but recognized by him, such that when relationships are sought one is not risking the admixture of incompatible entities—which would be as pointless as trying to breed different species—but seeking to discern relationships already immanent. Operating within such a cultural frame—where there is no contradiction between the internally differentiated and the externally discrete, and where the pieces that comprise an orderly social world require human assembly, science holds meaning only to the extent that it facilitates the establishment of those human relationships that alone transform a world unassembled into one that conforms to the capacity for reason with which men have been divinely endowed. The risk of admixture, of association across boundaries that neither conform to the true categories of the world nor recognize the fundamental relatedness of those things that properly may be related, is felt with great intensity. Research that does not reveal relatedness would be akin to inventing a singular truth about all relationships that would transcend local custom and the construction of the person, and thus limit freedom by limiting relational resources themselves. In a universe of relational logic the very meaning of science may turn on the expectations of what the world of relationship is itself like. The pursuit of knowledge holds no meaning if it does not conform with such relational orientations.

Comprehending this idea of connections, as seen through the lens of Arabo-Islamic culture, requires distinguishing between a series of entities that are regarded as discrete yet capable of being connected and an array that may appear divided but is inherently fraught with connections. It is as though you had a bunch of things that you could, within the limits of their construct, put together like so many building blocks and a bunch of things you regard as already connected in a number of ways (as vast as the moves in chess) whose inherent connec-tions you could make manifest. Those things that appear to have no in-herent divisions, those "unsegmented imponderables"—like time and volume and even love—that await a modern Westerner's quantification ("let me count the ways") are, for the Arabs, rendered meaningful when seen for their effects on human social networks, indeed when they ex-press the nature of relationship itself. What many Westerners may seek to break down analytically and put back together in the same or a very different way is, for many Arabs, the subject of a search for knowledge about their extant relatedness. What may then seem a contradiction to one is not for the other. My enemy *is* in no small way my friend be-cause implicit in our tie is our mutual ratification as leaders and hence common benefit in not utterly destroying the other; I may side with members of my clan or tribe on many occasions, but the moment the sources of constructing my own identity are threatened, I may identify with my prior adversary. Causal linkages, then, are relational strings, not unconnected parts. Indeed, from the Arabs' perspective the fail-ure of Westerners to see the logic that binds commercialism, aggressive politics, sex, and popular culture is simply an example of our larger failure to appreciate the inherent connectedness of things. Whether it is the Quran, which is viewed as seamless to Arabs and as shot through with narrative disconnects to many Western scholars, or the image of causality in the physical and social world—which for many Arabs still implies no necessary relation between cause and effect since God can intervene at any moment—the logic of assemblage marks a subtle but very significant point of divergence in Arab and Western orientations that cannot but affect the approach, among others, to science, ritual, morality, and political alliance.[56]

Just as we can see that the style of education may replicate the con-textualized and socially oriented aspects of Arab culture, so, too, we can see why attitudes toward women would, for most men who iden-tify strongly with Islamic fundamentalism, form a logical component to their overall orientation. To such men, as to the large proportion of Arab men generally, women are propelled principally by their pas-sions and therefore pose a threat to the social order; in the phrasing of the Quran, women need the oversight of men. However much the status of women in Islam improved over that of the pre-Islamic period, the strongly paternalistic viewpoint of men toward women and their place in society is only reinforced by the notion that justice consists not of equality but of treating each according to his or her nature. So-cial chaos (fitna) is seen as being implicated by the inherent nature of women. As one fundamentalist organization has evocatively phrased it, "Flames of passion rise from the naked bodies of immoral women and burn humanity to ashes."[57] Islamic law must keep women in their "natural" place, and hence a quest for orderliness easily melds into a position that seeks to avert social harm by avoiding the prospect of women being out of place. Many of the conflicts between fundamentalists and comparatively secular governance thus turn on the question of the treatment of women within society and the state. To the extent that a scientist seeks a sense of the orderly that is beyond human invention, the retention of women in a clear place in the social order becomes as vital as any other element of a physical world governed by determinate rules.

———

The fact that science and technology in its present form did not develop in Islam is not a sign of decadence, as is claimed, but the refusal of Islam to consider any form of knowledge as purely secular.

SEYYED HOSSEIN NASR

In Islam there is no science for the sake of science and there is no knowledge for the sake of knowledge. Everything is for an end, which is using scientific knowledge for the good of humanity at large.

M. A. KAZI, SCIENCE ADVISOR TO THE LATE PRESIDENT MUHAMMAD ZIA OF PAKISTAN[58]

The Nobel Prize laureate Isadore Rabi once quipped that "two kinds of people go into physics: those who have trouble with their car, and those who have trouble with God." Few Muslims may fall into the latter category—or at least openly acknowledge that they do—and many more probably fit more comfortably into the former. Even in the classical ages of Islamic science this may well have been the case. The relation between an educational background in the sciences and an attraction to fundamentalism, whether peaceful or violent, is necessarily speculative. Intelligence agencies may have more elaborate profiles; Islamists may have a keen sense of their own recruitment success. It is just as likely, if not more so, that a scientist will be drawn to secular and democratic affiliations, or that a deeply believing Muslim will indeed support substantial equality for women. Absent more data our conclusions can only be tentative. But if we set aside the need for statistically verifiable correlations and look instead to the rationales that link literalist faith and scientific background, the history of Islamic science and the concerns of the contemporary world, we see that attitudes toward science are consistent with those that inform other domains of Arab culture, including the formation and perpetuation of negotiating relationships in the world, the logic of literal faith as an expression of the unity of natural phenomena and the articulation of a life of faith lived through a community of believers, the focus on the need to preserve social order against the chaos that may arise from things being out of category, and the concern that without enactment neither an idea nor an association rises to the level of reality. As a vehicle for insight into the nested set of meanings that comprise the cultural variants of the Islamic world, the relation of the scientist to the terms of a literal faith, like understanding the meaning of property or portraits, genies or outsiders, affords a window into a world of significance that Westerners ignore only at their peril.

ELEVEN

Expecting the Unexpected: Cultural Components of Arab Governance

Discussions about governance in the Arab world often revolve around the prospects for democracy. One of two models tends to dominate these discussions. Either it is assumed that an electoral model based on competing political parties must cast up leaders whose legitimacy stems from the process itself, or a middle class must develop whose eagerness to affect the distribution of power coincides with those enlightened self-interests and unseen market forces that conduce toward representative government. It is not that these models lack merit, but they tend to exist in a partial cultural vacuum. To understand the relation of democratic forms and contemporary Arab political life—bearing in mind always that a general reference to "Arabs" is in no way to deny the range of variation—it may, therefore, be useful to explore some aspects of Arab culture more broadly conceived and to consider how they interact with the forms of governance that have been developing.

I come at these issues as both an anthropologist and a lawyer. While some scholars seek to derive, by historic or contemporary comparison, the "foundations" of a given political form like democracy, an anthropologist like myself is concerned more with the ways in which seemingly unconnected social and cultural factors may contribute to the development and perpetuation of a particular political pattern. Thus, I consider factors such as the ways in which concepts of person and time affect the idea of power, the nature of reciprocity and ingratiation in the development of bonds of obligation and institutionalized ways for leveling difference, and the relation between Arabs' concepts of "chaos" and their views of the moral and religious underpinnings of human nature. As a legal scholar I am also interested in the ways in which cultural assumptions inform the institutions through which power is distributed and differences are addressed. I will, therefore, with full recognition that there are significant differences within the Arab world, try to show how such cultural concepts and institutional forms are vital to any understanding of Arab governance and how they may be drawn upon in fashioning culturally responsive constitutions.

Cultural Components of Arab Social Life

In the Arab world, to recapitulate my earlier argument, persons are identified primarily in terms of their networks of obligation. Envisioning the world as a terrain for interpersonal negotiation—and supported by the Islamic view that central to human nature and divine injunction is the need to govern one's passions with reason—individuals are defined largely by their ability to marshal dependencies and to overcome opponents on behalf of themselves and those with whom ties have been formed. Since one's local community operates within the broader community of believers, to fabricate a network of associations is to connect one's own actions with a world whose universal vision of humankind and its proper organization appear consistent with nature and common sense. Successful construction of a network of dependents thus implies both self-mastery and worldly effect. As elements of the cultural paradigm emerge in distinctive contexts, the synergistic quality of each upon the whole reinforces the sense of a universe that is both orderly and consonant with the structure established by God. Consider some of the specific cultural correlates through which this pattern is expressed.

We have seen that, by contrast to the West, where property ownership primarily expresses one's relationship to a thing, in the Arab world it expresses one's ties to others as they concern that thing. We have also seen that it is vital that a man be able to move freely, forming attachments wherever they prove most advantageous. To be tied up is, both metaphorically and literally, to be unmanned, indeed to be rendered less than fully human. To acquire knowledge is to be able to move in the world, hence, in the words of an early writer, "Knowledge lifts the lowly person to the heights/Ignorance keeps the youth of noble birth immobile."[1] Rituals may heighten this emphasis: in some marriage rites, for example, a man is bound with a cord and then released, demonstrating his progression from a female-like position to that of a man. Similarly, an apprentice's situation is often analogized to that of a woman, and being freed from the master to become a master in one's own right is to be unbound.[2] (The equation of the feminine with the lack of free movement is captured in a common North African saying: Never trust a man who does not move about or a woman who does.) Jews, too, were characteristically analogized to women, unable to move with genuine freedom in the world of men. These two aspects—of property as relationship and the freedom to move to effect in the world—are vital to the Arab understanding of one's ability to navigate the world of reality.

Because free movement and property as relationship are linked, so long as one can establish oneself in a place and replicate relationships there, the specific site at which one may once have established such ties carries little in the way of mystical or romantic meaning. One may, therefore, hypothesize that where networks of relatedness can be moved, as Rémy Leveau has noted in Morocco, attachment to a home territory is not particularly intense. A person's name may be associated with a given place from which one's predecessors are said to have originated. But the combination of genealogical amnesia and genealogical manipulation frequently yield identifying family place-names that are either of recent creation or simple fabrication.[3] Attachment to a particular territory may, however, be intensified if people are not in fact free to reproduce in one territory the network of associations enjoyed in an earlier one. Thus, as we have also seen, Algerians and Palestinians, who have been hampered in their ability to re-create social ties in another place, may have an unusually strong attachment to particular places. The idea, therefore, that the state must safeguard property as personal possession in order to establish legitimacy may be less central than the need to ensure freedom of movement and the ability to enact one's capacity to forge interpersonal ties wherever they prove most beneficial. Put differently, any attempt to restrict movement—whether through educational or economic opportunity—cuts deeply into the Arab sense of justice, maturity, and legitimate authority.

In the West we see a kind of fractionation of the self that contributes to the separation of one's personal viewpoint from the role one might be playing at a given moment. In Arab cultures, by comparison, conceptual unity is emphasized, and the idea that a person may play a role in one context that is wholly separable from other roles is largely inconceivable. It is as if every association, every social tie, adheres to the individual who, in turn, can use any of these points of attachment to connect to others as circumstance and ability provide. Since connections are not mutually exclusive, the sense of freedom is maintained so long as the coherence, the integrity, of one's multifold persona itself remains intact. While fractionation of the self is certainly not a prerequisite to democracy, its counter—the focus on the unity of the person—does, however, downplay institutions as the foundation upon which to build a political system and emphasizes political office as an aspect of a person's multiple attachments.

Time, as we have seen, also plays into this pattern. Events are commonly categorized not by strict chronology but by whether they have an ongoing effect on relationships. Events that occurred in the more distant past but are perceived as having a continuing effect may be far more important than recent events that are seen as having no continuing relational impact. Particular years may be designated by a special name—the year of the ration coupon, the year of the "voluntary" donations for building the extravagant mosque, the year of the death of a particular big man—because those were years in which the arrays of negotiated relationships were being recast. Aspects of the colonial period may seem very current to people in some Arab cultures, but not, as some of the Orientalists would claim, because they are constantly mired in a past from which they cannot shake free or because they look to this past as a way of blaming others for their present circumstances.[4] Rather, if one looks at the highly selective references to the past that are being made, one can see that the principle of selection is not one of self-justifying misrepresentation of the past but of whether persons or events are seen as having a continuing impact on current relationships. Thus, if one sees the French, say, as still having an impact on the politics and culture of Morocco because the French language is used in texts and lectures at the university level, people may understandably feel that colonial pressures are still being brought to bear since anyone who hopes to go on to higher education will effectively have to learn French in the earlier grades. The old saw that colonialism has never worked so well as since its demise is, then, not a departure from reality. Time and context are perceived not as mere duration and setting: rather they constitute additional cultural support for the focus on the continuity or discontinuity of people's relationships to one another.

The ways in which memory is manipulated by the state, or the ways in which time is used to legitimize or delegitimize by characterizing the past as relevant or not to ongoing structures, may bear on the course of political development. If, for example, one looks at monuments or pictures of current or past leaders in the Arab world, some common elements emerge. Historic monuments are particularly noteworthy for their absence: one sees rather few memorials to the past. In some instances, of course, this is connected to the Islamic prohibition on idols, to which statues may be easily equated. But it is also, perhaps, connected to the points made above, namely that if what is vital for one to know is how a person fashions his or her relationships and how those relationships continue to have effects in the world, an acceptable mode of monumental portrayal may never have been a priority. Instead, it is in various utterances that such memorials may be found—the stories told, the words identified with a given leader, the allusions to a powerful man's continuing effect in the world. Graveyards commonly have either no markers or extremely modest ones: people are usually buried in rows ordered only by when they died, and though people visit cemeteries on particular occasions and even eat a meal at the site of a relative's grave, after forty years a cemetery may be bulldozed and turned to another purpose altogether. The common saying in North Africa, as we have seen, is that three days after one's death, one's property dispersed and the mourning rituals complete, one no longer exists. Thus, the emphasis found in other domains of Arab culture—the emphasis on continuing social impact in the world—is shown even in the rituals of death to reflect the focus on worldly social ties rather than their transcendental implications.

The way politicians, among others, draw upon and manipulate cultural forms sheds light on what is perceived to have effects in the world of relationships. We have seen, for example, that portraits are uncommon because they cannot tell the viewer what he or she needs most to know about another person—how that person goes about arranging associations with others.[5] By contrast, film and television are readily accepted modes of representation precisely because one can see the individual moving in a world of relationships, creating ties wherever desired. The use of photographs of leaders in the Arab world might seem to contradict this proposition. But if these images are not portraits as that medium is commonly regarded in the West—not merely an identifying image but an entry point to an understanding of the personality of the figure represented—then such portraits must be seen in the Arab context as signs of the persons rather than insights into them. The latter could be gained only from a moving figure operating in the world. Every mode of representation thus accentuates the view that each person stands at the center of a web of associations of his own making, and each new form of representation makes sense to the extent that it accords with this cultural emphasis.

Several aspects of social organization also correlate with this pattern of relationships. Although most Arabs do not belong to actual tribes, these political forms have features that continue to affect many perceptions and relations. That is why I have suggested that one think in terms of a "tribal ethic" separable from its initial source. This ethic has several components. First, tribes themselves are a distinct set of political forms, but their shapes are not the defining or constant feature about them. Indeed, they are political forms that are capable of shifting shape. Elsewhere I have analogized them to amoeba, whose distinctive quality is captured by looking not at their shape but at the way they vary in response to changing conditions.[6] Similarly, tribes do not manifest their characteristic qualities by their momentary organizational form. Their foundational quality lies not in the form they take on at a given moment but in their ability to take on a range of variations while retaining certain capabilities. Indeed, tribes commonly coexist with other political forms. It has been shown, for example, that tribes often come into existence only in response to the formation of states, not as some "evolutionary" precursor to that more elaborated form.[7] Bands, defined as extended families that operate as producing and consuming units, may be the form out of which a broader identity may precipitate under various circumstances—ranging from predatory expansion and common defense to spiritual unification in the face of religious competition or threat. But if the organizational form is not the central feature of tribes, two other features mentioned earlier may be vital to their identity, namely the existence of mechanisms for internal leveling and the moral equivalence of constituent units.

Leveling keeps too much power from flowing into too few hands for too long a period of time. It may take many institutionalized forms, such as teasing others to knock them down to size or avoiding others (as when Arab men keep a distinct distance from their fathers but expect emotional support from their maternal uncles, who are not part of their lineage). These leveling devices, which undercut rank based on descent or role, may limit certain forms of collective action, but, more important, they work to dispel the felt disadvantages of hierarchy. If we connect this first point about leveling to the second, that of moral equivalence, we can see the synergy that results. For if one regards every social unit as standing on the same moral footing—that no one family or person or lineage is inherently and permanently of greater moral worth than any other—then leveling devices can be seen as supporting the moral equivalence of each social unit.[8] The result is a political and social form of enormous resilience, one that may even appear and re-appear at different moments, as the stimulus of other political entities operates to bring them into action. And if we see the features of leveling and moral equivalence as no longer necessarily connected to the existence of actual tribes—any more than one must be a Protestant concerned about one's soul to evince the Protestant ethic—then the forces of this tribal ethic may still pervade much of Arab political culture.

For example, the legitimacy of any leader may be primarily a function of his effectiveness in putting together a network of dependents, a constellation of others who owe him support and whom he must support through his much larger network of connections. The flip side of this "big man" pattern, in the context of a tribal ethos, is that anyone who can put together a competing, indeed superior, network will ipso facto be legitimate. It is the process of demonstrating such effective movement in the world that is the indispensable index of legitimacy, not some inherited or elective position. Since, as we saw earlier, roles are not segregated but coalesced, legitimacy lies in the fabrication of culturally recognizable capabilities and social consequences. If every unit is morally equivalent, anyone can try his hand at the game.

We have even suggested that this notion of the tribal ethic (to continue poaching from Max Weber) is related to what might be called the spirit of reciprocity—that all obligations are interchangeable and subject to bargaining. Power, as we have seen, tends to be both personal and susceptible to limitation. It is accumulated by getting others indebted and then, given the ability to convert debts formed in one way into obligations that may be called up in quite a different domain, to be able to play the expectation of reciprocity to advantage. Thus a "favor" done to help another raise a bridewealth payment may be drawn upon when one seeks help in a political election, or help offered in an economic venture may be called up in asking another to serve as one's intermediary in a dispute. It is this interchangeability of reciprocal obligations, and the constant quest for information about others' networks of obligation, that forms a central component of the political cultures of the Arab world and the changes that may be taking place in them.

Limiting Power: Culture and Democracy

For democratic forces to work successfully in the context of Arab political structures, it may be essential that they perpetuate leveling devices, reinforce morally equal social units, and support the interchangeable nature of obligations. For example, discussions of democracy in the Arab world often refer to several classic modes of collective decision-making, or at least decision-ratification. *Shūrā*, or consultation, generally describes some group either sitting with the ruler as an advisory panel or being contacted by the ruler for their input and/or approval.[9] The group itself, however, does not have a clear, universal, institutional definition. It may be as unspecific as the "notables" (*ʿayan*) of the area—usually men of substance, education, and familial connection—or it may refer to those regarded as particularly learned in the sacred texts (*ʿulamāʾ*).[10] As is the case with political leaders and important persons in all other domains, it is by taking on the qualities ideally associated with a given position that one comes to be treated as someone in that position. Proof of position is by worldly consequent acts rather than formal induction. Thus, when consultation does occur it is predominantly with those who have acquired the status of being acknowledged rather than ex officio occupants of particular roles. Such consultation can also vary quite widely, from mere rubber stamping by those picked by the ruler to a far more profound, indeed sometimes courageous, willingness to tell the truth to the powerful, or at least to oppose the powerful on some personal or principled grounds. Stories are told, for instance, of a big man who would try to steal land by having the local religious officials ratify his duress only to find that such figures were willing to risk prison or death to oppose the theft on religious grounds.[11] Proponents of modern democratization who point to the practice of shura, however, should not expect that by its constitutional formalization alone it will act as a counterweight to executive power: as always, it is to a great extent the person who makes the institution—whether political or juridical—not the other way around.[12]

The institution of the *baiʿa*, or ratification of the ruler in his position, is also seen by some as a practice on which one could build democratic institutions. Here, too, however, the acknowledgment is traditionally made not by a group whose membership is prescribed, much less institutionalized, but by a far more amorphous grouping of those regarded as knowledgeable and worldly. Even if one were to claim that the election of the leader constituted the *bayʿa* of "the people" or that it was effected by the endorsement of a body of elected or appointed persons, the question of legitimacy would still remain. Can one acquire legitimacy in this cultural system merely by garnering the necessary votes or group ratification, or must one demonstrate through favor and obligation that one can indeed construct an effective network of obligations that stands above and beyond institutional position alone? When one hears a Bahraini prince say that "as traditional Arabs, I don't think democracy is part of our nature," but still hear him assert that some accountability is required, is it a mistake to think he has in mind the constraints of mutual indebtedness rather than of a separation of powers?[13] If, in sum, this is a system in which persons make institutions, rather than vice versa, one will have to address the process by which legitimacy is ascribed and whether such personal proofs of effectiveness can actually be transformed into impersonal institutions.

Corruption forms an important indicator of the concept of power itself. Surveys by Transparency International and others show just how extensive corruption is in many Arab countries. But these studies seldom explore the meaning of corruption in people's everyday lives. Arabs tend to characterize corruption not as abuse of some formal set of criteria associated with a given position but as the failure to share whatever largesse comes one's way with those to whom one has forged ties of obligation. To be told, as some informants only half-jokingly put it, that "bribery is our form of democracy" because it means one can undercut an autocrat by bribing a person below him to disregard the superior's direction, is but to suggest the way corruption, however ironically expressed, implies a limitation on power.

Identifying certain moments as ones of "chaos" may also fit this patterned emphasis on the relational and the negotiable. As we noted earlier, after the invasion of Iraq in March 2003 we were told that there was a period of anarchy, chaos, and looting. The implication of these terms was that there was no order to people's acts beyond the personally expedient. But such moments always have a distinctive set of characteristic features—whether it is the "anarchy" of Russia at the time of the Bolshevik Revolution or the mayhem wrought in seventeenth-century Britain by such "libertine" groups as the Ranters. As we have seen, the Arabic term for chaos, *fitna* (far more than its milder corollary, *fauda*), calls forth notions of the social universe not holding together.[14] But it also implies (to employ Western metaphors) a reshuffling of the deck, a leveling of the playing field so that others may have a chance at the game. From other examples we know to look at such practices as new marital arrangements, the revitalization of voluntary associations, and the redistribution of wealth to see how people are achieving a measure of security for themselves in an uncertain social environment. To understand acceptable order one may, therefore, need to understand the meaning and structure of acceptable disorder.

Language is central to the ability of any Arab to maneuver in such a world. A person of importance is said to "have word": a person who can capture the definition of a situation can turn it to advantage. The structure of Arabic is itself important in this context. Arabic may be thought of as organized like a kind of periodical chart: there are elements (composed of three, and more rarely four, consonants) that can be varied by the use of prefixes, infixes, and suffixes—especially through vowel variations—to produce words whose theoretical places in the chart are known but whose specific overtones may be open to variation. Thus, a root applied in a given verb form may mean "to cause or be caused by that action," but specifically what this causation means will vary with the contexts and uses to which it may be put.[15]

The result is that control of language as an instrument for capturing the terms of discussion is an enormous asset to be used in forming relationships. If someone can define a situation as one of commonality rather than hierarchy, or as one in which collective duty takes precedence over monetary advantage, he can control the repercussions of the relationship. It is for this reason that political rhetoric, which to outsiders may at times seem extravagant and out of touch with reality, may more accurately be seen as trying out a concept that, if it takes, will capture the situation in a particular way. Like a price mentioned in the marketplace, it is not inherently true; instead it becomes "true" only when relationships get formed in and through it. Poets are vital to Arab political culture precisely because they are the ones who, above all others, explore language and create terms that forge a new reality. In the realm of politics itself this means, among other things, that the man who wishes to build a following must not only "have word" (in the sense that his words have an impact on relationships) but demonstrate, directly or through surrogates, his ability to capture relationships through words. An anthropologist of the Middle East who was looking at the period following the invasion of Iraq, for example, would want to learn what was happening in the coffee houses: Were poets using words in new ways? Were they speaking about relationships in a language of "democracy" or "insurgency"? Were they expanding the use of standard references to reconceptualize the meaning of the property that had been "stolen" or "liberated" or "reallocated" during the period of "chaos"? Indeed, did they refer to this period as fitna or in some other way? Just as one would like to know if items that were "stolen" were ever returned (perhaps with the expectation that the hospital or school from which they were taken would be expected to favor the allies of the person returning the items should the latter have need of medical or educational assistance) and how this recirculation of items—like the recirculation of words—was used as an instrument for rearranging relationships of interdependence.[16]

Even Islamic law, when seen against this cultural backdrop, appears somewhat different than it is often portrayed. The practice of Islamic law (as opposed to its theological and scholarly renderings) tends to focus on the local. Judges use experts and witnesses from the area to inform them of both the facts and the customs relating to various actions, and even where national codes apply they are commonly informed by these local fact-finding mechanisms. Just as political and religious leaders build followings, so, too, judges establish credibility not simply by virtue of their office but by cleverly applying their learning to complex relationships. While this may be true in almost any legal system, it is particularly important in Islamic law. Moreover, every Islamic legal variant has a proposition that basically asserts that, short of violating one of the very few clear prohibitions in the Quran, custom takes precedence over shariʿa. Judges have very wide discretion, even in the modern context of an appellate structure. The personalistic element in fashioning believability, the use of the local in the calculation of consequences, and the enormous creativity of the courts in fashioning approaches to the cases before them are all consonant with a system that displays similar features in many other cultural domains.

Within this cultural context, the Arab variants of political culture are also enormously flexible: people are not simply held to category, nor are events reducible to prefigured occurrence. Rather, like an elaborate game of chess—again, that most theologically correct of games Arabs may play—the moves can be infinitely alluring without additional pieces or altered rules being essential to variation. The old saying that a man can be poor in the morning, a vizier of the king in the afternoon, and hanged in the public marketplace the next day is only one way in which many Arabs underscore the need to maintain this flexibility and its promise at all times. Yet it may also be true—and here as a proposition of universal import—that at times when the world seems disorderly, people have a strong tendency to revert to role expectations. What parent has not insisted at a frustrating moment on a child doing what he or she is told simply because "I am your father (mother)"; what individual has not felt more prone to revert to expected behavior when challenged by uncertain circumstance? The key, of course, is to understand what constitutes such challenges in different cultures as well as for different personalities. But if this argument has merit, then we must also ask, for example, whether Arabs who feel they are living in a continual state of disorder and injustice are, like any others, prone to revert to traditional roles—to claims of honor or paternalistic authority or exaggerated solidarity, all elements that under less stress are occulted by the advantages of ambiguity and ambivalence. We need to understand what constitutes disorder in these cultures if we are to ask what actions may prove most effective when Arabs change the structure of political/religious leadership or fashion such foundational documents as a new constitution.

Indeed, the failure to see how such key ideas as time and person, property and "chaos" play out in the context of political culture may lead to a view of future Arab politics that is far too dependent on ideas of democracy and legitimacy derived from the Western experience.[17] This view leads commentators like Thomas L. Friedman to make the untenable assertion that all Arab regimes are regarded as illegitimate by their people and that if these regimes were to be removed truly legitimate ones could take their place.[18] Whatever else may be said of such autocratic regimes, one cannot responsibly assert that they are utterly devoid of legitimacy: one can detest one's president but still recognize him as the legitimate holder of power. In the Middle East every Arab leader must put together his following in a highly personalized way, and anyone who fails to accomplish this through culturally recognizable ways will not be legitimate. Put differently, legitimacy comes not from the ballot box or other institutionalized mechanisms alone but from the fabrication of networks of indebtedness that demonstrate a person's ability to marshal allies in the real world. And whoever does that will, by definition, be legitimate.

As a thought experiment, let us take some of these cultural issues and try to relate them to the building of democracy in a hypothetical Arab country. Let us also assume in this exercise that the keystone to democracy is not the presence of elections or political parties but the recognition that a democracy is a government of limited powers. Then, given the emphasis on personalism described above, it can be argued that it is indeed possible to construct a government of structurally balanced powers even in the absence of a clear set of institutionalized roles, i.e., even though people do not fragment themselves into roles through which they might act contrary to their own private beliefs. Moreover, the balance of powers need not be a static one, in the sense that a formal list of the powers accompanying a given position articulates the limits of their range. To the contrary, the limitations may be at the margins, rather than at the core of each position. There is a saying that constantly recurs in the Quran: These are the limits of God; do not trespass them. Islam makes a clear distinction between the "rights (sing. *ḥaqq*) of God" and "the rights of man," and it is part of both religious doctrine and the concept of humankind that God intended humanity to control all those aspects of life through their God-given reason that are not fully and clearly proscribed by divine ordinance. Since these latter are very few in number—the Quran not being an intensely law-like document, as are portions of the Hebrew Bible, for example—a very great deal is left to humans to determine. Thus, limitations may be forged at the boundaries in terms that are consonant with those that are actively prescribed by Islam. We could even specify some of these restraints on personalistic power more precisely. For example, courts might take cases for purposes of issuing advisory opinions, truth and reconciliation mechanisms could expose abuses of power without threat of conviction, supermajorities might be required for the passage of certain types of legislation (thus requiring some cooperation across ethnic or regional boundaries), and military leaders may have a specified term of office (as do members of the Joint Chiefs of Staff in the United States). Each of these modes of limiting power may have greater hope of success because it is consonant with the cultural and religious assumptions that give meaning to relationships in social life at large.

Creating Culturally Responsive Constitutions

Since the late nineteenth century, many Islamic countries have adopted constitutions, usually based on specific Western models. Frequently, these constitutions have been changed at the whim of autocratic rulers or ignored when their tenets were regarded by a ruler as inconvenient.[19] In response to the Iraq war that began in 2003 a new round of constitution writing was initiated. The question arises as to how one develops a constitution that is in accord with the sentiments of the people. If constitutional provisions are to be responsive to cultural concerns, several foundational notions may be worth keeping in mind. In the West, if one asks people to name the opposite of freedom, most would probably respond that it is tyranny. In the Arab world, as we have seen, the opposite of freedom is chaos (fitna). Thus, in order to avoid the threat of social chaos as the people see it, protection from abusive power might need to be grounded in particular cultural freedoms. At the risk of sounding a Wilsonian note—with all its attendant hubris—we might think of these as the four freedoms of Arab governance:

(1) *Freedom of movement.* We have seen how vital mobility is to Arabs—in the sense of being able to freely negotiate their networks wherever advantageous. This mobility incorporates both spatial and relational elements. Spatially, it would be important that people be able to own land wherever they are able to purchase it, and that the government underscore its desire to supply adequate housing for each family.[20] It is also very important in some Arab countries that collective ownership of land and resources be placed on as sound a footing as private property titles. Tribal lands, in particular, could be specifically protected as the private property of a group—the internal divisions and uses of the land being entirely a matter of their own organization—thus merging whatever laws apply to collective land with that of private holdings as a way of securing the former through homology with the latter. The seizure of any property by right of eminent domain should be permitted only when it is done with a clear public purpose, the owners receiving full compensation for the taking. Securing open markets, rather than intense central regulation, would also be consonant with this sense of free movement. Relationally, it is also important that there be clear definitions of what constitutes corruption, as, for example, when parents have sacrificed enormously for their children's education only to encounter forms of bribery that advance some students over others, or where the state itself arbitrarily changes the level of passing grades for a diploma in order to claim fewer people with degrees are actually unemployed.[21]

(2) *Freedom of law.* From its earliest days the central government in Islamic countries had control over criminal law, but each confessional community or school of Islamic law followed its own approach to marriage, divorce, and other matters of personal status. This pattern was continued in the Ottoman lands and was common even beyond that empire's borders, as for example in Morocco and Mauritania. To Arabs, local control involves more than mere jurisdiction: it is a matter of being free from the potential chaos that may be engendered by having to follow a legal regime that is not locally responsive. Addressing this legal and cultural concern, Arab states might constitutionally authorize local confessional groups to apply their own laws of marriage, divorce, filiation, and inheritance, but with two provisos—that if either individual chooses to opt out of the local system, jurisdiction will rest with a national court operating by national codes, and that such laws shall not be inconsistent with the equivalent of a "cultural repugnancy

clause" of the constitution.[22] To put this latter proposition in context: much of the debate about Islam and democracy concerns the role of Islamic law in the state system, and often the discussion is set in terms of whether Islamic law shall govern or whether laws shall only be consistent with the general principles of Islam. To get away from this divisive perspective, one might say that no law shall be inconsistent with such Prophetic values as balance, moderation, and proper intent. Alternatively, it could be said that laws must demonstratively further the Quranic principles of avoiding evil and doing good.[23] A repugnancy clause places the burden on those proposing a law to show that it is not inconsistent with these religious and cultural values. Like "the limits of God" it emphasizes that the constitution is a vehicle for drawing outer boundaries more than prescribing details of life that may vary with locality and custom. Despite appearing to some Westerners as antithetical to a unitary "rule of law," the simultaneous availability of alternative legal forums, coupled with support of the local through limited appeals, may for at least certain issues allow a substantial degree of competition among courts for socially acceptable approaches to the law.

(3) *Freedom of the local.* Islamic law is only one manifestation of the importance of the local in Arab cultures. As we have noted, the tribal ethos incorporates a strong component of building local networks that sometimes may coalesce into larger groupings. This ethos is also coupled with an emphasis on personal identity (origins, *asl*) as deeply informed by the relational practices of the localized group with which one is identified. To build on this ethos, it may be appropriate to make use of regional, devolved legislative bodies. Models to be studied may include those of Spain or the United Kingdom. There should be no fear that semi-autonomous zones would be coincident with ethnic or confessional boundaries. To the contrary, concern about local groupings should be replaced by support for them. A brief comparison may be informative here. The writers of the Federalist Papers were greatly concerned about "faction" as a threat to an independent America, worrying that competing groups would threaten the new republic by their inherent divisiveness. In fact, the fear was largely misplaced. Political groupings, if roughly balanced or required by the structure of legislative decision-making to rely on one another as allies for various endeavors, may actually fortify democracy rather than undermine it. We have seen how, for the Arabs, the acknowledgment by one's enemies was often vital to one's own legitimacy. In a similar spirit, the structured interdependence of local groups may strengthen emergent Arab democracies, and that localism should be encouraged rather than

feared. Obviously, a balance of local and national must be sought, and the former may, as in the constitution of Iraq, be vital to holding the entire apparatus together.[24] But federalism need not imply the dissipation of power; rather, it simply underscores the need to consider that without the local the national may either fail to cohere or fail to accord with a felt sense of how limited power is acceptable within Arab political culture.

(4) *Freedom of personality.* For the Arabs, force of personality is key to navigating the world. Everyone, therefore, should be assured of an identity. This means that immigrants, women, and illegitimate children, like all others, should be entitled to civil identity documents and passports drawn in their own name, not drawn in the name of a husband or, as is sometimes the case for the illegitimate, denied documentation altogether. Similarly, the right to privacy—to a home immune to invasion without warrant, to the retention of information about oneself that is not available to the government—has particular relevance insofar as the quest and control of knowledge about others is vital to building alliances. Indeed, the sense of fair play here includes the need for protecting confidential knowledge. At the same time, public places—which are often those terrains for which no one feels any individual responsibility since they are not involved in the development of people's bonds of affiliation—should be reconceptualized as joint space for which some investment of personality becomes at least possible.

———

Of the twenty-two Muslim countries in the Middle East, none is commonly regarded as a democracy. Yet if the keystone to democracy is not elections or parties as such but a government of limited powers, then we may hypothesize that institution building where personalism informs relationship, time, memory, and property may very well follow a different course than in the West.[25] There is (it should go without saying) nothing inherent in Arab cultures, much less Islamic thought, that is antithetical to the development of democracy. It may be true that the introduction of new political parties has merely replicated the autocracy and nepotism of their predecessors, and that those who are well disposed to some form of democracy—republican, liberal, or Islamic— draw back from further democratization after the first steps for fear that it will result in one of the other forms they wish to avoid.[26] But simply drawing constitutional models from the West, as if those documents were without cultural and historical foundation and were the manifestation of some natural phenomenon, is to court failure or meaningless legislation. Constitutions that not only reflect underlying cultural assumptions but are built analogically from 'the limits of God' and the 'rights of man,' that serve less as the scaffolding for the construction of a state than as an exoskeleton that protects vital organs, and that recognize the continuing force of personalism over institutionalized roles, may have far more meaning in Arab nations than some artificial construct imposed from above or outside. The idea that democracy can only follow on a certain level of economic advancement fails to grasp that democracy has many forms, and as a limitation on power it is not necessarily linked to any specific level or type of economic structure.[27] What we in the West need to understand, as we watch these developments at a distance, is that fundamental aspects of person, time, and relationship will deeply inform whatever changes take place, and that treating democracy, legitimacy, or institutions in a cultural vacuum is, at the very least, to diminish our own chances of being better prepared for the unexpected.

TWELVE

Power and Culture in the Acceptance of "Universal" Human Rights

Given the enormous variation in the world's cultures, is it really possible to generate a set of shared, indeed universal, human rights that are substantively meaningful? In the Arab world—where the situation of women or illegitimate children may vary widely from practices in the West, or where the publication of comments deemed insulting to a ruler or the Prophet may bring severe punishments—can common standards be framed without doing violence to one or another of the cultures involved? And if attempting to codify human rights within a single culture at least helps spark conversation among its own citizens, how can meaningful enforcement follow if the very idea of "rights" is itself incompatible with the local culture's approach to law and social relations?

These questions are by no means new, but they are usually put in terms of what common political factors support universal rights or what functional equivalents may replace one of the prerequisites thought necessary to their acceptance. Missing is the analysis of the circumstances under which the movement of human rights across frontiers is effective. Of course, the transregional acceptance of universal rights may depend on the context of local history. The reach of Roman citizenship or the Barbarians' acceptance of Christian morals is not the same story as the introduction of democracy to postwar Japan or the conversion of many African Americans to Islam. When we think about weaving Islamic and Western concepts of human rights into a single framework, therefore, we first need a clearer and more realistic understanding of the circumstances under which such combination may take place generally. This chapter attempts to set forth some of those circumstances, rather than explicating the range of particular human rights conventions drawn up by Western or Muslim nations, as a necessary step to further discussion about establishing standards across cultural lines.

Crossing Cultures—in Theory

Academic discussions about the formulation of universal standards of human rights tend to focus on three sets of concerns: the philosophical foundations for asserting general standards or specific propositions, the reasons one culture may legitimately assert its principles over those of another or must defer to the variant nature of human values and practices, and the debate over group versus individual rights and the consequent impact for the relatively powerless members of a community if their voices remain unconsidered. Vital as these discussions are, it may also be useful to look candidly at the circumstances in which the precepts, which are said to be universally applicable, are extended across cultural boundaries. For while human rights precepts may arise out of international accord, quite commonly they emanate from a particular cultural background and are extended abroad mainly by enticement or force.

"Universal" formulations—whether put in terms of human rights, attributes of intrinsic human nature, or manifestations of natural law—not only challenge our capacity to view realistically the prospects for extending rights across cultural borders, but they test some of the most central theories of culture and power with which we approach the whole question of fabricating a regime of rights that is both universal and locally responsive. Asking under what circumstances human rights proposals may achieve, and not merely assert, universality challenges us to rethink certain aspects of the concept of culture itself. For if we wish to formulate human rights that traverse borders, we need to think about the ways in which culture facilitates or defeats this goal and to reconsider the conditions that support it. Thus, instead of focusing on general standards or specific propositions, we may ask whether it is possible to formulate human rights in procedural rather than substantive terms, whether some principle of equivalence rather than equality may in some instances suffice to further universal human rights, and whether it is possible to tap into the diversity of views that exists in any culture to facilitate greater representation by those who are relatively powerless.

That the bases on which different cultures ground their own visions of human well-being vary enormously hardly needs documentation. Within a single culture, standards that have been adopted from another culture may (at least to some members) be ambiguous or contradictory. Is it a violation of equal human rights when men have access to religious practices or properties that are denied to women, when male circumcision is not child abuse but female genital cutting is, when only the state religion can be the subject of blasphemy, or when any level of corporal punishment is denied custodial parents?[1] What agreement can there be about universal human rights when a Native American tribe may deny membership to the children of women who marry outsiders while granting it to descendants of men who marry abroad?[2] What consensus is possible when one-third of American states regard first-cousin marriage as incest while two-thirds do not, or when private colleges rationalize gender exclusivity as not inimical to fostering equality?[3] Why do Arabs commonly perceive that the opposite of tyranny is not freedom but chaos; why is wearing a headscarf to school such a challenge to the secular state in France; why should the proposition that "those in need have a right in the property of those who are better off" not mean the same thing regardless of culture?[4] It is not that shared orientations operating under the rubric of universal human rights are not possible. But it is naive to imagine that merely hitting the right common philosophical chord will do the job. We have to look elsewhere if we are to have a realistic sense of when such accords may or may not prove effective.

The Power of Culture and the Culture of Power

Let me begin where an anthropologist might be expected to begin—with the idea of culture as an analytic device. Put briefly, I accept the proposition that cultural differentiation is central to the kind of animal that we are. We do not simply implement distinctions given to us by instinct; rather, we have developed, over the course of our evolutionary history, the capacity to create the units by which we make sense of the world. These categories are replicated throughout the diverse domains of any culture—the religious, the political, the economic, the familial, the artistic—such that they appear to its members as both immanent and natural.[5]

This theory of culture has extremely important implications for the creation of universally acceptable precepts. If the capacity to define our own experience of the world through differentiation is central to our being, then it is reasonable to assume that we will work to keep that capacity alive. Differentiation, or category creation, does not, of course, mean simple division. Units of experience can certainly be combined into ever more inclusive entities. But a constant propensity to create distinctions will ultimately challenge the success of so-called universal human rights conceptions. It may be very difficult, if not impossible, to maintain a unified application of human rights absent some way to avoid the tendency toward the locally distinctive.[6] Thus, it is not as though one need simply hit on the right set of features discoverable in every culture and then codify these shared features in a unitary list of attributes. Rather, what I am suggesting is that, for several reasons, one *cannot* articulate a common denominator of shared conceptualizations—because they simply do not exist, because uniformity can be achieved only through the expression of some form of power that one culture exercises over another, and because shared propositions will have no lasting quality if they do not knit together the different domains of a culture in ways that make everyday experience appear both comprehensible and beyond individual design.

Two forces may affect the universalization of human rights: the power of culture, which tends toward new category creation (largely local but potentially incorporative), and the culture of power, in which the fissioning tendency of new categorizations may, under certain circumstances, yield to the ever more inclusive. Under what circumstances, we may ask, have the concepts generated by one or more cultures been extended beyond their original source to affect other societies? The most salient instances would include physical conquest, attraction to the categories of another culture engendered by trade, religious and cultural conversion precipitated by the breakdown in coherence of the cultural categories of the subject culture, or the sheer intellectual persuasion to a different way of viewing one's place in the order of things. In each instance, one would find the intrusion of some form of power by which the boundaries of cultural differentiation are traversed and society comes to see the world in a different light. Some examples may be instructive.

Sheer force may, of course, involve the imposition of new values. It may involve the extension of "citizenship" to all or some of the conquered, or it may destroy the political or religious elite and thus forever alter the society's worldview. Two features characterize the process of conquest. First, the effects of conquest are commonly reciprocal: the invader may be transformed almost as much as the defeated. In the realm of human rights the conquest may, either formally or effectively, result in the greater differentiation of the conquered population itself, so that rank and its privileges are exaggerated rather than lessened by the conquest. This may occur even in relatively "benign" conquests—done to "civilize" the subject population "for its own good"—as, for example, in opening the criminal courts to all but having so much greater a collective impact on the lives of the "natives" as to insure their inability to compete equally with the invading force.

Second, if the conquest does not so adversely affect the ordinary members of the defeated population as to "persuade" them to abandon the system that led them to defeat, they may merely adapt themselves to new masters for a time but not change their beliefs or behavior. Thus, it has been argued that German and Japanese civilians suffered so greatly in the Second World War that their links to the sociopolitical ideas of the defeated regimes were thoroughly broken and their receptivity to new concepts and values rendered far more possible. By contrast, the comparatively lesser civilian casualties of the two Iraq wars involving the United States may not lead to a fundamental break with the preexisting system of Iraqi political culture, and as a result Iraqi society may remain relatively unreceptive to outside standards couched as universally applicable human rights.

Physical conquest may or may not result in cultural domination. Whether it is through the direct extension of the colonists' culture in education, language, or the arts of government, or whether it is through hooking others on one's opiates, one's hamburgers, or one's pornography, two factors may bear on the culture of universal human rights . First, the presence of a foreign power usually involves opportunities for segments of the indigenous population to shift their place in the order of society. As such shifts occur among classes, castes, and categories, they are likely to produce new forms of naturalized knowledge. What had been the natural order of social placement must be re-naturalized, and the bases for asserting the new positioning must accord with the criteria of identity and the rationale for social alteration. Human rights, drawn from an outside culture, may therefore become one of the bases upon which mobile social groups establish their new positions. The success of this change will depend on the extent to which such a conceptual shift is integrated with other aspects of the culture, such as the pattern of economic exchange, the idiom through which the state is envisioned (e.g., as parent or divine design), and the extent to which change is seen as emanating from the choice of the people or some natural progression.

The sheer attraction of power—of allying oneself with the winners—may lead to kaleidoscopic shifts in the way existing cultural propositions are themselves configured. When, for example, the Khomeini regime came to power in Iran in 1989, many Americans were surprised to learn that the Iranians linked American imperialism to American pornography. Similarly, the widespread antipathy of the French to McDonald's restaurants struck many Americans as genuinely irrational.[7] But it could be argued that both the Shah's Iran and late twentieth-century France had allied themselves with American culture to the point where many people began to feel their own identities slipping away. Given their own cultural configurations, they made connections among features of American culture and politics that Americans did not make. These cultures felt the threat of their own attraction to Americanism, in no small part as a result of their unwillingness or inability to alter many domains of their own cultures to adequately absorb the connections American culture appeared to entail. Given the ambivalent nature of such associations, the introduction of professedly universal human rights into these cultures from an American source may not sit well; conflicts might arise, for example, between a kind of First Amendment view of freedom of religion versus the abolition of religious symbols in French schools, or freedom of speech versus restrictions on "blasphemy" in Iran.

The adoption of a human rights paradigm that is not entirely homegrown may also come about through trade contacts, and in this case the question for the adopting culture is whether the benefits outweigh the disadvantages. Inclusion in the Roman orbit through acceptance of Roman law, access to markets that accompanied acceptance of the Muslim faith, incorporation of additional nations such as Turkey or China into the European Union or the World Trade Organization, and the conferral of "most favored nation" status by the United States may well be worth the price of accepting the more powerful nation's standards. For while trade may insinuate attendant cultural concepts—like, say, those of equality of opportunity and hence equality of persons—the process of adoption may be subtle and unseen or, like other forms of culture change, conscious and desired. In any event, history is replete with instances in which changes in the view of humanity follow the routes of trade even more than they follow the sword. When they do so, however, one may fairly question whether a kind of cost–benefit analysis is being run by the affected culture or whether, as a correlate of Western capitalism, particular changes are likely to occur in the views of personhood and relationship that advance or retard the acceptance of transnational human rights.

Changing views of human rights may also occur through wholesale conversion to a new set of religious beliefs, possibly after the disintegration of existing elements of the culture caused by military defeat, cultural disorientation, or environmental disaster. Before such large-scale change occurs, there is often a high degree of cultural incoherence as the various domains of a cohesive worldview no longer seem to hold together.[8] And whether the conversion is sudden and systemic or involves a change of manners without a major change in social position and views of humankind, the acceptance of new views of humanity and society prompted by the conversion will almost certainly imply a different configuration of cultural features than would be the case as the result of trade or cultural contacts of a more gradual nature.

Intellectual persuasion as a means of extending human rights is understandably emphasized by intellectuals. But only the most deterministic of historians would argue that in all such instances ideas simply follow self-interest. Intellectual roots of changing cultural concepts can hardly be underestimated, even in the overtly political way they may be applied. Thus, President Carter's insistence on speaking in terms of human rights when discussing the Soviet Union played a vital role in legitimizing those seeking change: they were not to be written off as *refuseniks*, dissidents, or proponents of a particular form of political change but were to be seen as embodiments of a transcendent move toward human rights. Such a change in the terms of the discussion was undoubtedly a significant factor in the eventual downfall of the Soviet system. Yet it is difficult, without turning deterministic, to see such conceptual shifts as existing in some pure realm of idea. For new concepts such as "universal" human rights to take hold, two mechanisms are necessary. The first is described by Stephen Toulmin when he comments that "patterns of conceptual change reflect the presuppositional structures of conceptual systems," i.e., the "logic" of change is not disconnected from the logic of the preceding pattern of concepts.[9] And second, the combination of new and old concepts must integrate the diverse domains of a society with sufficient clarity that a new way of conceiving the old becomes part of a new common sense. Consistency,

far from being the hobgoblin of little minds, is essential to a naturalized view of the world. The acceptance of a new way of viewing human
rights—whether within a given cultural tradition or as an expression
of a claimed universal—depends for its very existence, to say nothing
of its missionary success, on attaching a form of consistency to one tradition that originated in the worldview of another.[10]

In each of these instances one cannot look for laws that will com-
prehensively explain the nature of cultural change, resistance, or reciprocity. But a careful study of the expansion of cultural concepts, such
as those of modern universal human rights, may help us to think sys-
temically, to see the connections any such expansion may require if it
is to take effect in a given culture. It has often been noted that there
may not be any invariant basis on which we can explain to others why
they should accept our values as universal.[11] But we do know that the
constituent elements of a culture must possess enough coherence for
new concepts to reach across cultural boundaries. It is to several of
these aspects of cultural integration that we must return if we are to
understand how human rights conventions are incorporated into cultures, such as those of the Arab world, that did not give them birth.

Universal Rights and Particular Cultures

The theory of culture described above suggests that it is difficult to integrate human rights concerns into a subject culture in a piecemeal
fashion. The often Westernized elites of a recipient nation may attach
themselves to the universal standards promulgated by an international
or transnational body, but absent further force or incentive, the effect
of such rights in the people's daily lives is frequently nil. The Bangkok
Declaration and even the United Nations Universal Declaration of Human Rights, for example, employ exceptionally vague terms and have
very limited repercussions for everyday life. Those who see in "globalization" a vehicle through which the advantages of accepting such
standards may be furthered might consider that where principles do
take root it is less by intellectual persuasion than by economic compul-
sion. And even in the presence of worldwide economic and cultural
diffusion, local meaning and local circumstance commonly render the
impact of the seemingly universal highly distinctive indeed. Blue jeans
or rock music may signify youthful exuberance in the West but political
rebellion in the Soviet Union or China. If one ignores the integration
of an outside feature into the pattern of the recipient society, one may

be surprised later to discover that people who seemed to have become so alike are in fact so different. Clare Boothe Luce (though for her own purpose of asserting American exceptionalism) may have overstated the case when, in 1943, she called globalization "globaloney," but the local does indeed have a way of coming back at the unprepared.

That said, the theoretically troubling problem remains. For if what is vital to a culture is the reverberation in numerous domains—social, religious, familial—of a distinctive set of related ideas, the truth is that our theories are quite inadequate for telling us the precise nature and extent of this process of integration. At the margins we know that people have died when their cultures no longer provided them with a sense of the orderliness of their world. People removed from their island homes in the South Pacific by atomic testing or exiled from their tribal regions under the force of colonial expansion in North America have literally died of meaninglessness, while "suicide" bombers in the Middle East may kill themselves when doing so is the only way to make sense of the world. Away from the limiting cases, however, there are a number of analytic problems that directly affect our thinking about the acceptance of universal human rights.

Specifically, over the past generation anthropologists had come to see culture as largely a matter of "shared symbols": thought, being extrinsic, operates through shared conceptualizations so that people can orient their actions toward one another in a way that gives a sense of comprehensive reality to their everyday relationships. For a long time, however, the problematic feature of this expression was the part about "symbols"—what they are, how they operate and change, how their failure as "material vehicles of thought" has both caused and reflected the breakdown in certain social relations.[12] Less problematic—and hence less studied—has been the "shared" part. For if conceptual and relational change—whether from within or without—is to occur, then it is vital to have some basis for asserting, say, that only a limited degree of shared orientations—mere "passing acquaintance"—is sufficient to hold a society together. Alternatively, replication of a new concept in only certain domains or a certain number of domains may be sufficient for the worldview of one culture to affect the entire way of life of another. It is here that grand theory—Marxist, structuralist, economistic—has failed, while particularist explanations, though insightful for distinct situations, seem inadequate to predict what notions will succeed—what it is, for example, that may make a view of gender equality or the right to a specified level of income meaningful in a sociocultural system that had not previously subscribed to such a notion.

Yet if general theory eludes us, a basic understanding of culture as we have described it does alert us to certain possibilities. Although we may not be able to generalize about the extent to which new concepts must suffuse different domains of a culture so as to appear obvious, we do know that some degree of integration is necessary. Short of being imposed by force or filling a void occasioned by internal disintegration, the adoption of substantive human rights principles may be less effective at achieving integration than the adoption of procedures that track transnational goals without being exactly identical in every culture. To achieve what Richard Shweder has called "universality without uniformity," a shift toward procedural forms rather than substantive rules may prove more effective.[13] Thus, couching human rights in terms of access to a forum in which anyone is free to make his or her argument, or encouraging the involvement of community representation from which no group is excluded, may tap into cultural assumptions that, while different from one place to another, involve elements already present within those cultures themselves. A concept such as the presumption of innocence, which may very well be present in some domains of a given culture, may gain additional legitimacy—especially for the less powerful members of a society—when reinforced by the international discourse of human rights.[14] Studies in a number of countries show that people often regard procedural justice as more important than the specific outcome of a dispute, and that if people identify with both the subgroup to which they belong and a larger political entity, it is often through a sense of procedural fairness that the two may be seen as mutually reinforcing.[15] Thus, women may need to see other women in the act of asserting a specific substantive right at least as much as they may need the right itself.[16]

Indeed, the recognition that the same features may take on radically different meanings in different cultures is vital to any attempt to extend human rights norms across cultural boundaries. When they have not been either ideologically imperialistic or purveyors of the vacuous, proponents of universal human rights have often failed to consider the nature of culture in their accounts.[17] Robert Cover, in his oft-cited essay *Nomos and Narrative*, claimed that there was a "tragic limit" to the peace any state could expect to extend even to its own citizens, but that the violence done by the state to minority views could be overcome by forming a shared world of legal meanings and goals.[18] Although Cover failed to grasp the nature of culture, speaking in terms that were vague and sociologically naive, he did at least acknowledge that multiple meanings can exist alongside shared orientations—in short, that difference is tolerable—so long as people regarded as essentially fair the process by which they won their argument on some occasions and lost on others. In the human rights context we might consider how such a notion may operate when the emphasis is, for example, on equivalence rather than equality. Let me explain.

In many societies the differences among various categories of people and groups are regarded as so natural as to be commonsensical. Whether it is a matter of women versus men or one socioeconomic or ethnic group versus another, in certain instances we may be dealing not with differences that are ranked as superior and inferior but with distinctions that are seen, by the ideology of the culture itself, as simply natural. To most Westerners the notion of natural distinction violates the precept of equality and—even when coupled with notions of equivalence—smacks of a theory of "separate but equal," a concept we have come to regard as an oxymoron. But even many Western religions operate according to such a principle. Women cannot become Catholic priests or Orthodox rabbis, yet neither religion overtly asserts the inferiority of women. In Islam, too, we have seen that the idea of justice does not promote equality of all individuals but equality of freedom to develop within category. The result in both cases is a vision of justice as equivalence, not equality.[19] Now if one started with such a standard for international human rights—one that seeks local versions of equivalence as forms of equality—might the specific content of local orientations be more flexible, more likely to capture the terms of discussion, more capable of actually integrating elements in culturally compatible ways than by simply attempting to impose a concept of strict individual equality? Or would such an approach merely emphasize that the differences in "universal" human rights, shorn of the power that may force their acceptance, are little more than justifications for the status quo? Perhaps no single answer is possible, but the very idea of justice as equivalence rather than equality is not one that Western proponents of human rights should dismiss out of hand, particularly since, as we have noted, many Western religions themselves embrace the idea.

Thus, if one focuses not on substantive rules but on access to the process of change itself, one might cast human rights with a somewhat different emphasis. Here the goal would be to give a place at the table to the full range of voices that are undoubtedly present in any given culture to begin with. For if we eschew the sociologically suspect assertion, so common to studies of an earlier generation, that in order to function at all cultures had to be characterized by "shared" concepts, then we can recognize (even though our theories are not fully up to the task) that multiple orientations are not necessarily destructive of social order. In other words, to encourage processes by which the various voices present in any culture may be expressed is to place emphasis less on substantive results than on processual themes, the processes through which multiple perspectives that may already be present can be given voice.[20] Of course, entrenched powers may do all they can to keep the less powerful from participating in any process of reform, or the indoctrination of the powerless may skew their ability to partake in their own cultural conversations.[21] But if one starts with the assumption that the goal is unity in diversity, not uniformity of all content, and if one builds on the range of views we now know are present in all cultures and proceeds to encourage their articulation, then one may, at the very least, be building on a foundation that current theory tells us is applicable to any culture and its actual history. How these features may play out in the particular context of the Arab world is especially intriguing.

Human Rights and Arab Cultures

To many Westerners, the treatment by Muslims of women, religious minorities, and alleged criminals may seem to contravene "universal" human rights.[22] In principle, human rights and Islam are in no sense incompatible. Many Islamic nations do, however, find the specific terms of Western-based conventions to be biased in favor of Western cultural standards even when the human rights conventions Muslim nations have created are themselves couched in universal rather than culturally specific terms. Indeed, a number of documents produced by Arabs and Muslims articulate human rights from their perspective rather than that of the West. The documents emphasize, for example, "the protection of the community over the autonomy of the individual" and state that human rights must not be inconsistent with divine law.[23] Without reviewing the specifics of these documents, we can make a few remarks about distinctively Arabo-Muslim concepts of human rights that might be at once culturally responsive—and hence more likely to receive implementation—and that may, at the end of the day, only underscore that successful acceptance of transcultural standards may depend far more on power, trade, and internal discord than international agreement.

One intriguing approach to human rights generally, and to Muslim versions of human rights in particular, shifts the conversation from one of rights to one of duties.[24] Simply put, the idea is that whatever rights individuals ought to possess, they must carry out certain correlative duties. These may be as general as a duty to attend to the needs of the environment, maintain tolerance toward others, or engage in negotiations that further the cause of peace. The emphasis on duties can find legitimacy in various cultural and religious ideas. In Islam, for example, each person must perform certain duties on behalf of society so that it remains a proper community of believers in the sight of God; this idea can be extended from specific ritual obligations to ones that touch more generally on the well-being of all. Thus, individual charity can be extended to an obligation to support the disadvantaged or to provide adequate education to dependents or neighbors. The problem, of course, comes both in the specificity of the duties and the extent to which they merely support traditional authority.

Let's take the latter point first. A major reason for shifting to a language of rights in the West was to free individuals from the need to remain in their designated traditional positions in the social order. Whether set in terms of feudal ideology or Lutheran doctrine, perpetuating the idea of staying in one's place—a place said to be designated by God and violated only at the risk of utter chaos—cast duty in so restrictive a manner as to violate the rising sense of individuality in the West. At the other extreme, a language of duty can be so vague as to have little substantive content. One needs to know, in each instance, what the constraints will be for violation of a duty, who will decide when and how it is enforced, and what interests will be served by formulating it one way or another.

Perhaps more appropriate would be the approach suggested in the preceding chapter of this book, namely asserting as individual rights those actions that also benefit society as a whole. The right to freedom of movement, the right to one's confessional laws of personal status (or to opt out of them), the right to formal identity, or the right of locales to decide many issues for themselves could be articulated as societal duties rather than Westernized individual rights. The operative word here, of course, is "could," for the very act of putting these values in a rights–duties context may render them foreign to many people in the affected region. The idea of duties is no more self-executing or divorced from aspects of power than any formulation that comes from an international or foreign source.

Human Rights in Perspective:
Muslim and Non-Muslim Encounters

Ultimately, power is all but ineradicable from human rights discourses, even when the apparent persuasiveness of ideas has been the key factor in their ability to transcend cultural borders. One can speak, as Joseph Raz does, of using multicultural measures not to "preserve the pristine purity of different cultural groups [but] to enable them to adjust and change to a new form of existence within a larger community, while preserving their integrity, pride in their identity, and continuity with their past and with others of the same culture in different countries."[25] But difficult as it is for any of us to avoid well-intentioned generalities or partisanship over issues of specific rights, it does not help resolve how to balance the general and the specific if we fail to note how such changes and accommodations may be affected by those features of human culture to which I now want to return more directly.

Nearly half a century ago Joseph Wood Krutch argued against those who seemed to suggest that, since what one culture condemns another might regard as a virtue, there simply are no universal moral standards. He cautioned against losing our sense of the specific by relying too much on general philosophical categories:

[I]f there is anything to be learned from anthropology it would appear that the only really deadly social philosophy is that which holds that one way is as good as another. At the present moment we are hardly more sure than we were a generation ago where to look for a valid "ought." But we are growing notably less sure that we can get along without one.[26]

Krutch, like many to this day, mistook a method for a claim when he equated relativism with moral anarchy, instead of seeing relativism as the suspension of judgment needed to understand other social and cultural systems. Anthropologists may not have helped their own case when, to the confusion of many, they opposed the adoption of the United Nations Universal Declaration of Human Rights in 1947.[27] But anthropology certainly supports the proposition that one does not have culture, but some particular culture, and that the capacity for possessing culture does not change the fact that it is only manifest in some specific form. That said, the way in which apparently similar features may integrate with other elements of a culture will doubtless vary, and the assumption that even "universal" standards means the same thing everywhere is simply insupportable. The measure of successful movement of standards across boundaries may, as I have suggested, be more appropriately accomplished by generalized means than by substantive propositions. Only if they fit with other elements of the culture—whether by peaceful means or violent, by gradual inclusion or cataclysmic shift—will such human rights concepts likely take root.

Human rights need to be specific to the local level, therefore, even though the process of discussing them can be universalized.[28] But the question becomes, how much difference is any of us prepared to accept? Are we prepared, in our own society and law, to treat those who come from a minority cultural heritage differently when they commit acts regarded as criminal in the dominant culture but not in their own?[29] Are we to draw the conceptual boundaries of, say, marriage widely enough to include same-sex unions and to regard access to such state ratification as a fundamental freedom? Or do we try to finesse particularly problematic issues for which local answers vary widely by concentrating on procedures that serve to unite people in a common discourse? Indeed, would people be more willing to accept greater difference and more inclusive concepts if they recognize as fair the process by which norms will be reconsidered and concrete situations addressed? If, to amend Krutch, anthropology teaches us anything in this regard, it might be that just as we do not have religion but some particular religion, so, too, we must always embrace specific cultural norms; but because a significant degree of open-endedness—indeed of indeterminacy and ambiguity—remains vital to any culture's survival and extension, we can never expect a universal code to resolve all issues for all time.

Bringing Westerners and Arabs together within a single framework of human rights cannot be a simple matter of finding a few common sources of morality within the Abrahamic tradition or of asserting values at so general a level as to have no real meaning. Discussion and negotiation may indeed produce documents that express general values, but they are unlikely to result in protocols that can be implemented directly into such varied cultures. The emphasis on the process of addressing claims and greater inclusion of diverse segments of each population in the formulation of standards may prove the most fruitful level at which each can prod the other. Underscoring the positive elements in each religious tradition—whether couched in terms of compassion and mercy, love and forgiveness, or duty and holiness—may be essential to the development of any common rules. Ultimately, however, history and theory would suggest that successful adoption of common standards is more likely to depend on specific equations of power than on some effervescent global reach.

In sum, the question whether human rights can be universalized is inseparably linked to power and culture, the qualities of integrative meaning demanded by the latter often being accomplished only through the exercise of the former. People will undoubtedly continue to address human rights concerns as the expression of our own cultures' values, and, given the naturalizing quality of all cultural assumptions, each scheme will be put forth as if it were indeed both natural and self-evident. Only the force of circumstance will determine which systems will be capable of extension across existing cultural barriers, and perhaps only an emphasis on process and equivalence, multiple voices and open forums will keep the more unrestrained forms of power at bay. The global will not replace the local; it never has. But as the experiment in shaping relationships in terms of human rights takes on local implications, we will, at least as scholars, be called upon—whether in the Muslim world or elsewhere—to rethink the nature of culture and power alike if we are to understand whether, and why, any of these "universal" rights is likely to take root.

Afterword

I often feel as though I am just one metaphor away from understanding the Arabs. It is, of course, an illusion, a professional conceit, an ever-alluring mirage, but I remain susceptible to it despite myself. I do not for a moment think there is some essence of any culture—some key to its mysteries or source of all its manifestations. To structuralists that essence may lie in the coded oppositions that inform everything from kinship to house style; to functionalists it may reside in the pragmatic ability to keep things working; to evolutionists it may hide in the replicative force of a population's institutional variance. But to those of us who practice a more interpretive form of anthropology—where the joinder of orientations and meanings across multiple domains never recedes from the imaginative into the exclusively organizational—any grasp for a single essence evaporates in a cloud of significations. Nevertheless, the temptation to capture if not the essence of a culture then a shorthand image for its qualities is almost irresistible.

At times I have thought of Arab life—and of Islam more generally—as being like an arabesque, that labyrinth of interconnections where stylized life-forms and reified utterance surround and entice the faithful into a realm where the generation of never-ending meaning encounters ever-renewing association. At other times I have imagined Arab culture as being like an elaborate web—formed of symbols, relationships, event orientations, and spatial arrangements—whose inhabitants may possess greater or lesser knowledge of its pitfalls but from which they can never fully extricate themselves. At still other times I even imagine that Arab society is similar to the physical world of string theory—all teased-out arrays of energy, each wriggling unit's properties responding to its own vibrations—or that Arab lives are like some kind of cultural quanta—packets of energy and matter that cannot be seen in one guise without being changed into the other, one more manifestation of a natural world in which each new instance of disorder stimulates a further exchange or creation of information. But then I draw back, knowing that I will only embarrass myself through my feeble grasp of science even though I continue to imagine that a unified theory of culture would be a wonderful thing to behold. The attraction and the conceit may never end. But if one understands that it is not a matter of progressing to the ultimate metaphor but submitting to the allure, if only to see what it reveals, then perhaps one can achieve insights that even this illusion might otherwise have left unmasked. False propositions, it has been said, can produce true results. The trick, perhaps, is in knowing which one you are dealing with at any given moment.

As non-Muslims in the West continue to encounter the Arab and Muslim worlds, the willingness to make errors of interpretation without imagining we will ultimately get to some clear essence may, from our own cultural starting point, be as much as we can hope to achieve. Humility in the face of our ignorance is vital, but it is not enough. It is by our engagement with one another's difference—and by putting private thought into personal action—that we see analogues in our respective worlds. Life (as many Arabs say) is a matter of living by analogy. Interpretation is a collective act, and a moral one, and only as we try to understand what is happening in our meeting of another will we find out more about what we encounter in ourselves. We are the Arabs, and they are us. Almost. We may be just a metaphor away.

Notes

1. Allen amplifies her interpretation of the proposition that "laws exist to be broken" in the following terms:

> In life things break. While sometimes they can be repaired, they are never the same again, and many injuries are irreparable. But law is different, for laws are made to be broken. . . . [L]aw substitutes a symbolic-metaphoric world of doctrine for real-life conflict and damage, and with the resolution of the doctrinal conflict enacts a social triumph over disorder and injury. . . . Generally speaking, in the physical world when things get broken they become less themselves, at least temporarily, sometimes losing their identity altogether. With laws it is just the reverse. A law that is never broken ceases to exist. . . . This is most obvious with common law, where no written statutes exist in books ahead of time to draw a line between legal and illegal, where the determination of the law is in some sense always retrospective, arising out of someone's claim that breakage has occurred. Even legal codes, though, lose authority when no one breaks them. For laws that go unbroken go unenforced and unnoticed and eventually fall into obsolescence. At the very least they will only be revived as significant in anyone's mind at the point that someone breaks one.

J. Allen 2005, 127–28. See also Peckham 1965.

CHAPTER TWO

1. Lewis 2002; United Nations Development Programme 2004.
2. Makdisi, for example, notes that "what occurs in the inner recesses of the mind is not relevant in terms of the legal effects of the contract. Rather it is the external circumstances of the declaration that are important" (1985, 335). On intention and Islamic law, see L. Rosen 1989, 51–53.
3. The poets of pre-Islamic Arabia were the object of great antipathy by the Prophet (Sura 26:224–27), who no doubt appreciated that their capacity to beguile and mislead by capturing a false sense of reality was a power of enormous import.
4. Indeed, hypocrisy (*riya'*) is regarded as a cardinal sin in Islam precisely because it disrupts the reliability of witness testimony—including that of sacred text and Prophetic utterances—upon which reputation and trust, so central to this system of interpersonal ties, depends. On hypocrisy as "a minor form of heresy" (*al-shirk al-asgar*), see M. Carter 1998, 235.
5. See the opinion of Justice Felix Frankfurter in *Louisiana ex rel. Francis v. Resweber*, 329 U.S. 459 (1947) (Frankfurter, J., concurring), and the opinion of Justice Harry Blackmun in *Furman v. Georgia*, 408 U.S. 238 (1972) (Blackmun, J., dissenting).
6. See Gimaret 1993; Leaman 1985.
7. Early Islamic wine poetry provides a good example. Drinking is disparaged not because it causes one portion of the self to dominate another portion but because, as one writer puts it, drunkenness "undoes the vestments of selfhood. Rather than returning the drinker to a pre-existing, innocent nature, wine produces a nature that is the undoing of culture." Noorani 2004, 351.
8. When Asma al-Akhas gave up a career as an investment banker in the West to become the wife of Syrian president Bashar al-Assad, she was struck, as she told a reporter, by the fact that "Syria lacked institutions. Every ministry was a 'one-man show.'" Bennet 2005, 34. T. E. Lawrence's formulation—"Arabs believe in persons, not in institutions"—is characteristically blunt and broadly true, provided one understands him to be referring to the nature of personhood rather than whether such institutions as the mosque-university or the mortmain/charity organization (*waqf, habus*) have any existence beyond their momentary occupants.
9. Chess, rather than a game apparently played with dice called *nar*, early on became the proper game for Muslims to play since it involves the exercise of reason rather than reliance on chance. See Rosenthal 1975.
10. Friedman's (2005) "basic rule no. 4 for Middle East reporting" thus holds that "if you can't explain something with a conspiracy theory, then don't try to explain it at all—people there won't believe it." Friedman's error is to confuse conspiracy with the social foundations of the Arabs' concept of causation in numerous domains.

11. Gittes 1991, 40, 48, and 50 respectively.
12. Ritual reversals often confirm the arrangements of daily life. Thus at the time of the pilgrimage to Mecca one should cancel all debts and thus be prepared for death, the true end of all obligational bonds. See Hammoudi 2006.
13. Caton 2005, 32–33.
14. The proverbs are noted and explained in Bailey 2004, 223–24.
15. On the possible introduction of concepts of probability in recent Arab cultures, see L. Rosen 2002, 108–29.
16. See Rosenthal 1970, 300–308 ("Doubt in whichever way indicated became the true pariah and outcast of Muslim civilization." For a fuller version of this passage, see below, chapter 10, note 23.) See also L. Rosen 2002, 158–73. T. E. Lawrence, who characteristically captured and overstated the case, also wrote, "Semites had no half-tones in their register of vision. They were a people of primary colors, or rather black and white, who saw the world always in contour. They were a dogmatic people, despising doubt, our modern crown of thorns. They did not understand our metaphysical difficulties, our introspective questionings. They knew only truth and untruth, belief and unbelief, without our hesitating retinue of finer shades." Quoted in Lewis 2000, 17.
17. Ahmed 2004, 13.
18. Langer 1957, 287.
19. *Fitna* also conveys the idea of rebelliousness against the divine law and the moral chaos that follows threats to the purity of Muslim belief. See Gardet 1965. See especially the discussion of fitna in Pandolfo 1997, 89–93 and 156–62. In some colloquial usages it also implies an ordeal faced by the community. See also Kamali 1993; Williams 1995.
20. Pandolfo 1997, 56.
21. Sura 2:189 is translated by A. J. Arberry thus: "persecution is more grievous than slaying." The Bedouin of the Sinai and the Negev culturally translate *fitna* in this verse to mean that "incitement is worse than murder," thus underscoring their emphasis that inciting another to commit a crime or take revenge risks uncontrollable social disorder. In each case any regularities of a system of retaliation or limiting reciprocity are disrupted. On the Bedouin sayings, see Bailey 2004, 105.
22. The primary architect of contemporary Islamic fundamentalism, Sayyid Qutb, has written, "A girl looks at you, appearing as if she were an enhanting nymph or an escaped mermaid, but as she approaches, you sense only the screaming instinct inside her, and you can smell her burning body, not the scent of perfume, but flesh, only flesh. Tasty flesh, truly, but flesh nonetheless." Quoted in Wright 2006.
23. Quoted in Hegasy 1997, as cited in Newcomb 2004, 271.
24. "[O]ne man put it to me straight: 'Who is the government?' he asked. The question was only two words long in Arabic [presumably, *shkun*

al-ḥukuma], but I had to ask him to repeat it a couple of times before I understood what he was getting at. Who was the government? Who was in charge in Iraq?" Feldman 2004, 77–78.

25. Thomas L. Friedman consistently makes the mistake of referring to most Middle Eastern leaders as illegitimate. Referring to the potential role of U.S. troops as midwife to Middle East peace, he observes that "[t]he Arab leaders don't want to face this fact . . . because most are illegitimate, un-elected autocrats who are afraid of ever speaking the truth in public to the Palestinians." Friedman 2002. As noted above, his failure to realize that legitimacy comes from the process of building dependencies in a recognizable way leads to the dangerous implication that if one simply displaces the present leaders, truly legitimate ones will be able to emerge, when in fact replacement leaders will almost certainly have to prove their legitimacy in exactly the same ways as their predecessors. Similarly, the UN report formulated mainly by Muslims, which says that in the Arab world "[o]bsolete norms of legitimacy prevail," is clearly a value judgment, not a descriptive fact. Fergany et al. 2002, 2.

26. This interpretation of time is more fully developed in L. Rosen 1984, 172–77.

27. Tribal identity does remain enormously important in certain parts of the Arab world. As one Saudi who holds a doctorate in the humanities from the Sorbonne put it: "I am a member of a tribe. That identity and connection is crucial to me. And no matter how I might feel about it, I can tell you that if I were to let my wife drive, the next day I would no longer be considered a part of my tribe. That is how strong the societal pressures are." Another informant, described as "an influential Saudi prince," told the same reporter, "If we had elections, there would be only two kinds of people on the Majlis (Parliament): tribal chiefs, no matter how uneducated or bad, and businessmen" (Sachs 2000). Indeed, only when American forces built up a map of tribal and other relationships were they able to find the weak link in Saddam Hussein's network who informed on him. Schmitt 2003.

28. Some commentators on the Arab world, however, fail to understand how fluid tribal structures are. Friedman (2004), for example, perpetuates an uninformed stereotype: "Democracy-building is always a work in progress—two steps forward, one step back. No one should have expected a utopian transformation of Iraq. Iraq is like every other tribalized Arab state, where democracy is everyone's third choice. Their first choice is always: 'My tribe wins and my rivals lose.' Second choice is: 'My tribe loses, so yours must lose too.' Third choice is: 'My tribe wins and so do my rivals.'" A more accurate statement is that made by General Wesley K. Clark (2005): "The American approach shows little sense of Middle Eastern history and politics. As one prominent Kuwaiti academic explained to me, in the Muslim world the best way to deal with your enemies has

always been to assimilate them—you never succeed in killing them all, and by trying to do so you just make more enemies. Instead, you must woo them to rejoin society and the government. Military pressure should be used in a calibrated way, to help in the wooing." Friedman's question-begging assertion that one can mostly explain Middle East politics on the basis of tribalism is in Friedman 1989, 87–105. For a detailed argument on this subject, see L. Rosen 2002, 39–55.

29. On freedom and its antonyms, see Rosenthal 1960.

30. On ambivalence to power in Arab cultures, see L. Rosen 2002, 21–38.

31. In truth, if one is to generalize about the Arab world it may be necessary here to think in terms of a sliding scale. There may be more of a middle class in Tunisia or Lebanon than in some other Arab countries, for example. Nevertheless the vital aspects of most definitions of a middle class, which includes not simply income level but the perpetuation of a position in the social order, suggest that such a characterization does not fit Arab countries nearly so well as it does those in many other parts of the world.

32. An interesting variant on this tradition of genealogical isolation may be seen in the rise of slave-dominated governments, such as the Mamluks, for a time in Arab history. For what might seem an inversion may really be just a variation on retaining "the game" as an open-ended array, if not an actual recruitment, of strong successors from wherever they may come. As one scholar notes, "It is remarkable that even in the Mamluk kingdom, where the slave often rose to the throne over the murdered body of his master, the tradition of genealogical isolation, of not passing one's status on to one's children, and of recruiting only from persons alienated from their community and kinsmen, persisted with only a few strongly frowned-upon exceptions." Patterson 1982, 331–32. The implications for the recruitment of fundamentalist terrorists is also intriguing in this regard.

CHAPTER THREE

1. On "unit solidarity" as an explanation for terrorist self-destruction, see Sageman 2004b; on nationalism rather than religion as the source for such acts, see Pape 2005, 22–23; on terrorist activity as simply another version of frustrated individualism akin to that experienced in the West, see Roy 2004; on Islam itself as the source of terrorism, see Bukay 2006; on self-destruction as ritualized redemption and the fulfillment of a religious obligation performed on behalf of society, see Hafez 2006. See also Hafez 2007, Heffelfinger 2005, Krueger 2007.

It goes without saying that no one has ever interviewed a successful suicide bomber. Studies that involve failed (or reluctant?) bombers include Bloom 2004, Hassan 2006, Kimhi and Even 2004, and the documentary *Suicide Bombers: Inside the Minds of Failed Martyrs* (Princeton: Films Media Group, 2004).

2. It is true, of course, that Middle Eastern Muslims are not the only ones who have engaged in suicide bombings. Some of the first to do so in the region were Christian Arabs, including several women. See, e.g., Davis 2003, 67–84. And one finds suicide bombers in India, Sri Lanka, and elsewhere, both at present and in various epochs. It is, however, no criticism of the present analysis that non-Arab Muslims or Christian Arabs have engaged in such practices. Indeed, personal motivations aside, the sociological basis for both Christian and Muslim Arab suicide acts may very well share the common base of their common social life. The point, therefore, is not to claim universal explanation but to see how Arab social organization and Muslim conceptual categories bear on each other in this domain, and to invite the reader to consider in what ways the analysis offered here might enlighten our understanding of the acts of people coming from related groups.

3. For an analysis of women bombers see Bloom 2005. While there are some notable instances of women martyrs, they are not only comparatively rare but frowned upon by many Muslim commentators. One possible reason that women may not be favored for such tasks is that most Arab Muslim men regard women as creatures of passion rather than reason, and if women were to engage in suicidal bombings as a matter of course the act itself may come to be viewed as a thoughtless act of passion rather than a rational act of network consolidation.

4. See, e.g., Taseer 2005. See generally Hashim 2006.

5. See Gerges 2005, 142–43, 237. Since suicide is forbidden by Islam, such acts are called al-'amalīyat al-istishhadiya, or "self-martyrdom operations." On the history of Islamic martyrdom see D. Cook 2007.

6. This is the simplistic and completely acultural explanation given in Sageman 2004b. It is an explanation that cannot account for the decision to choose this particular form of death. Unit solidarity is every bit as strong in military settings as among jihadists, but in most instances it does not take the form of killing oneself. Indeed, many of the young jihadists do not spend substantial amounts of time in schools or camps forging strong bonds of unit solidarity with others, but are moved quickly from recruitment to action. Even the 9/11 bombers were not all engaged in intense face-to-face relations with one another.

7. Strathern 1999, 254. See more generally Strathern 1988, 134: "[I]f in a commodity economy things and persons assume the social form of things, then in a gift economy they assume the social form of persons." In a sense, too, the corollary of an individual expressing his network is met by the community itself expressing its vested interest in the bomber. Strathern's account of a New Guinean's initiation has interesting resonance with the suicide bomber's final taped envoi: "When a male initiate steps forward all decked out in his transformed body, a new member of the clan, his clansmen own, so to speak, the concept of this person as 'a

male clansman'. He has to look, act, and behave like one. His clan mates acknowledge him by claiming him; they see him, at that moment, the embodiment of a concept. What they own is that concept or image of him manifest as his 'body', and they own it as they own themselves" (2004, 218).

8. On the cultural construction of relationships as if they constituted a face-to-face "chain of consociation," see L. Rosen 1989. Parallel to the martyr's demonstration of his social network are the events surrounding grief and illness. In both cases Arabs commonly act in highly emotional, expressive ways—crying, falling into the arms of others, expressing enormous pain or suffering—all of which trigger supporters to demonstrate their attachment to the one afflicted. As a vehicle for precipitating one's network and revealing it socially—in short, as reinforcing elements of a single cultural pattern—both grief and illness replicate the approach to the martyr. Indeed, just as the martyr is not prayed over, so too the normal grief shown to a deceased is commonly masked in the case of a martyr, thus further demonstrating that he no longer has need to precipitate his social network, his act of self-sacrifice having trumped the issue altogether. On the absence of grief in such situations, see Carr 2006, 262–63.

9. Foucault 1973.

10. There is, as in all such matters, a range of variation on this theme among various Arab and Muslims groupings. In one such variant those who die of plague are also placed in this category. Plague, some say, was seen as an expression of the wrath of Allah in the times before the advent of the Prophet, but after his arrival plague should be regarded as a blessing because people who stayed patiently in their homes submitting to the will of God, whether surviving or dying, would be like martyrs and hence in no need of prayer. See Dehlevi 1990, pt. 1, 2 and pt. 2, 63.

11. In his study of the al-Muhajirun movement of Muslims in Great Britain, Wiktorowicz (2005, 105) notes that 31 percent of those studied—the highest proportion having background factors in common—had recently suffered a death in the family. While his emphasis on a "cultural opening" begs many questions, he makes a relevant observation that a quest for inclusion in a social group is a vital ingredient for many potential martyrs. In this case, it should be noted, the group disbanded itself in 2004. For profiles of Palestinian suicide bombers, see Hafez 2006, 79–86; for additional statistics, see Pape 2005, 253–67; see also the work of Nicole Argo cited in Hafez 2006, 101 n. 5.

12. Such a process is hardly limited to Muslim terrorists, but even when the expression of power differs the propulsion may be similar. The Hassidic Reggae superstar Matisyahu, for example, says of his transition from being a drug-ridden and rebellious middle-class secular Jew to pop music icon: " 'It's an amazing thing, a phenomenon, when a person is willing to give themselves over to something else,' Matisyahu says softly, in a lilting

voice that reflects both his White Plains roots and the accent of the rabbis he studies with. 'That's what real passion is . . . and that passion comes through a divorce of self . . . And the way to do that is to give yourself over to something greater'" (Wiltz 2006, N4; ellipses in original). The problematic issue, of course, turns on the concept of the self that is operative in any particular culture.

13. The absence of social networks is noteworthy in the description Brigadier General Nizar Ammar of the Palestinian General Security agency gives in the following profile of a Palestinian suicide bomber:

> Young, often a teenager.
>
> He is mentally immature.
>
> There is pressure on him to work.
>
> He can't find a job.
>
> He has no options, and there is no safety net to help him.
>
> He would try to work for the PA [Palestinian Authority] but he doesn't get a job because he has no connections.
>
> He tries to get into Arafat's army, but again, he doesn't have the right connections. He doesn't have "vitamin W." (*Vitamin W* is an expression for *wasta* in Arabic, which refers to political, social, and personal connections.)
>
> He has no girlfriend or fiancée.
>
> On the days he's off, he has no money to go to the disco and pick up girls (even if it were acceptable).
>
> No means for him to enjoy life in any way.
>
> Life has no meaning but pain.
>
> Marriage is not an option—it's expensive and he can't even take care of his own family.
>
> He feels he has lost everything.
>
> The only way out is to find refuge in God.
>
> He goes to the local mosque.
>
> It's not like in the United States where they just go to church on Sunday. He begins going to the mosque five times a day—even for the 4 a.m. prayers (An average devout Muslim will not attend the early-morning prayer.)
>
> Hamas members are there and notice him looking anxious, worried, and depressed and that he's coming every day. It's a small society here—people tend to know each other. They will ask about him, discover his situation.
>
> Gradually they will begin to recruit him.
>
> They talk to him about the afterlife and tell him that paradise awaits him if he dies in the jihad. They explain to him that if he volunteers for a suicide bombing, his family name will be held in the highest respect. He'll be remembered as a *shaheed* (a martyr, a hero).

He'll become a martyr and Hamas will give his family about $5,000, wheat flour, sugar, other staples, and clothing. The most important thing is that his family's status will be raised significantly—they too will be treated as heroes. The condition for all this: he is not allowed to tell anyone.

They will take him away from home forty-eight hours before the operation so there is no chance for him to reconsider. During this period he will write his last letters and sign his will, making it difficult to turn back. (Stern 2003, 50–51)

14. Erlanger 2006.

CHAPTER FOUR

1. Gould 1985, 160–61.
2. Planhol 1959, 43.
3. See the sources cited in Leveau 1985. This definition tracks that of Aristotle: "An object is 'our own' if it is in our power to dispose of it or keep it. By 'disposing of it' I mean giving it away or selling it." *Rhetoric* 1361a. 21–23, as cited and discussed in Pipes 1999.
4. Other schools of Islamic law gave different emphases. Followers of Shafi'i would have conquered lands divided among the conquerors; the Hanafi school would leave the decision to the newly formed government.
5. This proposition is often supported with the hadith, according to which the Prophet said, "Land belongs to God; whoever leaves it uncultivated for three consecutive years will have it taken away and given to someone else." Cited in Behdad 1989. Naturally, not all adherents of even a single school of Islamic law have seen matters identically. "Whoever cultivates waste lands with the permission of the Imam obtains a property in them; whereas if a person cultivates them without such permission he does not in that case become a proprietor, according to Abu Hanifa. The two disciples (of Abu Hanifa) maintain that in this case the cultivator becomes proprietor, because of a saying of the Prophet, 'Whoever cultivates waste lands does thereby acquire the property of them.'" Williams 1962, 127. A modern version of the proposition that anyone may use land that no one is using is to be found in the practices of squatters across the Muslim world. See, e.g., Bukhari 1982; Agoumy 1994.
6. Real property preemption (*shuf'a*), while generally considered a "weak" right in Islamic law and hence not indispensable to correct practice, may have originated in the desire to maintain certain relations (of co-ownership, proximity, or kinship) over any strict sense of a personal tie to the property. See generally Ziadeh 1985–86. The right to buy adjoining property was initially without reference to any specified period of time

in much of the Muslim world, but various time limitations were subsequently imposed. Gerber 1999.

7. Schacht 1964.

8. For a brief overview of land law in classical and modern times in a variety of Muslim countries, see Liebesny 1975.

9. On the history of the habus in Morocco, see Luccioni 1982.

10. Grey (1980) thus argues that we should dispense with the idea of property as things because, at least in the West, it is now entirely a function of relationships. By contrast, see Strathern's (1996) argument that, at least in the context of Melanesian society, social relations do not simply exist between persons because persons can be substituted by things.

11. Harris 1996. The analysis of ownership as an array of reciprocal capacities is particularly associated in modern jurisprudence with the schema of Hohfeld 1919.

12. Cilardo 1993, 32. Cilardo is referring here to the Hanafi jurist al-Sarakhsi, but on this matter there is little difference among the legal schools. It is precisely because the manumitted slave is able to possess, Sarakhsi says, that he is brought back to life, revivified (*ihya'*). Ibid.

13. For the argument on human possessiveness, see Pipes 1999.

14. For a brief summation of these issues, see C. Rose 1985.

15. The owners of extensive tracts in Lebanon in the early twentieth century, rather than specifying the size of their holdings, were reported by ethnographers thus: "When one asks the extent of his fields, the proprietor immediately gives the number of villages on their surface." Gilsenan 1996, 81.

16. Hence the key concept of *asl*, whereby place and custom, network of ties and characteristic ways of forming them become so crucial to any person's identity. See L. Rosen 1984, 21–29.

17. On the concept of *mul*, see generally ibid., 23–24; L. Rosen 2000, 137.

18. Pandolfo suggests that the idea of *roh* (or *ruh*), that which gives the quality of life to a thing, needs to be understood in this light:

> The term *roh*, hastily translated as soul by scholars quick to assimilate difference to Christian metaphysics, colloquially indicates, quite technically, articulation, an extension, or better, a consequence of the closing of a *rbta*, which "gathers up" something in existence and creates a body of movement. Contrary to Western common sense, it is not running water that has roh, but water that has been obstructed and detoured into another flow, neither flowing, nor stagnant. Roh is generated by something coming in between. Something is brought to existence that did not exist before and comes thereafter apart. Roh exists only in the interim, actualized by the closing of an obstruction. The transient body of a garden is similarly brought to being by the forced circulation of water, as is the human body by the system of "closed" articulations (*mfasil*) and liquid circulation. A diseased body is described as open or loose (*mhelul*), and an opening of the

articulations (mfasil) is what happens at death. Conversely, when a person gathers up strength or energy to begin some work or endeavor, she or he is said to *hzem*, literally, "tie the belt," the paradigmatic rbta of the body, a belt which is said to *shidd roh*, literally, "hold roh together." (1989, 14)

19. Donahue 1980.
20. On the idea of life as a game in Arab cultures generally, see Khuri 1990.
21. The quoted phrase comes from Lewis 1988, 95. See also L. Rosen 2002, 34–37.
22. See the development of this idea of privacy and tolerance in L. Rosen 2000, 187–99.
23. See L. Rosen 1984, 60–70.
24. For the contrary view, see Pipes 1999.
25. See generally Grey 1980.
26. On irrigation and water rights, see L. Rosen 1979, 113–22.
27. Leveau 1985, 71.
28. Ibid., 81. The emphasis on mobility was also a factor in the struggle for independence, when many Moroccans saw the end of colonialism as removing the barriers the French had set up to movement around the countryside:

   As one informant [a schoolteacher from Azrou, speaking in 1990] told us: "After 1956 there was freedom to settle wherever you wanted. People therefore looked for a fertile location to earn a living; that was the only important thing." From then on nobody could be prevented from settling because the reply would be: "I'm a Moroccan; I now have the same rights as you." Our informants made the point that they fought for Moroccan independence so that everybody could live and go where they choose. (Venema and Mguild 2003, 40)

29. As Leveau remarks, "[T]oday a passport has greater market value than a hectare of irrigated land" (1985, 81).
30. See generally Decroux 1977. See also Parcheminal 1985.
31. Several of the comments that follow are prompted by comparisons drawn from the analysis of land title, memory, and mapping in Pottage 1994.
32. A detailed example of this moment for a Berber from the Middle Atlas Mountains appears in my forthcoming book *Drawn from Memory: Moroccan Lives Unremembered*.
33. See L. Rosen 1984, 172–77; L. Rosen 2002, 89–93.
34. See the contrast between the Muslim saint in Indonesia who gains legitimacy by sitting still, rather Buddha-like, versus the Moroccan saint who must be moving to be recognizable, as described by Geertz 1968. See also L. Rosen 1984; L. Rosen 2002, 21–38 (in a form of ritual reversal the groom is tied up, his manly ability to move temporarily frustrated).

35. This also connects with the idea that the self cannot be fractionated into a series of discrete roles such that one could be expected to act one way in an institutional role and believe quite differently "as a person." See L. Rosen 1984, 2002.

36. Johnstone (2003) thus argues that invisible property in Athens, with its dependence on interpersonal trust, was (because of the fragile nature of friendship itself) dependent not on legal enforcement but on the effective arrangement of interpersonal ties, whereas the security of visible property often depended on rhetorical skill in convincing the large public jury of the merits of one's claims.

37. See my essays "Whom Do You Trust? Structuring Confidence in Arab Law and Society," in L. Rosen 2000, 133–50; and "The Circle of Beneficence: Narrating Coherence in a World of Corruption," in L. Rosen 2002, 3–20. See also L. Rosen 1984, 148–63. Such ties were already common in the Middle Ages, as documented most notably by Goitein 1967–83.

    As recently as 2002, in Fez, residents were reluctant to allow the property of former Jewish neighbors to be taken over by a Muslim. They said that their relationships had been close and personal with the departed Jews and that one should not take their property without their permission. Eventually, one of the properties was converted to use as a bakery, but the fact that these Muslims felt the relationship to the Jews to be so strong—a feature replicated in many instances and parts of present-day Morocco—underscores the interpersonal nature of this tie. (I am indebted to Rachel Newcomb for bringing this to my attention.)

38. See, e.g., Mehdi 2001; Maher 1974; and Cuisenier 1976, 142 (Tunisian women customarily give up their inheritance shares to their brothers).

39. Pound 1954, 133.

40. The phrase apparently stems from French revolutionaries such as Jacques-Pierre Brissot, who denounced property as theft, an idea that was further popularized by Pierre-Joseph Proudhon's declaration, "What is property? It is theft." See the citations in Pipes 1999, 47 and 49. For a study of how this idea has played out in an Eastern European context, see Shapiro 2000.

41. James 1918, vol. 1, chap. 10, 291, 293.

42. Examples abound in the anthropological literature of "things" being capable of the act of ownership or ownership itself being founded on propositions that may seem strange to Westerners. When, for example, Maning (2001) sought to buy property from the Maori in the mid-nineteenth century, one man offering land claimed title from the fact that his grandfather had been killed on it, another man from the fact that his grandfather had done the killing, and still a third from the fact that he had the right to catch rats on the land—a claim, he cheerfully asserted, that was perfected by the fact that there were no rats on the land. Intangibles are often capable of exclusive control in nonliterate societies: "No Greenlander or Andaman Islander ventures to sing the song of another

without his permission" (Lowie 1940, 282). And of course to many Native Americans the idea that anyone can "own" mother earth is as unimaginable as was the ownership of air rights at one time in American law. For Arabia and Yemen, see respectively Meeker 1979 and Caton 1990.

43. Other useful sources for rethinking the meaning of ownership and property are Ryan 1984; Singer 2000; Pennock and Chapman 1980.

44. Personal communication. On land politics in postrevolutionary Iran, see Bakhash 1989.

45. The use of checkpoints and the changing legal status of those who cross national borders reinforce the Palestinians' perception of themselves as unable to move freely within boundaries that are meaningful to them. See Kelly 2004. See also the discussion of "Land Day," which memorializes the Palestinian loss of territory, in Sorek 2002 and in Ben-Zeev and Aburaiya 2004, especially the references in the latter (at 652–53) to memoirs, films, oral histories, and village ethnographies of the sites that Palestinians lost during the Arab-Israeli wars. In the fall of 2005, when the Israelis left Gaza, Palestinians poured across the border to Egypt. Some undoubtedly did so to visit relatives, others to smuggle back goods that cost considerably less in Egypt. However, there may also have been an element of finally feeling free to move in the world and to rebuild one's sense of integrity and identity through such movement. See generally Wilson 2005.

Also, I am told that in Palestine a judge will always ask litigants about their *asl* (their origins, the place that nurtured and characterizes them). In this case the answer is couched in terms of the place in Israel from which they originated. Moreover, in marriages the *mahr* (bridewealth transfer) is "guaranteed" by the land now within Israel. One could see this as a kind of special purpose money: it symbolizes attachment to the lost land and the replication of that tie into the next generation by marriage. It may also seem to secure the marriage since payment via the lost land is not feasible. On the concept of *asl* in both cultural and legal settings, see L. Rosen 1984, 2000.

46. Darwish 2002, 77. Neither Darwish nor I am in any way suggesting that Palestinians have no attachment to the lands they claim. It is the meaning of land as a terrain of relationship, whatever its other implications, that must also be taken into account. On some of the legal aspects of land holding by Palestinians, see Grossman 2003–4.

47. Of relevance here may also be the Islamic aversion to the juristic person: there is no emphasis on the attributes of personhood being extended, whether culturally or legally, to entities such as corporations, guilds, or public institutions.

48. Some of the important earlier sources remain quite valuable. See, e.g., Goody 1962. See also the analysis and sources cited in Hann 1996, 453–54; Hann 1998.

CHAPTER FIVE

1. "[W]hereas Christianity is primarily the religion of love, Islam is above all the religion of justice. This does not, of course, mean that Christians are necessarily better at loving than Muslims, or that Muslim society lends itself more successfully to the realization of justice. . . . Nevertheless . . . the two watchwords, love and justice, can usefully act as signposts to a wide range of differences between the two religions in terms both of their acknowledged practices and dogmas and of the unconscious prejudices of their adherents." Ruthven 1984, 227–28. See generally Kassem 1972, 81–108; Khadduri 1984. This emphasis on justice in Islamic discourse, broadly applicable throughout the Arab world, has been applied specifically to the Egyptian case in the following way: "While the West speaks of democracy and freedom, Muslims [in Egypt] tend to speak of justice. There is widespread feeling that the region's governments deny their people justice. . . . 'It has reached to the point where Egyptians do not feel entitled to anything, and all they want is justice,' said Ibrahim Aslan, a leading Egyptian writer. 'Across history, in literature, Egyptian peasants asked for justice, not for freedom or democracy. Just justice. Social justice.'" Slackman 2006, 1.

2. Lewis distinguishes between substantiating an argument by showing the common denominator among examples and proving the rule by showing how it may be superseded:

    > Here I may draw attention to a rhetorical device very common in classical Arabic usage—an argument by the absurd. It is, however, very different from that device which we call the *reductio ad absurdum*. The purpose of the reductio ad absurdum is to demonstrate the falsity of an argument by stating it in its most extreme and therefore absurd form. The Arabic rhetorical device to which I refer has the opposite purpose—not to disprove but to emphasize and reaffirm; it is not thus a reductio ad absurdum, but rather a *trajetio ad absurdum* (if I may coin a rhetorical term). A principle is asserted and an extreme, even an absurd, example is given—but the purpose is to show that the principle still applies even in this extreme and absurd formulation. (1990, 34)

3. See bin Laden 2005, 160–72.
4. Both quotations are to be found in Bulliet 2004, 62–63.
5. Quoted in Dalrymple 2005, 16.
6. Khuri 2007, 126.
7. Bulliet (2004), like many scholars, largely equates justice with fair taxation, adherence by rulers to the sacred law (shari'a), and recognizable

moral precepts. This view still begs the question whether there is greater cultural content to "justice" inasmuch as each of these notions replaces one vague concept with another.

8. "The justice, or 'giving what is due' and 'establishing the true' (*haqq*), turns out to be the 'preservation' and 'maintenance' of this needed-in-order-to-exist assemblage of huquq. . . . Consequently, justice is deviated from when the exactness of 'preserving the middle' is lost, through a twist this way or that." Smirnov 1996, 345.

9. Compare this perspective with the discussion in Daube 1951.

10. For more on this topic, see L. Rosen 2000, 153–75.

11. Even in modern cartoons one sees "the notion of justice as appropriate exchange." Douglas and Malti-Douglas 1994, 98.

12. See Geertz 1968 on the way a saint or mystic may be represented quite differently in such contrasting Muslim cultures as Morocco and Indonesia.

13. Even so conservative a thinker as Sayyid Qutb argues that the Quranic declaration that "men are the overseers of women" arises from convention rather than nature, since as men move outside the household they have greater opportunity to develop their reason, while "due to the nature of family duties, the emotional and passionate side of the women [is what] grows and develops" (1953, 55).

14. Gallaire 1990, translated and quoted in Box 2005, 125.

15. This is not to suggest that women are not kept separate for much of the haj. To the contrary, especially when the pilgrims are not in the ritually pure state of *ihram*, women are not permitted to pray with men or be relieved of their oversight, particularly under the keen eye of the Wahhabi Saudi regime that "hosts" the pilgrims. See Hammoudi 2006, especially at 42, 62, 71–72, 94, and 150.

16. What has been said here of women could largely apply to Jews and Christians, the idea being that other peoples of the Book can also be members of a given category and transcend that category on the basis of their personal attributes.

17. The reference to right hands is commonly thought to refer to one's slaves.

18. See chapter 6 for a fuller discussion of this passage.

19. See Ziadeh 1957.

20. Quran 4:128–29 says, "You will not be able to act equitably (*ta'dilu*) to all your wives, however eagerly you may wish to do so. But yet do not be altogether partial (*la tamilu kull al-mayl*) so as to leave one in suspense." This recognition that there will doubtless be some favoritism further supports the idea of justice as equivalence, implying close attention to the person involved.

21. For this and similar hadith, see Kamali 2002, 52.

22. "The higher estimation of knowledge is, for instance, expressed in the constantly cited Prophetical tradition showing preference for the man who knows (*'âlim*) as against the pious worshipper who fulfills all the religious duties (*'âbid*)." Rosenthal 1970, 248.

23. Rahman 1966, 321. As Freamon notes, taqwa is not a universal but "an active and virtue-based human character trait." Freamon 2006, 12. See also Izutsu 1966; Izutsu 1964, 234–39.

24. For some of the different readings of 49:13, see Mottahedeh 1976.

25. Some, however, link fitna and differences among men and women less in terms of potential chaos than as an indispensably generative natural force. Pandolfo quotes a Moroccan informant who put it this way:

> They say this is a land of fitna, but fitna is difference [*l'fitna hyia l'ikhtilâf*], without difference there can be no life! Think only of the difference between languages, between nations: if there is no difference there is no movement, nothing, everything is petrified [*jâmed*] . . .
> A society is like a loom, it must be articulated. If you make the threads go simply straight, there can be no rûh [vitalization], the textile opens up and everything unravels [*ghâdi thell kulshî*]. Society is born from disagreement! If I disagree with you, if there is a discrepancy between us [*ilâ tkhalfnâ*], a gap is open and the textile, the society, holds up together. It is like a knot, like the stitching of a bag of flour . . . Take just the example of those ropes made with palm leaves: if you want to tie something using a whole leaf, it breaks; if instead you split the leaf and knot the two halves by way of a third, it'll never break. (1997, 125; brackets in original)

26. Quoted and discussed in Maddy-Weitzman 2005, 409. The Quranic passage generally cited for men's governance over women is Sura 4:38: "Men are the managers of the affairs of women for that God has preferred in bounty one of them over another, and for that they have expended of their property."

27. See, e.g., the case of Pakistan in Mehdi 2001, 20–26.

28. Even the command that one should do right and avoid wrong implies much about the way one must fashion relationships toward this end. See M. Cook 2000.

29. See generally Crosby 1997.

30. See Geertz, Geertz, and Rosen 1979.

31. See Pandolfo 1997. The idea that justice is a personal attribute rather than an abstract, disembodied concept appears to be one of the differences between Muslims and Jews living in the Arab world. For Muslim Arabs, justice is inseparable from the persons who manifest it. For Jews, justice comes from cutting off words from deeds, and deeds from those

who perform them; one awaits justice by being disconnected from context and the judgment of events. Anidjar explains the Jewish perspective this way: "the essence of justice is that virtue be abstracted from its performer, and knowledge be removed from its servant or implementer" (2002, 224); "Justice . . . is never done. It is . . . the cutting off that separates, ineluctably, words from contexts, and deeds from doers" (ibid., 245).

32. Quotation at Hampshire 2000, 17; see also ibid., 37, 45–46.

33. Quoted in von Grunebaum 1953, 236–37.

34. Franz Rosenthal has written, "It can be asserted with considerable assurance that in the Muslim view, knowledge by and large ranks higher than action" (1970, 248). My argument is not inconsistent with Rosenthal's inasmuch as I am suggesting that at least for modern Arabs, while mere action carries no inherent merit, knowledge itself cannot be truly meaningful without enactment, in whatever form fulfills the need to support the community of believers.

35. It is also important to emphasize the moral element in action as well. Indeed, the predominant philosophical orientation in Islam, notwithstanding the place of mystical orders, is that one must act in order to be moral. As Rahman has put it, "The orthodox impulse is activist; it does not reject intellectualism but subordinates it to the end of moral dynamism. The philosophers' reality is an immobile eternal truth; the orthodoxy's ultimate reality is also eternal truth, but being primarily a moral truth, it must result in moral action. The orthodox conception of truth is therefore not of something which merely is but essentially of something which 'commands'" (1958, 110).

36. On honor, see generally F. Stewart 1994. There are also studies that simply reduce the issue to some flaw in Arab personality or rationality, as in Patai 2002. See generally Gregg 2005.

37. See Hammoudi 1997. The idea that one needs to be both cautious and moderate in the treatment of friends and enemies alike is contained in many sayings, among them: Be moderate in your love of your friend, lest one day he become your enemy. And be moderate in hating your enemy, lest one day he become your friend (Ibn Hamdun); Beware of your enemy, and beware a thousand times of your friend; for often a friend becomes an enemy, and then he knows best how to harm you (anonymous poet, cited by Ibn 'Abdun; both quoted in Lewis 2000, 403).

38. For an example of the nature and meaning of corruption in daily life, see L. Rosen 2002, 3–20.

39. Ibn Khaldun 1967, vol. 2, 107. See also ibid., 107–10, on those who are capable of injustice.

40. Sen 1992, 23–26. See also Soroush 2000.

41. See, e.g., Mernissi 1991; Barlas 2002; Manji 2004.

42. Rawls 1999. See also Nachi 2004; Ricoeur 2000.

CHAPTER SIX

1. Three editions of the Quran actually became best-sellers for Amazon.com in the days following the attacks.

2. To doubt that the Quran has never been changed would, in the eyes of Muslims, place one on a slippery slope, like the one that led the popular religious writer and scholar Bart Ehrman to argue that since the Gospels were often rewritten, he could no longer retain his Christian faith. "[I]t would have been no more difficult for God to preserve the words of Scripture than it would have been for him to inspire them in the first place. . . . The fact that we don't have the words surely must show, I reasoned, that he did not preserve them for us. And if he didn't perform that miracle, there seemed to be no reason to think that he performed the earlier miracle of inspiring those words" (2005, 11). The common Muslim belief is also that the Prophet was illiterate, and hence could not have been the author of the miraculously revealed Quran. But some scholars, both Muslim and Western, argue that the reference in the Quran (7:157–58) to the Prophet as *al-ummi* should be rendered not as "illiterate" but as indicating one whose people have not previously received a "book" in their own language. See Günther 2002. It may also be noted that one of the great blasphemies many Muslims found in Salman Rushdie's novel *The Satanic Verses* concerned the surreptitious changes made in the Quran as the Prophet dictated it to his scribe, Salman.

3. Carlyle 1966, 64. Carlyle, it is only fair to note, expresses considerable admiration for the Prophet and strenuously defends him against charges that he was a fraud or that Islam was some form of quackery.

4. Rahman 1979, 32.

5. Quoted from Barr 1978 in Ruthven 2004, 61.

6. For a brief overview of the disputes surrounding the compilation of the Quran in the years after the Prophet's death, see Rippin 2001, ix–xix.

7. See Gardet 1976, 197–227; L. Rosen 1984, 172–77.

8. Each of these positions (the former represented by the work of Gerd-Rüdiger Puin, the latter by Patricia Crone and John Wansbrough) and others are most accessibly presented for nonspecialists in Lester 1999. Puin, described as a specialist in Arabic calligraphy and Quranic paleography, is quoted as saying, "The Koran claims for itself that it is *'mubeen*,' or clear. But if you look at it, you will notice that every fifth sentence or so simply doesn't make sense. Many Muslims—and Orientalists—will tell you otherwise, of course, but the fact is that a fifth of Koranic text is *just incomprehensible*. This is what has caused the traditional anxiety regarding translation. If the Koran is not comprehensible—if it can't even be understood in Arabic—then it's not translatable. People fear that. And since the Koran claims repeatedly to be clear but obviously is not—as even speakers of Arabic will tell you—there is a contradiction" (Lester 1999, 54 [em-

phasis in original]). It should be noted that the positions of many of
the Western Orientalists, aside from being greatly disputed among
themselves, are particularly contested by a number of Muslim scholars.
Compare Wansbrough 2004 and Crone and Cook 1977 with al-A'zami
2003. See also Baljon 1961. For a critical set of essays concerning Quranic
interpre-tation, see Ibn Warraq 2002b.

9. N. O. Brown 1983–84. Rahman notes a similar effect for the Quran when,
in regard to its apocalyptic style, he observes, "The Qur'an often states
that when He removes a people/community from power or destroys them,
He makes a whole new start with a new People (14:28; 6:6; 21:11; etc.)"
(1983, 182).

10. N. O. Brown 1983–84, 169. Interestingly, Joyce himself makes innumerable references to the Quran in his work, and may have been building on
the style of the latter. See Yared 1990; Atherton 1954.

11. N. O. Brown 1983–84, 169–70.

12. "If you are in doubt of what we have revealed . . . then bring [a verse]
like it. But if you cannot—and indeed you cannot—then guard yourself
against the Fire, whose fuel is men and stones" (2:23–24, also 16:101). This
doctrine of inimitability, known as 'ijaz (literally "impotent," in the sense
that no mortal has the power to produce such verses) is to this day an academic subject in many Islamic institutions, where grammar and syntax
are elaborately deployed to demonstrate that no Quranic sentence could
be the product of a human hand.

13. For an application of this argument, see L. Rosen 2002, 158–73.

14. Recent scholarship has demonstrated that a wide range of interpretations
of the Traditions and the sacred law have been current throughout much
of Muslim history, but that (as in Christianity) these were occulted by
the interpretations that became part of the accepted canon. Mohammad
Akram Nadwi, for example, has collected more than eight thousand instances of women hadith scholars, dating back as far as 1,400 years, whose
writings have been lost sight of in subsequent consolidations. See Power
2007.

15. Shi'a readings are something of an exception to the orthodox Sunni pattern described here, inasmuch as some concern with "inner meaning"
has long formed a part of Shi'a theology, particularly as it might support
the claim for descent through the line of Ali, the Prophet's son-in-law,
and his kin. On Quranic interpretation generally, see Gätje 1976, 30–44;
Rippin 2005. Underscoring the importance of communal unity, Muslims
commonly believe that it was for the sake of unity that Aaron (Haroun)
permitted the construction of the Golden Calf while Moses (the only
figure in the Quran to whom God speaks directly) was away from the
people.

16. Rosenzweig 2005, 134. Internal divisions are regarded as undesirable,
whereas differences among such entities as tribes or nations are thought

to be both realistic and beneficial insofar as they require people to use reason to negotiate relationships.

17. For the possible effects of this attitude on the acceptance or rejection of scientific experimentation, see chapter 10.

18. On the concept that later versions take precedence over earlier ones, see Wheeler 2002.

19. To avoid misunderstanding, it is worth emphasizing that here, as elsewhere in this work, juxtaposing the history of different religious traditions is in no way intended to suggest some failure on the part of one system as compared with another. It is not that one religion possesses certain qualities and the other lacks them; it is that, as noted at the outset, Western readers are likely to have a comparative baseline as they approach any other religious system, and it is useful to acknowledge and build on those comparisons for purposes of clarifying what this less familiar system may be like.

20. These points often escape the notice of those who read only scholarly commentaries or think of Islamic law as a variant of civil or "religious" law (rather than being typologically a kind of common law system). For a more extensive discussion of these issues, see L. Rosen 2000, 38–68.

21. Obviously, many Westerners have converted to Islam, finding in it a far more congenial terrain than they experienced in their prior affiliation. It is intriguing, nevertheless, to consider which elements, and what reasons, they find most attractive. Studies of African American converts are particularly revealing in this respect. See Rouse 2004.

22. Rippin 2005, 8950.

23. For another example of highly variant ways of translating a passage, the phrase *qawwamuna 'ala an-nisa* can mean "watch over," "support," or "be in charge of," such that the passage about men's oversight of women can yield quite different interpretations. See Aslan 2006, 69–70. Comparisons of numerous translations can be found in http://www.kavalec.com/Quran/default.htm.

24. The suggestion is that the word *hur* (appearing, for example, in suras 55:72–74, 56:12–25, and 76:12–22) is not actually the Arabic *houri* but, like many terms in the Quran, a word based on early Aramaic. This point is argued by the pseudonymous German scholar Luxenberg 2000. The author does not, however, indicate whether *white raisins* might simply be a metaphor for virginity, just as the crude term *cherry* is in English. See generally Stille 2002; Ibn Warraq 2002a. The approach Luxenberg draws upon is described in Reynolds 2004.

25. The example is borrowed from Ehrman 2005.

26. See Rippin 2005, 8951.

27. Sura 10:37, for example, asserts that no one but God could have created the Quran.

28. As an indication that the reference to orphans is not seen as a restrictive clause in this passage, one recent commentator, citing this verse, lists as its three "apparent meanings" that it shows marriage to be a legal state, that multiple marriage is limited to four wives, and that one should remain monogamous if one fears doing injustice. The potentially limiting reference to orphans is not part of the consideration, perhaps because it is thought that if one marries an orphan just to do good but without wishing her as one's sole wife it is simply better to take several others than to resent the orphan wife. Regardless, what is commonly not stressed is the same sort of elucidation of the passage that Westerners might expect given their own legalistic tradition of biblical interpretation. See Ramic 2003, 7–8. At present the term *orphans* has additional problematic effects that may have applied in the past as well. For it can refer not just to one who has no living parents but to one whose father has never stepped forward to acknowledge the child. The result is that an individual may, in a number of contemporary Arab nations, be unable to obtain identity papers because the father never acknowledged the person. And if the father has since died it may never be possible to obtain such papers, which are vital to getting into a school, obtaining a job, or applying for a passport. Being an "orphan" can be a state of permanent social and legal limbo—a person alone, truly without attachment to a line of descent or specific kin group.

29. It has been argued, however, that in the early years of Islam there was a type of hadith that contained quoted words of God, which may have been taken as supplementary to the Quran. Later orthodox thinking rejected these traditions as unauthoritative. See Graham 1979.

30. Virtually anyone can claim to issue a *fatwa*, an authoritative reading of proper Muslim behavior. Though many regimes and nations have sought to restrict or legitimize their promulgation, it remains a vital—if highly contentious—aspect of Islam almost everywhere that fatwas can emanate from an astonishing array of sources, as witness the number of fatwa Web sites in existence. See, e.g., http://www.Islam-online.net. In a law case, it is still quite common to shop around for favorable opinions.

31. Graham 1984. See also Tritton 1972. The Quran is not believed to have been transmitted to the Prophet by God—who, again, spoke only to Moses—but through the angel Gabriel.

32. The first evidence of the Quran that survives actually dates to about 691, some fifty-nine years after the Prophet's death, when verses appear as inscriptions on the newly built Dome of the Rock in Jerusalem. The recent discovery of fragments of early texts in Sana'a, Yemen, may also affect the study of this period.

33. See Hofmann 2004, 21. See also Rippin 2001, ix–xix. There are multiple recitation possibilities for the Quran, but these are thought to be insignificant differences, even though it may extend the learning process for

a reciter to become proficient in all variations. See the discussion of this concept of *qirā'at* in Paret 1986.

34. On how to listen to the Quran, and for a discography of various recitations, see Sells 1999, 145–219. For a specific example of Quran recitation in its cultural context, see Nelson 2001. For a speech act approach to Quran recitation, see Martin 1982.

35. Some of that familiarity may also come from the Quran's incorporation of a number of folkloric modes that are found as well in other texts. See Dundes 2003.

36. See Spellberg 1996. It is also said by many that the black stone that marks the most sacred spot in Mecca was actually white until it was touched by a menstruating woman. Hammoudi 2006, 176.

37. See Goldman 1995. For a case of a Muslim judge relying on this story to adduce circumstantial evidence favoring a woman litigant, see L. Rosen 1989, 27.

38. See chapter 8 for the Prophet's protection of the image of Jesus and Mary.

39. See generally Khalidi 2001.

40. On fear as the result of personal failing, Fazlur Rahman writes:

> Taking the element of "fear" to be the main constituent of taqwa, Professor Izutsu [1959] has advanced the theory that since the pre-Islamic Arab was a haughty and proud man, the Qur'an came forth with the concept of taqwa ("fear of God") in order to break his haughtiness and humble his pride. But as our examination and analysis of this all-comprehensive concept will show, the element of fear conveyed by this term has a very complicated nature and the only translation that will do justice to it is perhaps "the fear of responsibility" which is very different from a fear someone might have, say, of a wolf, or a fear that a guilty person might have of police. In its possibly earliest use in the Qur'an (91:8), it most probably means righteousness. (Rahman 1983, 176–77)

41. There have, of course, been Muslims throughout history who have expressed fundamental doubts, but they have almost always been regarded as heretics. See Stroumsa 1999; Hecht 2004.

42. The reference to monkeys and pigs has figured prominently in the statements and wall posters of Hamas and Fatah. See Oliver and Steinberg 2005, 101–3 and illus. 31.

43. Not only is there a chapter in the Quran entitled "Mary" (19: esp. 16–38), but there are numerous positive references to her elsewhere; see, e.g., 3:30–45, 4:155, 21:92–94, and 46:12.

44. See Delong-Bas 2004.

45. Broadly speaking, contemporary Muslims argue that slavery, while permitted in the Quran, is disfavored and should wither away as attitudes and incentives change. The Quran strongly recommends indi-

vidual emancipation (5:89, 58:3, 90:13) and directs believers to allow slaves to purchase their freedom over time (24:33). It is worth recalling that it was not until the end of the nineteenth century that the Vatican finally condemned slavery. See generally Clarence-Smith 2006; Freamon 2006.

46. See, e.g., the characteristic passages at 55:14 and 72:1.

47. See Macdonald and Massé 1991.

48. For example, before his death in 1998, Sheikh Mohamed Mutwali al-Sharawi, a very popular religious television commentator in Egypt, frequently emphasized the verses in the Quran that asserted the existence of the genies. Many popular Muslim newspapers and magazines, like Egypt's *Hadith al-Medina*, contain advice columns in which people inquire about the illnesses from which they are suffering and whether their problems may have been caused by genies. For an example of the problems caused when a home that was purchased was thought to be occupied by genies, see Shah 2006.

49. See Leemhuis 1993.

50. See the cases described in Dupret 2003, 15–44; Drieskens 2004, 2006. On the related issue of claiming insanity due to spirit infestation, see Arabi 2004.

51. On the psychodynamics of genie possession, see Crapanzano 1975; Khatibi 1984; and Younis 2000. It is by no means only poorer people who believe in the powers of genies to make them ill: Many of the people who went to a famous Egyptian curer/exorcist were reported in the leading newspaper *Al-Ahram* to be scientists and engineers. See Drieskens, 2008.

52. Rothenberg 2004, 103–8.

53. Muhammad 'Abduh, for example, wrote, "The *'ulama'* say that the *Jinn* are living bodies which cannot be seen. The *'Manar'* has said more than once that it is permissible to say that minute living bodies which today have been made known by the microscope and are called microbes, may possibly be a species of the *Jinn*. It has been proven that the microbes are the cause of most diseases" (quoted in Livingston 1995, 226).

54. On the training of Roman Catholic priests in the art of exorcism, for example, see Associated Press 2005.

55. Arkoun 1982.

56. Taha 1987. See generally Mahmoud 1998, 105–28.

57. See Hirschkind 1995. Of particular concern to those attacking Abu Zayd was that he appeared to deny the existence of the genies.

58. See Barlas 2002; Wadud 1999; and Manji 2004.

59. Cornell 1995, 393. See also the interesting discussion in Fisher and Abedi 1990.

60. Martin 1982, 383.

61. Quoted in Lester 1999, 55.

CHAPTER SEVEN

1. Figurative art was almost entirely of and for kings, many representations
    suggesting allegorical relations between the monarch and the divine.
    See Barry 2004. Western knowledge about Islamic representational art
    remains rather limited. In the words of the director of Oxford's Khalili
    Centre for Art and Material Culture of the Middle East, "While we are
    relatively well informed about the various Christian attitudes to represen-
    tational art, we remain profoundly ignorant about the arts produced by
    Islamic societies, and about Islamic doctrine on the arts and its interpreta-
    tion. We are accustomed to the kaleidoscope of arts produced by Chris-
    tian societies, but still look at the arts of Islamic societies through the
    wrong end of the telescope, reducing them to a single and lesser unity"
    (quoted in Jones 2005, 14).
2. Sura 5:90, for example, says, "Intoxicants and gambling, sacrificing to
    stones, and (divination by) arrows, are an abomination." The stones no
    doubt refer to the "idols" of pre-Islamic Arabia, but they do not appear to
    have been figurative, so, as one writer states, "It is not figuration as such
    that is targeted" (Besançon 2000, 77). Indeed, the term used in 5:90 is
    ansab, which appears to refer to poles of an uncertain nature that were
    the subject of worship in pre-Islamic times, a fact that may account for
    different translations of the term as "idols" and as "decorated pillars." See
    Melikian-Chirvani 1987; he also writes, "Ce n'est pas la figuration qui
    est un sujet de preoccupation en islam mais l'adoration de la matière et
    l'association à Dieu (*shirk*) de toute notion extérieure à Son Essence, de
    toute personne, perçue comme une manifestation du polythéisme"
    (ibid., 91) [It is not figuration that preoccupies Islam but the worship of
    the inert and the admixture with God of everything separate from His Es-
    sence, of any being, perceived as a demonstration of polytheism].
3. Alternatively, it is God who does the creating through Jesus since God
    alone is described in the Quran as the "the Creator, the Maker, the
    Shaper" (59:24). This image of Jesus and the bird of life, created out of his
    breath, is an artistic and literary theme that is not uncommon to Islamic
    art of the medieval period. See Barry 2004. The Quran also refers to the
    genies who, at Solomon's command, could fashion likenesses (34:13). As
    Ghabin remarks, "Many exegetes argued that from the time of Solomon
    until the advent of Islam making figures was permitted. This permission
    was rescinded by Muhammad for two reasons: first, Muhammad said
    that God would command those who made figures of living creatures to
    breathe life into them: they would fail, and then He would torture them.
    The second reason was to prevent the return of paganism to the memory
    of Arabs" (1998, 213). Other Quranic passages, being more explicit about
    the prohibition on idols (e.g., 5:90, 5:33, 22:31, and 70:43), are read to
    imply that forming any object that casts a shadow is impermissible. For a

classical statement of the role of idols at the time of the Prophet's life, see al-Kalbî 1952.

4. The Prophet was more negatively disposed toward poetry, which he regarded as capable of misdirecting relationships to the point of leading people to venerate beings other than God. His opinion on representational art, by contrast, appears less certain. As one commentator writes, "[W]hile views on Muhammad's attitude to representational art and to music must . . . remain conjectural, views on his attitude to literary art are not" (Shahid 1965, 563).

5. The earliest of chronicles, that of Abu'l Walid Muhammad ibn 'Abdallah al-Azraqi, tells how the Prophet ordered the destruction of all the frescos on the pillars of the Ka'ba except those of Jesus and his mother. See Melikian-Chirvani 1987, 92. See also Creswell 2002, 102. It may be in relation to this story that the Tradition also says, "Woe to him who has painted a living creature! At the day of the last Judgment the persons represented by him will come out of the tomb and join themselves to him to demand of him a soul. Then that man, unable to give life to his work, will burn in eternal flames." See Whishaw 1910, 1068. Another Tradition suggests that the Prophet permitted cushions decorated with human figures in his house, but not curtains—perhaps because the breeze would give figures on such draperies the appearance of being alive. For additional examples of human representations in early Islam, see Blair and Bloom 1999, 230–36. On the place of Jesus in Islam generally, see Khalidi 2001. Allah was probably the first among equals in the pantheon of pre-Islamic Arabia, with Jesus represented as a lesser figure. As Leaman writes,

> As time went on, the original Abrahamic observances at the Ka'ba were progressively diluted by the influence of pagan features (perhaps arriving through the caravan routes that led to Mecca). The pilgrims of pre-Islamic times visited not only the house of Abraham and the sacred stone of Gabriel but also the display of stone idols (representing different deities) housed in and around the *Ka'ba*. There were said to be 360 different deities including Awf, the great bird, Hubal the Nabatean god, the three celestial goddesses Manat, al-Uzza and al-Lat, and statues of Mary and Jesus. The most important of all these deities was called Allah ("god"). This deity was worshipped throughout southern Syria and northern Arabia, and was the only deity not represented by an idol in the Ka'ba. (2004, 4–5)

6. In the hadith collected by Bukhari the reference to embroidery will be found at volume 4, book 54, number 449; the reference to the picture of Aisha at volume 5, book 58, number 235. A number of hadith concerning pictures are available at the University of Southern California database, http://www.usc.edu/dept/MSA/reference/searchhadith.html.

7. See Papadopoulo 1979, 52. For examples of the use of human representations in early Islam, see 'Isa 1955, 263–64. Some of the representations of the Prophet are said to have been placed on prayer rugs. For comparisons to the discouragement of human representations in Jewish art, see Rosenzweig 2005; Batnitzky 2000; Besançon 2000, 63–77; and Bland 2001. Islamic law also has had no clear prohibition on representations: "There is, in fact, no consistent tradition in classical Islamic law which specifies a penalty for Muslims or non-Muslims who portray the Prophet. In practice, it has been widely accepted that such images—while tragically underestimating the grandeur of their subjects—can be endured as long as the intent is not clearly insulting" (Winter 2006, 20).

8. One modern Muslim commentator offers this perspective: "If the question of *taswir* [making a picture] had been as important as other problems, such as those of strong drink, marriage, divorce, and inheritance, the Qur'an certainly would have dealt with it explicitly, as it did with other problems of conduct and worship" ('Isa 1955, 252). Although discussions about the use of human images may have been limited, the effect may nevertheless have been substantial. "[T]he influence of the Muslim theologians on art was of decisive importance. No Muslim artist has ever attempted to depict Allah, and with very few exceptions figurative works of art have never found their way into mosques or other religious buildings. The Koran has never been illustrated, and depictions of the Prophet Muhammad are rare. With the reforms carried out by the Umayyad caliph Abd al-Malik in 696–697 A.D., portraits of rulers disappeared for a long period from Islamic coins, to be replaced by calligraphic decorations. And even if there were a number of exceptions to this rule, the trend was clear. Figurative depictions were removed from public areas and were, where they existed, primarily found in the private sphere of the upper class and rulers, where they were unable to disturb the spiritual equilibrium of the common man" (Folsach 1996, 80). As Arnold observes, "In no mosque nor in any other religious building are there to be found either statues or pictures, and orthodox religious sentiment has always been active in the destruction of pictorial representations of human beings wherever such destruction was possible" (1928, 4). He concludes that "there has never been any historical tradition in the religious painting of Islam" (ibid., 91). On the unusual portrayal of the Prophet in popular Iranian images, see the text and references at chapter 8, note 5.

9. Quoted in full at Papadopoulo 1979, 53. For a critique of al-Nawawi's argument, see 'Isa 1955, 253–54.

10. A recent vice chancellor of Al-Azhar, commenting on a twelfth-century work, is quoted as saying, "It is not forbidden to make images of whatever is inanimate or has no model as in the case of a winged man" (El Kadi 1996, 10). Papadopoulo says, "The central idea, we see, is that of imitation of animate beings. 'Animate' is better than 'living' in this context because

it refers to creatures capable of moving of their own will, because for the Muslims, once again following Aristotle, plants are not alive in this sense. To the doctors of the faith it was the act of imitation on the part of the painter that was sacrilegious" (1979, 53).

11. Cited from Massignon in Papadopoulo 1979, 54. This admonition is probably connected to the oft-told story about the Prophet's uncle, Ibn 'Abbas, who advised a painter, "You must decapitate animals so that they do not seem to be alive and try to make them look like flowers." See the hadith collection of Bukhari, volume 3, book 34, number 428. See also Hillenbrand 1999, 195.

12. This was true particularly after the sixteenth century, when the Prophet was portrayed simply as a flame. Rulers such as the Turkish pasha who punished a book buyer for disfiguring the faces in an illuminated manuscript and the emperor Akbar, who supported portraiture on the grounds that it was not animate, are often cited as examples of monarchs who did not accept the common prohibition on representations of the human figure. See Papadopoulo 1979, 56–57. In some representations of human figures a line was drawn across the throat to symbolically suggest that it was not the artist's intention that the figure could ever be brought to life.

13. "There is one characteristic of the figure painting of the Muhammadan period which is deserving of special attention, viz. the infrequency of any attempt to give emotive expression to the faces of the living persons represented in these pictures" (Arnold 1928, 133).

14. "One of the commonest of these is the putting of a finger to the lips as a sign of astonishment, and it constantly occurs in cases where, without this characteristic gesture, there would be no indication that the persons concerned were under the influence of any feeling whatsoever. Another conventional sign was the gnawing of the back of the hand to indicate the emotion of despair. Even violent grief makes no change in the features of the mourner, but it is shown by the veiling of the face or tossing of the arms" (Arnold 1928, 134). Even in the late fifteenth-century paintings of the Timurid court, when far more active scenes rich in natural detail exhibit a new vocabulary of forms, the inner life of love and psychology "was left more or less unexplored" (Ettinghausen 1981, 259).

15. See Kühnel 1977, 698; Baer 1999. Not until the nineteenth century do more nuanced emotional representations begin to appear in Qajar Persian art. Ettinghausen 1981, 269.

16. For an online collection of images of the Prophet, see http://www.zombietime.com/mohammed_image_archive/islamic_mo_full/ and http://www.lacma.org/islamic_art/intro.htm (the latter is the site of the Los Angeles County Museum's Islamic art collection).

17. See, for example, the figure of dancers from the Fatimid period in Ettinghausen 1956, 253. Additional images can be found at the Metropolitan Museum of Art's Web site, http://www.metmuseum.org/toah/hd/figs/

hd_figs.htm. For an overview of the representation of human figures in Muslim art, see Boorstin 1992, 193–200, and his comparison to figural representation in Western art at 175–92.

18. Barry 2004. This is not, however, to suggest that Islamic images were solely a function of Sufi thought. See Leaman 2004, 8–9.

19. See Papadopoulo 1979, 52; Freeman 1955. See also Kifner 2006. The Prophet still appears on the north frieze of the United States Supreme Court building in Washington, D.C., between Justinian and Charlemagne in a grouping of great lawgivers. See http://www.supremecourtus.gov/about/north&southwalls.pdf. In Saragossa, Spain, however, a fresco representing the Reconquest by "The Moor Killer" was removed when Muslims complained, and in Bologna, Italy, the fresco in the main cathedral showing Muhammad in *Dante's Inferno* was similarly removed following objections raised by the local Muslim population.

20. The particular form of representation may not, of course, be universally recognized. Interpretations of a photograph, for example, may require sufficient experience with that form and its contexts to be "read" correctly. Thus, when some New Guineans were first presented with pictures of a colonist's family that showed individuals only from the neck up, the native peoples were horrified because they thought it meant that the white men had cut off the heads of their own relatives.

21. The role of acting thus presents many Muslims with a delicate distinction between mere imitation and the threat of potential idolatry. In the words of one writer:

> Another difficulty that Islam appears to have with the dramatic arts has to do with the ongoing debate about the nature of acting. Islamic and Arabic language scholars use two different words for "acting," *al-tamthil* [incarnation] and *al-taqlid* [imitation]. If acting constitutes *al-tamthil*, a word [Yemeni writer Abdul Aziz] al-Magaleh translates as "figural representation" and Lutfi Abdul-rahman Fazio renders as "incarnation," then some Islamic scholars declare that it is forbidden. [Egyptian literary critic Muhammad b. 'Abd al-Hamid Musa Mandur] asserts that "personification" is an affront to God. *Al-taqlid*, which is generally translated as "imitation," on the other hand, is a less serious matter. For many religious authorities, a realistic psychological portrayal of a character involves incarnating a human being, and thus is sinful. The portrayal of an obvious stereotype, or an impersonation such as a stand-up comedian might do of a well-known figure, is an imitation and may be accepted, though few religious authorities will applaud it. This may be why presentational techniques, such as narrators and audience address, and stereotyped stock characters are quite common to Arab audiences. As long as the actor stands both inside and outside of the character he is playing, and a frank admission is made that the production is not in any way "real,"

he stands a better chance of being religiously correct, or at least tolerated. (Box 2005, 30; citations omitted)

22. Sheik Abdul Aziz bin Abdullah al-Sheik, the highest religious authority in
the country, stated on September 28, 2004, that such cameras were being
banned because they were "spreading obscenity" and were being misused
to photograph women without their knowledge. Associated Press 2004.

23. I do not, therefore, entirely agree with M. G. Carter, who argues that for
the Arabs poetry "is removed from the context of truth and is freed from
the constraints of religious values. [I]ts very origin and form consign it
to the general category of fallible human discourse, and it contains no
absolute or necessary truth, merely an accidental congruence with truth"
(1998, 241). While I do not doubt that the poet's truths are not com-
parable to direct assertions by Allah, the poet nevertheless constitutes
the archetypal embodiment of that most human of requirements, the
fashioning of the terms of relationship through which a community of
believers is sustained. For the Arabs, poets are indeed (following Percy
Bysshe Shelley) the true legislators of the world.

24. On marionettes, see Papadopoulo 1979, 57–58.

25. See Gimaret 1997.

26. There may, of course, be an elaborate vocabulary of iconic representations
themselves. This would be true not only in political iconography but also
in other contexts—say, cartoon representations. See Douglas and Malti-
Douglas 1994.

27. The seemingly repetitious nature of the arabesque, which may imply
choice and relationship at every juncture, can also be found in Arab gar-
den and urban design. See Ruggles 2000.

28. See Gittes 1991.

29. Pamuk 2001. Though he does not base his novel on it, Pamuk may also
have had in mind that when the Sultan Mehmed II allowed Venice to sue
for peace he required that an artist be sent to paint his portrait. During
the two years he spent in the Turkish court (1479–80) Gentile Bellini
produced not only a highly realistic portrait of the sultan but numerous
other representations of his court. See Campbell and Chong 2005. Compare Pamuk's novelistic approach to human representation in Islam with
the novel by Chaim Potok, in which a Hasidic boy from Brooklyn must
combat his community's hostility toward art as he develops as a painter.
Here, too, the issue is often, as for some Muslims, whether one trenches
on the exclusive right of the Almighty to engage in creation. "I looked
at my right hand, the hand with which I painted. There was power in
that hand. Power to create and destroy. Power to bring pleasure and pain.
Power to amuse and horrify. There was in that hand the demonic and the
divine at one and the same time. The demonic and the divine were two
aspects of the same force. Creation was demonic and divine. Creativity
was demonic and divine. Art was demonic and divine" (Potok 1972, 348).

30. M. G. Carter 1998, 236.

31. See Rosenthal 1968.

32. Elsewhere Rosenthal says, "The lack of confidence in the ability of artists to penetrate the spiritual reality of things was an attitude congenial to Christianity. Muslims also felt this irrelevance of art vis-à-vis true human values and its inability to express them. The physiognomists' approach toward painting was based, it would seem, fundamentally on magical ideas and was not as such an artistic one. In Islam, the ancient belief that painting possessed the ability to see beyond the outward shell survived only for magical purposes" (1971, 9). By contrast, I am suggesting that Muslims were averse to portraiture not because of any supposed magical ability it had to create "a truer reality than mere outward appearance was ever able to reveal" (ibid.), but because it could never tell the viewer the important sociological information needed to place the subject.

33. On readers' imagining another's appearance, see Cooperson 2001, 8 and 17. I disagree with Cooperson's speculation on this matter; I think he is projecting the Western approach to a portrait and offers no original sources to support his assertion that, icons of status aside, Arabs are expected to impute character or construct the portrait for themselves.

34. One finds rather few descriptions of the appearance of the Prophet. An exception is that of ʿAbd Allah b. Masʿud, who met the Prophet prior to his own conversion. The description was much disputed, but, as Cooperson says, "Even more disturbing, perhaps, was the implication that one could see the Prophet without recognizing him as such" (2001, 12; the text of the description of the Prophet is at 11–12).

35. T. Allen 1988, 36.

36. As Allen notes, it should come as no surprise "that inscriptions do not generally explain the figural representations they accompany" (ibid., 32). How could words ever match pictures if the former bear on relationships and the latter cannot show one moving to effect in the world? Words and pictures can only be juxtaposed, as aspects of a thing, speaking at somewhat crossed purposes in their portrayal of another.

37. See Gombrich 1969.

38. On our skepticism about reading character from portraiture, Fendrich writes:

> The disheartening truth—a truth most often swept under the rug of aesthetic pleasure—is that while portraiture teaches us about the human range of emotions and character in general, no specific portrait can reliably be said to reveal the inner life of the subject. Instead, great artists have the daunting ability to deceive us into believing that they have painted the heart and soul of a person. When we are moved by a specific portrait, then, we are unwittingly moved by the artfulness of the artist rather than the personality of the sitter. . . . The way we best acquaint ourselves with someone's char-

acter is through their actions, not their looks. Only after we know a person do we accurately read character back into his or her face. The portrait is, in other words, devious by nature, fooling and charming us into believing, for the time we are transfixed by it, that appearance and character are one and the same thing." (2005, B10–11)

CHAPTER EIGHT

1. It has also been argued that the charge of idolatry in the Quran was aimed not at pagans but at Jews and Christians as a way of challenging their proprietary claim to monotheism, much as charges of polytheism were used against some Christians as a way of demeaning their belief in the Trinity. See Hawting 1999.
2. Quoted in Boorstin 1992.
3. Among the earliest surviving representations are those from the fourteenth century housed at the Edinburgh University Library. The miniature of Muhammad rededicating the Black Stone at the Ka'ba (ms. 20, fol. 55, dated 1324) shows the face and body of the Prophet completely, even though the artist resided some distance away in Mecca. Other portrayals of Muhammad include *The Ascension of the Prophet* (Tabriz, 1315) and a Turkish miniature from a religious biography of the Prophet completed in 1388. For a broad range of pictures depicting the Prophet, most of them from Persia and Central Asia, see the Mohammed Image Archive Web site http://www.zombietime.com/mohammed_image_archive/islamic _mo_full/.
4. Ibn Warraq 2006, 13.
5. For analysis of the picture, based on a photograph of a Muslim boy taken by two European photographers around the beginning of the twentieth century, see Centlivres and Centlivres-Demont 2005, 2006. Films that depict the Prophet's face have been roundly condemned by Muslim authorities, whereas films that render only his shadow come in for somewhat less criticism. At the time of the Danish cartoon controversy many Muslims reiterated the belief that any portrayal of the Prophet has always been forbidden. In the United States the imam of the All Dulles Area Muslim Society mosque in northern Virginia explained that "the ban [on representations of the Prophet] stems from early Islam, when Muhammad preached monotheism in a culture steeped in the worship of idols. To discourage such idolatry, he ordered Muslims not to draw, and religious leaders have interpreted this to mean that the Prophet was banning images of himself and those close to him so they would never become objects of worship for Muslims" (quoted in Murphy 2006).
6. Despite the broad prohibition on human representation, such images, often commissioned and kept private by Islamic rulers, were once very common, especially among non-Arab Muslims. See the images on

the Metropolitan Museum of Art's Web site, http://www.metmuseum. org/toah/hd/figs/hd_figs.htm. For a general overview of the portrayal of human figures in Islamic art, see Boorstin 1992, 193–200; for his comparison to the development of human representation in the West, see ibid., 175–92.

7. The Danish cartoons, along with a variety of Muslim and Western representations of the Prophet from before and after the present controversy, can be seen at http://www.en.wikipedia.org/wiki/Depictions_of_ Muhammad. Readers can also see the original cartoons (and may wish to compare his reading of them with my own) in Spiegelman 2006, 48–50. For my own assessment of the Salman Rushdie affair, see L. Rosen 2002, 158–73.

8. Some of these latter cartoons can be viewed at http://michellemalkin.com/ archives/004465.htm; they are also described in Spiegelman 2006, 46. See also Smith and Fisher 2006. According to several Danish colleagues, the extra cartoons were taken by the imam to the Middle East to demonstrate the broader range of anti-Islamic representations, and some of those who saw them then mistakenly assumed they were part of the original twelve cartoons published by the Danish newspaper.

9. Not all the deaths were necessarily related to the cartoons. According to one reporter, eleven people killed by police in Libya during a protest ostensibly about the cartoons may really have been protesting against unemployment or were protesters hired by Qadhafi's regime who simply got out of hand. Solomon 2006, 60. In Germany a Pakistani student who carried a knife into the offices of the publisher who reproduced the cartoons in *Die Welt* was subsequently found hanged in his prison cell; in Britain several men were arrested under the Public Order Act for protesting without police notification outside the Danish embassy. See generally Ammitzbøll and Vidino 2007.

10. Four of the cartoons appeared in the magazine *Free Inquiry* only in May 2006, vol. 26, no. 3, pp. 8–11, where the editor also quotes a comment Art Spiegelman made to *The Nation* (repeated in Spiegelman 2006): "The banal quality of the cartoons that gave insult is hard to believe until they are seen." Two booksellers, Borders and Waldenbooks, refused to stock the issue of *Free Inquiry* in which the cartoons appeared because of concerns, as a Borders Group spokesman stated, about "the safety and security of our customers and employees." The editor of *Free Inquiry* replied, "To refuse to distribute a publication because of fear of vigilante violence is to undermine freedom of press—so vital for our democracy" (Gelder 2006). Later, all of the cartoons were reproduced, with commentary, in Spiegelman 2006.

11. F. Rose 2006a; see also F. Rose 2006b. For a basic chronology of the early months of the dispute, see Shadid and Sullivan 2006. The original children's book later appeared with illustrations of the Prophet, but without notice or comment. See the Web site mentioned above at note 7 on the

fabricated cartoons and the children's book. At other times portrayals of the Prophet have simply been ignored. See Winter 2006.

12. See Kotek and Kotek 2003; Lewis 2006.

13. Some of the Iranian cartoons can be seen in Spiegelman 2006, 51, and "The Israeli Anti-Semitic Cartoons Contest," http://www.boomka.org.

14. See Karimi 2006.

15. Goldberg 2006, 16. For more on the conflict between Danes and Muslim immigrants leading up to the controversy, see Pipes and Hedegaard 2002; Klausen 2005. On cartoons in the context of Arab politics generally, see Douglas and Malti-Douglas 1994.

16. This has also been translated as "Prophet, you crazy bloke! Keeping women under yoke." For this and other explications of the cartoons, see Asser 2006.

17. See generally Wensinck and Pellat 1971; Serjeant 1954; and Wheeler 2002. The absence of a long tradition of assessing prophethood among the Arabs may also account in part for the following, which comes from a fourteenth-century Arabic jokebook: "A man claimed to be a prophet. They asked him, 'What are the proofs of your being a prophet?' He said, 'I shall tell you what is in your mind.' They asked him, 'What is in our minds?' He said, 'You are thinking I am a liar and not a prophet'" (Lewis 1974, 284).

18. See generally Rahman 1958. On changing views of Muhammad, especially revisions of his biography as a model for various sociopolitical ideologies, see Tayob 1995.

19. See Aslan 2006, 58. Muhammad may also have incorporated aspects of the pre-Islamic seer, or *kahin*:

> The mantic knowledge [of the kāhin] is based on ecstatic inspiration. . . . They are interrogated in all important tribal and state occasions—especially before warlike enterprises, razzias, etc. in which they take part themselves as a rule, indeed, they sometimes lead them in person. . . . In private the kāhins especially act as judges in disputes and points of law of all kinds, so that the conception of kāhin is closely connected with that of *hakam*, judge. . . . At the same time, they interpret dreams, find lost camels, establish adulteries, clear up other crimes and misdemeanours, particularly thefts and murders, etc. . . . The prophet Muhammed disclaimed being a kāhin. But his earliest appearance as a prophet reminds us strongly of the manner of these soothsayers. He was an ecstatic and had "true dreams" like them. [E]ven the forms which he was still using for administering justice and settling disputes in Medina during the early years of his stay there correspond in their main features to those of the pagan kāhin and hakam. (Fischer 1987, 625–26)

See also Wolf 1951.

20. On the master–disciple pattern in Arab culture, see Hammoudi 1997. On ambivalence to power and an extension of Hammoudi's argument,

see L. Rosen 2002, 21–38. Sir Francis Bacon, who had reason to know, put the matter this way in his *Proficience and Advancement of Learning* (1605): "[D]isciples do own unto masters only a temporary belief and a suspension of their own judgment until they be fully instructed, and not an absolute resignation or perpetual captivity."

21. In the past women would even come out on the battlefield to shower a man who was insufficiently brave with the henna women used to adorn their hair and skin. Songs and gossip can do much the same to affect men's views of themselves at present.

22. Although the Ten Commandments of the Hebrew Bible are not replicated in the Quran, many of the propositions they embrace are recognizable in Suras 6:151–54 and 17:22–39, which include, among others, that one should have no other God than Allah, that one should be good to one's parents, and that one should not kill one's child because of poverty. On the commentaries of al-Tabari and others on the Ten Commandments, see Günther, 2008.

23. This may account for the common interpretation that although a father is responsible for the support of a child, he will not be subject to a punishment legally specified in the shari'a (known as a *ḥadd* punishment) for killing his child even though he could be subject to a discretionary punishment (*ta'zir*) at the hands of a local judge. See Ramic 2003, 13.

24. Dante places the hypocrites in the sixth level of the eighth circle of hell, where they walk around in lead-lined habits. The "sowers of discord" (the hypocrites) are farther down, in the ninth level of the eighth circle, which is the same level in which Dante places both Muhammad and his son-in-law, Ali. On the question of Islam's influence on Dante's *Divine Comedy*, see Palacios 1977; Olschki 1951; and Silverstein 1952.

In one popular Islamic account, which begins by detailing how each person will walk through the Plain of Doom over the bridge to Paradise with a candle appropriate to his fate, the plight of the hypocrites is described in the following terms: "Those who are hypocrites and are deprived of their personal light and hence will walk under the light of others and when they shall approach the edge of Hell they will observe that there is a narrow bridge over Hell which is thinner than a hair and sharper than the edge of a sword. It will be ordained: 'Walk over it into Heaven.' . . . On that occasion huge hooks rise forth from Hell. These hooks will injure some people a little, and they will drag down some into Hell. Similarly, relationships and trusts will now appear alongside the people and those who had not cared for them in the mortal world, these hooks shall drag them down into Hell" (Dehlevi 1990, 136–37).

25. The quoted phrases are borrowed from Schillinger 2006.

26. The theory expounded by most Muslim theologians who permit photographs and other representations of leaders is that the images are simply copies of the person's appearance and are permissible so long as they are not venerated.

27. As Asad has put it, "[W]hat is really interesting . . . is the way *representa-tions* of questioning, doubt, and so on, *in* the text are read backward into an authorial intention (the 'spirit' of the writing) that *produced* the text" (1993, 275; emphasis in original). Even former president Jimmy Carter (1989) couched his criticism of Rushdie in terms of the author's inten-tion: "The author, a well-versed analyst of Moslem beliefs, must have anticipated a horrified reaction throughout the Islamic world." See also Chakravorty 1995, 2241. By contrast, Werbner's structuralist analysis of *The Satanic Verses* and the role of authorial intent concludes that "from a modernist perspective *The Satanic Verses* did not intend to defame Islam and mock Muslims and their Prophet" (1996, S69).
28. Rushdie 1991, 410.
29. See L. Rosen 2002, 158–73.
30. For background on the idea of intent in Islamic legal history, see Powers 2006.
31. In this respect an analogy can be made to American laws on statutory rape or investing in the subsidiary of a bank toward whose parent entity one has a fiduciary relationship: Saying you did not know the girl was underage or the company was owned by the parent bank is no defense, since the legislature has marked these as matters in such great need of protection that no aspect of one's intent can be asserted as a defense to their commission.

CHAPTER NINE

1. See, e.g., Olivier Roy, based on a lecture at Princeton University in 1990.
2. A useful description of Ibn Khaldun's life is found in Talbi 1971; his meeting with Tamerlane is described in Ibn Khaldun 1952 and further recounted in Marozzi 2006. Other writings are available in Ibn Khaldun 1984, Ibn Khaldun 1987, and Baali 1992. For a fictionalized account of his life see Himmich 2001.
3. This essay was originally prepared for the celebration in honor of Akbar Ahmed's inauguration as the first Ibn Khaldun Professor at American Uni-versity. It is a pleasure to rededicate it to him. See generally Ahmed 2005; see also Dhaouadi 2005.
4. Ibn Khaldun may have gotten some of his most important historical ex-amples wrong. For an argument that the Almoravids of eleventh-century Morocco were not, as he argued, displaced by groups with "stronger group feeling and . . . more deeply rooted in desert life" but were overtaken by the rival Almohads precisely because they remained too attached to their desert life, see Messier 2001.

It is tempting to note that in the Hebrew Bible, God's rejection of the offering of the agriculturalist Cain and his acceptance of that brought forth by the pastoralist Abel may imply His favoring the nomadic life because of the solidarity and justice that were thought to characterize those who had not settled in cities. Whether Ibn Khaldun was in any way himself influenced by this biblical story is unclear.

5.   Ibn Khaldun's relation of his general theory to particulars is captured in his statement about how one should write about history and culture:

> He who practices this science needs to know the rules of statecraft, the nature of existing things, and the difference between nations, regions and tribes in regard to way of life, qualities of character, customs, sects, schools of thought, and so on. He must distinguish the similarities and differences between the present and the past, and know the various origins of dynasties and communities, the reasons for their coming into existence, the circumstances of the persons involved in them, and their history. He must go on until he has complete knowledge of the causes of every event, and then he will examine the information which has been handed down in the light of his principles of explanation. If they are in harmony, this information is sound, otherwise it is spurious. (Ibn Khaldun 1967, as quoted in Hourani 1991, 20)

This is a good example both of the attractiveness of Ibn Khaldun's style of history for modern Westerners and the ease with which the distinctively Arab meaning of such a statement may be lost in cultural translation.

6.   Whether human actions are predestined or subject to human control was a related issue on which Ibn Khaldun was—perhaps for intellectual reasons, perhaps to avoid sterile debates—less direct. One scholar calls attention to Ibn Khaldun's ambivalence:

> Human nature is depicted by [Ibn Khaldûn] as flexible and as subject to the influence of external causes and as always being guided by reason. All this would seem to be contrary to Ibn Khaldûn's openly avowed belief that God predetermines all human action. Of this contradictory attitude Ibn Khaldûn himself once in a while seems to become aware, and to assuage his theological conscience he quotes appropriate verses glorifying the power of God. . . . The answer provided by Ibn Khaldûn . . . is only the adoption of an old answer given by Muslim theologians whenever they found themselves committed to two contradictory beliefs—an answer expressed by the Arabic words *bi-la kayfa*, which, freely translated, means, "we know the contradiction can be reconciled, but ask us not how." . . . Faithful believers know that the doctrines of their religion are true, and whatever objections may be raised against them are not real objections; and so why bother to answer them. . . . Or, perhaps, . . . in the age-old struggle between orthodoxy and rationalism in religion he saw nothing but a struggle between the suspension of reason and the perversion of reason and, like a goodly number of non-quibblers of

every religion, he chose to suspend reason rather than to pervert it. (Wolfson 1959, 595–97)

For the related argument that Ibn Khaldun was simply following the Greeks in his methodology and presaging the French scholars of the Annales school, see Dale 2006.

7. Rosenthal 1987, 566 (emphasis added). In a related vein Hourani goes beyond the common translation of *'asabiyah* as "group feeling" to speak of it as "a corporate spirit oriented towards obtaining and keeping power" (1991, 2 and 449). Rosenthal, like many others, uses the shorthand translation of *'asabiyah* as "group feeling"—see, e.g., Irwin 1996, 35, Mahdi 1968, 56—but the fuller definition that includes leadership is undoubtedly vital to an understanding of Ibn Khaldun's usage. This aspect is not always sufficiently stressed in assessments of 'asabiya as a factor in contemporary Arab political structure. See generally Volpi 2004, 1065.

8. Lacoste 1984, 102. Lacoste argues that Ibn Khaldun restricts his concept of 'asabiya to North African tribes, and indeed to those in which some form of hierarchy of chiefs has arisen: "'Asabiya does not therefore mean social solidarity in general, but rather a very specific form of social organization which allows a tribal aristocracy to control the forces of a military democracy" (ibid., 108).

9. Many of the points mentioned here were made in a lecture by Cheddadi titled "Ibn Khaldun's Theory of the Muslim State," delivered at Princeton University on November 24, 2003. See also Cheddadi 1999, 2002.

10. Mahdi 1957, 197.

11. "[T]he expected Messiah will not come to power automatically because of the cyclical motion of the stars. He will have to possess the qualifications necessary for a leader and must be born in circumstances conducive to the creation of a powerful state, which in turn must follow the natural course of rise and decline" (ibid., 256). The necessary qualities of leadership include being just, competent, and knowledgeable. See ibid., 242–48.

12. This issue is explored in greater detail in L. Rosen 2002, 56–72.

13. A number of the points mentioned here were made by Abderrahmane Lakhsassi in a lecture titled "Ibn Khaldun and Moroccan-Andalusian Sufism," delivered at Princeton University on April 12, 1988. On Ibn Khaldun's approach to Sufism see also Z. Ahmad 2003, 65–75.

14. See Lakhsassi 1996, 367. Ibn Khaldun also thought that religious jurisprudence (*fiqh*) was related to but not subsumed under Sufism. In this regard he can be contrasted, for example, to Sibt b. al-'Ajami (d. 1479), who argued that fiqh was always subsumed within Sufism and never the reverse. See quotations in von Grunebaum 1955, 123 n. 17.

15. Ibn Khaldun's belief that the political and the mystical, though linked, must be pragmatically dissociated may also account for his argument, contra al-Ghazzali, that Sufism and jurisprudence (fiqh) should be separated. Indeed, Ibn Khaldun argued that "it is possible for the jurisprudent

to possess both the exoteric and the esoteric fiqh" (quoted in Lakhsassi 1996, 357).

16. Toynbee puts his assessment of Ibn Khaldun's *Muqaddimah* in the following extravagant terms: "[H]e has conceived and formulated a philosophy of history which is undoubtedly the greatest work of its kind that has ever yet been created by any mind in any time or place" (1935, 322). See also Toynbee 1954, 84–87; Irwin 1997. For critiques of Toynbee's work, see Montagu 1956. Friedrich Engels and Karl Marx may have been influenced in their own thinking by Ibn Khaldun's vision of cyclical histories; the translation of Ibn Khaldun's work by De Slane is mentioned by Marx in his reading notes from the early 1880s. See Hopkins 1990. Among anthropologists, Gellner (1981) was most attracted to Ibn Khaldun's image of the oscillation of social solidarity and fission. On the uses of Ibn Khaldun by various anthropologists, see Anderson 1984.

Interest in Ibn Khaldun was, as Robinson notes, "the classic exchange of Orientalizing influence. Yet, we should be wary of those who wish to make his prominence entirely a function of the West. In the early twentieth century, the ulama [religious scholars] of Farangi Mahall, Lucknow (India), busily discussed Ibn Khaldun in the context of burgeoning ideas of Muslim Nationalism. The likely origin of their knowledge was the Egyptian Bulaq edition of 1874, or perhaps one of the earlier Turkish editions, but not anything emanating from Europe" (2006, 11).

17. Ibn Khaldun 1987, 181.

18. When President Bill Clinton, shortly after his inauguration, suggested raising taxes on the rich, Ronald Reagan (1993) made this observation: "Although it goes back well before the 1980's, may I offer you the advice of the 14th century Arab historian Ibn Khaldun, who said: 'At the beginning of the empire, the tax rates were low and the revenues were high. At the end of the empire, the tax rates were high and the revenues were low.' And, no, I did not personally know Ibn Khaldun, although we may have had some friends in common!"

19. On his view of chance versus necessity, Mahdi writes, "Ibn Khaldun's rejection of absolute necessity does not then mean that he refuses to give necessity a place in history, for that would have meant the reduction of all historical events to accidental events, i.e., to events that have no cause and, therefore, are unintelligible. Rather, he follows a middle course between two extreme and simple, though illusory, explanations: an explanation based on universal necessity and the negation of chance, and an explanation based on universal chance and the negation of necessity" (1957, 260).

20. A complete picture of Ibn Khaldun's view of human actions and the causes of social events would have to include his belief in such matters as the effectiveness of human sorcery (and his reasons for thinking that those who employed this power were unworthy of respect) and the reli-

gious science of interpreting dreams, those sleep-filled moments when the disclosures of ordinary sensation are suspended and perceptions that can only be gained in slumber may be retained in the imagination even after one awakes.

21. Ibn Khaldun, it may be remembered, is the one who stated, "In the Muslim community, the holy war is a religious duty, because of the universalism of the Muslim mission and (the obligation to) convert everybody to Islam either by persuasion or by force" (quoted in Lazare 2004, 30).

22. Ibn Khaldun's conception of theory as an act, and not simply as an idea, is not so different from its meaning in Western antiquity:

> [I]n one of the earliest known uses of the word *theory*, Herodotus describes the journey of Solon from Athens for the sake of theory. Theory at that time connoted the act of observing, seeing, witnessing; more particularly a theorist (*theoros*) was, as Sheldon Wolin, describes it, "a public emissary dispatched by his city to attend the religious festivals of other Greek cities." Over time, "theory" was linked to observation of different and often alien lands, institutions, and practices, a journey that not only produced knowledge of other political worlds, but also "could eventually issue in a critical sense toward the particularity, even arbitrariness of [one's] own culture and stimulate a drive to find a higher unity or reality beneath the particularity of appearances, whether in nature, Being or human nature." (R. Euben 1999, 10–11, quoting Wolin 1968, 319, and J. Euben 1977, 34)

CHAPTER TEN

1. Einstein 1954, 55. Einstein referred to himself, in a letter to a friend, as "a deeply religious unbeliever." When asked whether he believed in God, Einstein replied, "I believe in Spinoza's God," whom Einstein elsewhere described as having created a universe that "will make no exception to its natural laws on your account; it will work no miracles for you; it will tender no affection, show no sign of concern about your well-being; in short, it will give you nothing that you do not already have" (quoted in M. Stewart 2006). On Einstein as "scientist-priest" and self-described adherent to "Cosmic Religion" (which sheds anthropomorphism and free will, thus eliminating the antagonism of science and religion), see Sonnert 2005, 298–302, and 299 for the above-quoted letter. It is noteworthy, too, that for many years some 40 percent of American biologists, physicists, and mathematicians have said they believe in a God who actively communicates with humankind and to whom one may pray in expectation of receiving an answer. See, e.g., the work of the noted genetic scientist, former chair of the Human Genome Project, and self-described evangelical Christian Francis S. Collins (2006).

2. Kepel 1993, 137–38. Kepel offers no survey data to back up his statement, only a few anecdotes about such figures as the (unnamed) leader of the Egyptian group who called for Sadat's assassination and who was trained as an electrical engineer (169) or general comparisons to science-trained fundamentalists in the other faiths (186). Absent any source citations for Kepel's statement, scholars should be more careful than they have been about citing it.

3. Sageman 2004a. See also Sageman 2004b. Unlike the typical Palestinian suicide bombers, who tend to be young, poor, with little education, cloistered, and devout, the al-Qaeda suicide squads are older, middle class, educated, worldly, and frequently the product of more secular families. Bergen (2005), who studied the background of seventy-five terrorists, concluded that 53 percent were college graduates. See also the detailed analyses of terrorists in Forest 2005, Reuter 2004, and Holmes 2005, 131–72. For a study of Muslim terrorists who were born and reared in the West, see Wiktorowicz 2005.

4. Raman 2004. He goes on to note the changing makeup of the new recruits: "[T]he attraction of educated youth to terrorism is not a new phenomenon. [Before 1991] [m]ost of them were students or graduates or teachers of humanities. There were hardly any students of science or scientists in their ranks. What is new about jihadi terrorism is the gravitation of a number of students of science or working scientists to the jihadi organizations to help the terrorists in their jihad" (ibid.).

5. Markon 2005; Viorst 2006.

6. See Randal 2004.

7. McDermott 2005, 111–20 (Khalid Sheikh) and 14–19 (Atta).

8. Fisher 2001. One could also add, for Morocco, Abdelillah Benkiran, a former physics student who founded the Islamic Community, which later merged with the Justice and Development Party, and the former science teacher and present husband of Nadia Yassine, whose father founded the Association for Justice and Charity.

9. Hoodbhoy 1991, 28–49. See also the United Nations Development Programme 2003.

10. Benoliel 2003. Regime control of science may also play a role in its development. See, e.g., Siino 2004.

11. See Metlitzki 1977.

12. *Muqaddimah*, as quoted in Dallal 1999, 157. On Ibn Khaldun's relation of revealed-sacred knowledge (*naql*) and knowledge based on human reason, see Dhaouadi 2005. Jamal al-Din al-Afghani makes a similar point when he says that "our 'ulama' [religious scholars] these days have divided science into two parts. One they call Muslim science, and one European science. Because of this they forbid others to teach some of the useful sciences. They have not understood that science is that noble thing that has

no connection with any nation, and is not distinguished by anything but itself" (quoted from Afghani's "Refutation of the Materialists," in Keddie 1968, 107).

13. Sabra 1976, 186.

14. During the Middle Ages in the West, optics was sustained because it was on rays of light that God was thought to interact with human beings. Thus, churches had to let in light so that God could relate to man. Perhaps for many Muslims—especially Sufi orders—light was also equated with man–God relationships, in which case the relational nature of even optics may render it less an exception than might otherwise appear. Some experimentation also occurred in astronomy and medicine, though it is not clear that it contributed to an actual experimental methodology.

15. Abdelhamad I. Sabra, quoted in Overbye 2001.

16. Quoted in Lewis 1976, 184.

17. The work of Latour (1987, 1999) is exemplary in this regard; Orientalist scholars have yet to pursue studies of science along these lines. The idea that scientific inquiry stems from some human impulse or some indecipherable amalgam of forces hardly addresses the issues. A good example of the motivating force of human curiosity is the following: "[T]he enterprise of Islamic science and philosophy, with its high level of achievement and its marked interest in theoretical and abstract questions, can hardly be explained as the unintended consequence of the practical concerns of a few individuals, however powerful and influential. In Islam, as in other civilizations, nothing less profound than genuine curiosity, or less complicated than the interplay of social, cultural and deep human needs, can suffice to explain such an impressive and long-lasting enterprise" (A. I. Sabra quoted in Lewis 1976, 182). Clearly if it is true that some basic human curiosity propels humans to scientific inquiry, the quest would not have ended for Muslims in the Middle Ages, and if a complex array of social forces is at work, it is toward an understanding of these forces that the inquiry should lead but never does.

18. For a review of arguments for and against a distinctly Islamic science, see Negus 1995. See also Hoodbhoy 1991, 65–84. Seyyed Hossein Nasr, himself a graduate in mathematics and physics from MIT and holder of a doctorate in the history of science from Harvard, has argued that since no science exists in a cultural vacuum, one can see "Islamic science as an independent way of looking at the work of nature," particularly in the way it addresses the unity of all things and the reasons why physical phenomena occur and not merely how they occur. See S. Nasr 1987, and his talk, sponsored by the Muslim Students Association at MIT in 2005, initially carried at the following Web site: http://web.mit.edu/mitmsa/www/NewSite/libstuff/nasrspeech1.html. Others, like Abdus Salam, would argue that science is not about the why, and hence there is no such thing as Islamic science.

19. Rosenthal lists 107 definitions of *'ilm*, while a sixteenth-century scholar listed no fewer than 316 (Rosenthal 1970, as cited in Hoodbhoy 1991, 137).

20. For a number of these classifications, see von Grunebaum 1955, 116–17.

21. The Persian mystic Ali ibn Uthman al-Hujwiri (d. c. 1072–77) is characteristic of a great many thinkers when, in dividing knowledge into the classic categories of praiseworthy (*ferḍ*), blameworthy (*haram*), and neutral (*mubih*), he says, "Knowledge is obligatory only in so far as is required for acting rightly. God condemns those who learn useless knowledge [Quran 2:96], and the Prophet said, 'I take refuge with Thee from knowledge that profiteth naught.' Much may be done by means of a little knowledge and knowledge should not be separated from action. The Prophet said, 'The devotee without divinity is like a donkey turning a mill,' because the donkey goes round and round on its own tracks and never makes any advance" (1976, 11, quoted in von Grunebaum 1955, 118).

22. The aphorism is noted in Huff 2003, 87.

23. "Doubt in whichever way indicated became the true pariah and outcast of Muslim civilization . . . a sufficient manifestation of ignorance . . . man's mortal enemy, depriving him of the certainty that his religion was intended and equipped to give him. . . . The common belief was that necessarily and simply, doubt in God was unbelief. . . . Doubting as an epistemological tool and, even more so, as a way of life was banned from Muslim society" (Rosenthal 1970, 300, 301, 303, and 308). See also Rosenthal 1984, 17.

24. Huff 2003, 106–17. I do not agree with Huff in certain of his assertions. He overemphasizes Islamic law as the source of failure to develop impersonal institutions and universal concepts, whereas a close study of both early and modern Islamic law reveals that procedure and operative cultural assumptions did create many ideas that do not fit the Eurocentric view of how law must be constructed, ideas that suffuse the work of Joseph Schacht upon whom he relies. For further discussion along these lines, see L. Rosen 1989, 2000.

25. Hodgson 1974, 458.

26. The idea of "impersonal criteria," quoted from the work of Thomas Merton's *The Sociology of Science*, is elaborated in Huff 2003, 215–24. It is also a mistake to argue that since God could change the rules at any time Islam adheres to "fundamental assumptions antithetical to science" (Stark 2003, 155). Not only may the same theological point apply in the West, but Muslims do not imagine that God does, in fact, act in this way, having instead endowed humankind with reason to negotiate the world as He created it.

27. S. Nasr 1976, 79. See also Sardar 1989, 13–18; Qadir 1988, 122–34; and Huff 2003, 211–39. Hoodbhoy 1991, 118–33, includes among responses to the question "why didn't the scientific revolution happen in Islam?" the rejection of the idea that God operates secondarily through causal laws,

the extractive nature of the economies of the region, the fragmentation of urban institutions, and the weakness of political organization across time.

28. See the discussion above in chapter 2 on the Arab frame tradition.

29. Contrast this suggestion to the more common one given for the decline of Islamic science:

> By the end of the Middle Ages, there was a dramatic change and in a sense a reversal of roles. In the Muslim world the spirit of independent inquiry was stifled and died; science was reduced to the endless repetition of approved formulae. In the West, in contrast, the scientific movement, already discernible in the late Middle Ages, advanced enormously in the era of the Renaissance, the Discoveries, the technological revolution, and the immense economic, social and intellectual changes that preceded, accompanied and followed them. Those who had been disciples now became teachers—and their former masters proved recalcitrant pupils. As one might expect, the products of alien and infidel science were most readily accepted in medicine and warfare, where they could make a difference between life and death, between victory and defeat. The acceptance of the underlying philosophy and sociopolitical systems that made these scientific achievements possible proved more difficult. (Lewis 2000, 352–53)

Von Grunebaum notes that for many in the Middle Ages, the mathematical and medical sciences "never did shed the suspicion of bordering on the impious which, to the strict, would be near-identical with the religiously uncalled-for" (1955, 114). He goes on to connect this suspicion to the decline of Arab science in the medieval period:

> This is why the pursuit of the natural sciences as that of philosophy tended to become located in relatively small and esoteric circles and why but few of their representatives would escape an occasional uneasiness with regard to the moral implications of their endeavors— a mood which not infrequently did result in some kind of an apology for their work. It is not so much the constant struggle which their representatives found themselves involved in against the apprehensive skepticism of the orthodox which in the end smothered the progress of their work; rather it was the fact, which became more and more obvious, that their researches had nothing to give to their community which this community could accept as an essential enrichment of their lives. When in the later Middle Ages scientific endeavor in certain fields very nearly died down, the loss did indeed impoverish Muslim civilization as we view its total unfolding and measure its contribution against that of its companion civilizations, but it did not affect the livability of the correct life and thus did not impoverish or frustrate the objectives of the community's existence as traditionally experienced. (Ibid.)

30. S. Nasr 1994. Nasr's views are summarized in Hamdy 2006.
31. For a contemporary instance of credibility being based on people who have an effect on relationships rather than on abstract knowledge, see L. Rosen 2002, 112–13.
32. "Telling truth from falsehood thus depended, as did the science of Prophetic tradition, on knowing the chain of reliable transmitters, what [Brinkley] Messick calls the knowing 'of men by men'" (Gilsenan 2000, 605). Or, to recycle a phrase of my own, it is not so much the argument that makes the man believable but the man the argument (L. Rosen 1984, 117–33; L. Rosen 2000, 133–50). One place where the tension between the believability of the observer and the claims of science can be seen is in the determination of when the monthlong fast of Ramadan ends. Following the tradition of the Prophet are those who believe that a reliable witness must observe the waxing crescent moon before celebration of the end of the fast (*Eid al-Fitr*) can begin, while proponents of modern astronomy can predict the arrival of the new moon without any actual sighting. In many respects this is a perfect example of the question of personalism versus impersonal, even institutional, attachments, a question that we have seen informing every other domain of Arab culture from the nature of politics to the meaning of portraiture.
33. Hoodbhoy 1991, 39. He continues: "The social conditioning of an authoritarian traditional environment means, as an inescapable consequence, that all knowledge comes to be viewed as unchangeable and all books tend to be memorized or venerated to some degree. The concept of secular knowledge as a problem-solving tool which evolves over time is alien to traditional thought" (ibid.). In his remarks at the 2006 Davos conference, Hoodbhoy also noted that after the October 2005 earthquake in Pakistan, one-third of his graduate physics students blamed the occurrence on the moral laxity of the victims, while another third interpreted it as a divine warning. Very few thought of it as a natural event. He repeated his assertion that students are passive and unquestioning and that "Pakistan's public (and all but a handful of private) universities are intellectual rubble, their degrees of little consequence." For related comments see Hoodbhoy 2002, 2006.
34. L. Rosen 2002, 108–29.
35. See Hoodbhoy's remarks cited in Overbye 2001, F5. The overall approach to modern scientific discoveries varies greatly among contemporary Muslim thinkers. Some find that since the Quran is said to contain all knowledge, all modern scientific discoveries are presaged in the Quran. See, e.g., Bucaille 2003. At the other extreme, the chief mufti of Saudi Arabia, Sheikh Abdullah bin Baz, for example, threatened to excommunicate anyone who favored the Copernican view of the heavens, a view still taught at the Deobandi schools in South Asia. See Sikand 2006.

36. Evolutionary theory is, however, overtly rejected by a number of Muslim fundamentalists, just as it is by most American Christian fundamentalists. (The Gallup Poll of November 2004 shows that roughly four out of ten Americans, and all but a handful of born-again Christians, believe God created humans in their present form within the past ten thousand years.) In a typical fatwa, Muzammil H. Siddiqi asserts that since a day of creation could have any duration Allah could certainly have engaged in "some kind of evolution." But he goes on to say, "The theory of evolution that postulates that the whole creation came by itself and nature evolved itself by mutation, selection and fixation, et cetera, is not acceptable in Islam. This is an atheistic theory and it has no sensible rational and logical foundation. Everyone knows that nature has so many possibilities and variables; how could all these variables have selected, mutated and fixed themselves in such a way that an orderly universe came out and continues to exist and flourish? To say that all these things happened by themselves is nothing but absurd. It is like saying that words collapsed, mutated and then fixed into a wonderful encyclopedia by themselves" (IslamOnline. net 2003). On the anti-evolutionary attitudes of Muslim students in Holland, see Koning 2006.

    The numerous books of the pseudonymous Turkish writer Harun Yahya are especially well known in this regard. One recent title, for example, is "The Dark Spell of Darwinism: How Darwinists Twist the Truth to Turn People Away from God." See also Yahya 2000, 2001, 2007. Yahya, whose works contain innumerable errors of fact (e.g., all mutations are deleterious), attributes atheism, Marxism, and other forms of materialism to Darwinian thought. He has also forged alliances with such American creationists as the Institute for Creation Research. See his Web site, http://www.harunyahya.com. See generally Riexinger 2002. On the response of Arab Muslims to Darwinian thought generally, see Ziadat 1986.

37. See the examples noted in L. Rosen 2004, 158–73. A number of scholars equate modernity and doubt: "[M]odernity effectively involves the institutionalization of doubt" (Giddens 1990, 176).

38. Recall the finding that 31 percent of recruits to a British Muslim terror group had suffered a recent death in their family. Wiktorowicz 2005, 105. Likewise, 29 percent of the members of the Tunisian radical group the Renaissance Party of Tunisia (formerly the Mouvement de Tendence Islamique [MTI]), led by Rashid al-Ghannushi, came from families where the father either had died or was an invalid. Hermassi 1984. See generally Hoffman 1995.

39. Sageman goes on to say that in his survey of terrorists, "90% came from caring, intact families . . . 73% were married and the vast majority had children. . . . Eighty percent were, in some way, totally excluded from the society they lived in. Sixty-eight percent had pre-existing friendships

with people already in the jihad or were part of a group of friends who collectively joined the jihad together" (Sageman 2004a). See also Sageman 2004b. Roy, by comparison, stresses the desire of many to be part of Western society. See Roy 2004, and my review of the book at L. Rosen 2005. Pape argues that "suicide" terrorists are motivated not by religion but by nationalism. He and Sageman have collected a good deal of useful information but both writers have two fatal problems in interpreting the data: first, they take similarities of actions as the essential features that bind the actions into a single category, whereas such lumping is like classifying animals together because they have hair on their legs or assuming that two words that sound alike must actually have the same meaning; and second, their generalizations completely obscure the possibility of seeing information that does not fit their preconceived narratives of what must make sense. Pape 2005. Neither Sageman, who leaps from one island of information to another, trailing a scheme of narration (unit solidarity means the same thing in all situations), nor Pape, who aligns data that appear similar (people killing themselves in civilian settings) and assumes that "nationalism" or "fundamentalism" means the same thing for all cultures, is capable of bringing his characterizations back to specific situations. Like the economist who thinks perfect markets do not exist yet really thinks all markets are versions of perfect markets, or biologists who think all taxonomies are just heuristic devices yet believe their own schema actually reflect reality, the accounts offered by Sageman and Pape fail to meet reasonable standards for social science explanation.

40. This point was made in a lecture by Robert W. Hefner at Princeton University on February 18, 2002. See also Hefner 2005. By the early 1980s, student unions throughout North Africa had fallen under the control of Islamist associations. Already by that time, too, as the few interview-based studies of fundamentalist organizations had shown, "the majority of the students in the movement [were] in the most prestigious and competitive faculties of medicine, science, and engineering" (Hoffman 1995, 204, citing, among others, studies in Egypt by Saad Eddin Ibrahim and in Tunisia by Elbaki Hermassi).

41. This position confirms the victory of the Rationalists over the Traditionalists that occurred in the centuries after the Prophet's death. As Aslan notes, the Rationalists (Ash'arites) "often responded to the rational incongruities and internal contradictions that resulted from their rigid interpretation of religious doctrine by cultivating a formula of *bila kayfa*, loosely translated as 'Don't ask why.' This formula horrified the Rationalists" (Aslan 2006, 154–55).

42. The science institute director mentioned above also said that the students do not engage in theological discussions. Indeed, there are pressures for them not to enter into such discussions. Debates instead center on politi-

cal Islam (i.e., the ends to be achieved), with very little theological debate occurring even among the religion students. That discussions are so limited further averts any confrontation of science and religion. On putting aside contradictions, see the references in chapter 9 above.

Perhaps the most famous example of holding two propositions that to outsiders might seem contradictory is expressed in the story of the Bedouin who rode up to the Prophet's tent on his camel to learn of the new religion. When the Prophet invited him to descend and enter his tent, the Bedouin said that he was afraid his camel would run away. Should I trust to Allah, he asked, or tie my camel down? And the Prophet replied, Trust to Allah—and tie your camel down!

43. Paulo 1996.

44. Ruthven 1994, 19. Ruthven also argues, however, that "[t]he applied, unlike the 'pure,' scientist can use reason without having to adopt a position of epistemological doubt" (ibid.). This may be an idealized distinction even in the West; for Muslims it may be overridden by both the identification of doubt about fundamentals with loss of faith and, just as important, the idea that unbelief is the necessary accompaniment of the social chaos that is destructive of the community of believers. Thus, the relational implications once again may override a distinction that has greater currency in Western than in Arab cultures.

45. This is also the rationale I have heard from one American Christian fundamentalist who is a trained scientist.

46. "It is . . . an old answer given by Muslim theologians whenever they found themselves committed to two contradictory beliefs—an answer expressed by the Arabic words *bi-la-kayfa*, which, freely translated, means, 'we know the contradiction can be reconciled, but ask us not how'" (Wolfson 1959, 596).

47. Stern 2001; A. Ahmad 2003.

48. Salam [1996]. See also Salam 1989a; 1989b; 1991, xi–xii (where he argues that, regarding the absence of a Sunni Muslim priestly class, "Islam has had the worst deal of all the great religions of humankind. In most countries, a class of nearly illiterate men have, in practice, habitually appropriated to themselves the status of a priestly class without possessing even a rudimentary knowledge of their great and tolerant religion. The arrogance, the rapacity, and the low level of commonsense displayed by this class, as well as its intolerance, has been derided by all the poets and writers of any consequence in Persia, India, Central Asia, and Turkey"). Salam especially blames these ulama for the excommunication (*takfir*) of those with whom they disagree and argues that "Islamic science, as set out by the late President [Muhammad] Zia of Pakistan, was a fraud . . . its practitioners (whom Professor Hoodbhoy rightly mocks) are (or should be) ashamed of what they have wrought in the name of science" (1991, ix). Abdus was born into a Muslim family, but the Ahmadi

sect to which he belonged was expelled from Islam by the Pakistani parliament in 1974, thus rendering him a non-Muslim in the eyes of that government.

49. Gülen 1997, 309. See also Bakar 2005. The equation of science with atheism is no less a concern for many American Christian fundamentalists. Describing the debate over evolution versus intelligent design in his own Presbyterian congregation, for example, one pastor quoted a member of his congregation, a professor of electrical and computer engineering, as arguing that "most who believe in evolution deny the role and even the existence of God, making it come down to evolution versus God." To teach evolution in a way that it can "not even be questioned in the classroom," he concluded, "is atheistic" (Brinton 2005, B2).

50. See the discussion in Sardar 1989, 30–37.

51. See Livingston 1995. 'Abduh was also an ardent Spenserian social evolutionist who argued that the process of evolution was part of the Quran's assertion that God has power over all things. At times he also claimed that science, having been developed by Muslims, would only be returning to its true Islamic origins by being embraced by modern-day adherents. Afghani, however, reacted strongly against Darwinian evolution, arguing in *The Refutation of Materialists* that if evolution were true "it would be possible that after the passage of centuries a mosquito could become an elephant and an elephant, by degrees, a mosquito" (quoted in Keddie 1968, 15). Indeed, Afghani attacked Sayyed Ahmed Khan, who advocated the modernization of Islamic education, as a materialist, "naturist," and unbeliever because Afghani's own political and religious pragmatism led him to suspect that scientific thinking might jeopardize Islamic metaphysics as he saw it. Huff 2003, 369.

52. Quoted in Sardar 1989, 35–36. For a fuller discussion of Qutb's position, see R. Euben 1999, 49–92. Another leading writer on the relation of science to Islam is Maryam Jameelah, an American Jewish convert to Islam and spokesperson for Jamaat-e-Islam, the Pakistani fundamentalist party: "Modern science is guided by no moral value, but naked materialism and arrogance. The whole branch of knowledge and its applications is contaminated by the same evil. Science and technology are totally dependent upon the set of ideals and values cherished by its members. If the roots of the tree are rotten, then the tree is rotten; therefore all its fruits are rotten" (Jameelah 1983, 8, cited along with her other works in Hoodbhoy 1991, 53). Compare Jameelah's view of science to that of the hero of Naguib Mahfouz's novel *The Children of Gebelaawi*. The hero, a scientist, is the last person to be able to express hope for a crippled community but is seen by religious critics as an enemy of religion.

53. Ahmed 2004, 13.

54. Giddens 1990, 176. Compare this emphasis with that suggested by Hoffman:

The perception espoused by so many Muslim fundamentalists that, to the detriment of all spiritual values, the West is mechanistically and technologically oriented may derive in part from the particular nature of the contact these Muslim students of science have with Western culture. They come to see their lives bifurcated between an Islamic culture that provides moral values, community, and spiritual satisfaction, and a Western culture that provides access to the material improvement of their lives. On the other hand, Mehrzad Boroujerdi sees the absolute dualism of perspective regarding East and West as a type of "Orientalism in reverse," in which the West continues to serve as the standard by which Muslim intellectuals evaluate their own culture. In doing so, they abstract the West in opposition to all Islamic values, just as Orientalism once abstracted Islamic culture as the opposite of all Western values. (1995, 210)

55. Anidjar 2002, 238 (quoting the literary document the author is interpreting). Although Anidjar goes on to speak of "science" in the context of a general pursuit of knowledge (*ma'rifa*) and of the "sciences" of reason broadly conceived rather than something restricted to what we now think of as the sciences, the following observation of his is suggestive: "[E]ven though it breaks 'ties of relationship,' pure science, as the practice of argument, is an attempt to fix and settle (to the point that even Fortune cannot shift) objects and positions, much like it sets and ties down, indeed, 'fastens down tent ropes,' positions and oppositions such as being and non-being. It causes strife, perhaps, but it is also the most far-reaching attempt to escape Fortune and its shifting, untying motions" (ibid., 239). That this idea should be explored in the context of literature, philosophy, and indeed Arab Jewish scholarship, far from being proof of its irrelevance, should be taken as an element of support for the relational argument put forth here—just as the mercantile image is being employed in the context of a moral argument in Anidjar's text. To see such ideas as certainty and argumentation, as opposed to trade, as divisive and contrary to the realities of "Fortune" is consistent with the notion that science is a preeminently relational matter, just as a focus on relational consequences is central to a number of domains besides that of formal scientific investigation.

56. See Huff 2003, 108–13.

57. Cited from the Fedayeen i-Islam organization by Ruthven 1994, 20.

58. Quoted in Hoodbhoy 1991, 128.

CHAPTER ELEVEN

1. Cited from al-'Amiri, *I'lam* in Rosenthal 1970, 323.

2. See Hammoudi 1997.

3. Some groups, such as the descendants of the Prophet or particular saints, are the exceptions that prove the rule, inasmuch as their predecessor's shrine may be vital to both their claimed legitimacy and the income produced by their attachment.

4. Lewis 2002.

5. See chapter 7 above on portraiture in Arab cultures.

6. L. Rosen 2002, 39–55.

7. Fried 1966.

8. On the moral equivalence of tribal units, see Dresch 1990.

9. In the choice of early caliphs, however, shura may not have been a consultative institution but a group of viable candidates from among whom the candidates themselves had to choose a successor in order to avoid civil war; those who withdrew as candidates thus managed to save face and earn a significant debt of gratitude from the winner. Crone 2001.

10. Rahman was especially critical of the misuses of shura: "The 'mutual consultation' (shura) of the Qur'an was never institutionalized. Worse still, the 'mutual consultation' of the Qur'an was distorted by Sunni Muslim political theorists into 'the ruler's consulting people whom he thought fit for consultation'! As for the Shi'a, there never was any question of a shura-democracy, since the rule really belonged to the Absent Imam ('religious leader'), who is, for some reason, in hiding" (1983, 184). A much more idiosyncratic view was that of the Sudanese reformist Mahmoud Muhammad Taha, who, rather than equating democracy with shura, defined democracy as "the right to make mistakes, as we learn from the Hadith of the Prophet: 'If you do not make mistakes, and then ask for forgiveness, God shall replace you by people who make mistakes, ask forgiveness, and are forgiven'" (1987, 160). Taha's overall views were declared heretical by major Islamic academies, and he was ultimately executed by the fundamentalist government of Sudan in 1985. See generally Mahmoud 1998, 105–28.

11. See the story told along these lines in my forthcoming book *Drawn from Memory: Moroccan Lives Unremembered.*

12. The idea that such consultation insured that the classical Islamic state did not move from authoritarianism to dictatorship until it acquired the technology of the modern Western state, with its surveillance and indoctrination methods, is one that should be approached with great skepticism. See Lewis 2002. On the other hand, while establishing "depoliticized" commissions, panels, or ombudsmen would be a contradiction in terms to Arab political personalism, it may be that Arab governance, at least at the local level, is somewhat "depoliticized" inasmuch as popular sentiment, multiple avenues for building support, and even bribery (used to subvert the will of the powerful) may contribute to a kind of deliberative democracy called for by some political philosophers. See Pettit 2004.

13. The words are those of Sheik Muhammad al-Khalifa, head of Bahrain's Economic and Development Board, as quoted in MacFarquhar 2006.

14. The importance of the fear of fitna is strikingly revealed in an anecdote about one of the 9/11 suicide bombers, Mohammed Atta, who was taken by a friend to a crowded theater where they saw the Disney cartoon *The Jungle Book*. Atta "seethed in his seat, muttering over and over again in disgust, 'Chaos, chaos'" (Kakutani 2005; referring to McDermott 2005, 88). Some Arabs also see the Palestinian *intifada* as verging on fitna because sons are taking charge rather than their fathers. That the term *fauda* comes from a root meaning "to trust, empower, or negotiate" is, perhaps, indicative of that common Arabic tendency for a word to mean both something and its opposite, at least in the sense here that residing in such parleys may be the risk of social chaos. An example of how a well-respected Arab American can misunderstand the distinction between fitna and fauda is provided by Anthony Shadid, who quotes an Iraqi man: "'I say the Americans are better than the Iraqis,' he said, shaking his head, his expression wavering between a grin and anger. 'We live in a country that is impossible. The Iraqis prefer *fawdha*, "anarchy and chaos." They won't let themselves be helped'" (2005, 342). Shadid fails to realize that the milder *fauda* is poorly translated as "anarchy and chaos." Had the informant intended real chaos he would probably have used the term *fitna* and acknowledged that fitna is the worst of all possible conditions, less tolerable than tyranny itself.

15. For a series of examples related to the larger points of this essay, see L. Rosen 1984, 19–23.

16. "In Mosul, a call from the mosques stopped the looting. A second call brought the restitution of a large proportion of the goods stolen over the previous days." Burke 2006, 205.

17. For an optimistic view of the prospects of democracy in the Muslim world, see V. Nasr 2005. However, Nasr offers no examples of working democracies anywhere in the Arab (as opposed to the more broadly Muslim) world and does not consider the kinds of cultural factors analyzed here.

18. See chapter 2 above, note 25. See also Friedman 2001.

19. Nathan J. Brown (2002) argues that Arab constitutions are more commonly intended to improve governmental efficiency than to limit the powers of the head of state.

20. Many people in the Arab world are unable to marry unless they have a place to move to outside of the parental home. Egypt, for example, actually requires one to show that some dwelling place is available to a couple before the marriage itself may be authorized. The older pattern of residing with the husband's family is regarded by most men as highly limiting of their freedom to entertain and ingratiate in their own name.

21. Recall that corruption is commonly seen as the failure to share with those with whom one has bonds of interdependence whatever largesse comes one's way; it is not corrupt to do "favors" for friends, relatives, and political patrons or clients. Gilsenan's story of a Lebanese sheikh who

wordlessly dispersed expensive tobacco to men in a reception room as if there were no personal motivation involved may also be interpreted as a demonstration that the man was not corrupt (i.e., he shared his largesse) and an act of reciprocation for the men's choice to be dependent on him. Gilsenan 2000, 614 n. 7. The pervasive nature of constant and petty bribery and its effect on people's sense of civility is one of the primary obstacles to the freedom of movement and ability to negotiate in the world, in accordance with the accepted rules, that give "the game" a sense of fairness. Whether anti-corruption measures should involve alterations in the form of civil service organization or the like will have to be matters of local choice, but a clear commitment to the eradication of "corruption"—as it is conceptualized culturally by those concerned—is increasingly vital to the stability of many Arab nations. For a story of corruption and its local effects, see L. Rosen 2002, 3–20. Concepts of corruption also are closely related to those of justice and injustice. For more on my own assessment of Islamic ideas of justice, see chapter 5 above and L. Rosen 2000.

22. Allowing either party to force the case into a national, rather than religious, court may settle the issue left unaddressed, for example, in the Iraq draft constitution of August 2005. Other conflict-of-laws possibilities may develop: a country might employ the principle of renvoie, under which the local court has jurisdiction but must apply national law; another country might choose compulsory conciliation to try to conduce out-of-court arrangements. Whatever the possibilities, it would be well for Western commentators and politicians to take note of the fact that even in an Islamic republic like Iran Islamic law is very flexible; that if women carry their cases to judgment, they actually win most of the time; and that while custom can indeed be the instrument of the status quo, it can also be a vehicle for enforcing changes in social position. For an elaboration of a number of these issues see L. Rosen 1989, 2000.

23. See M. Cook 2000.

24. See Makiya 2005.

25. Jamal (2005) argues that Muslims in the Detroit area who are young recent migrants are getting into the American political process, but that the characteristics that matter most in their involvement are those of gender, mosque attendance, and participation in civic organizations. Alternatively, one could argue, these Arab immigrants may be showing signs of emphasizing institutions over persons, and the differences indicated by category may be somewhat differential responses to this reciprocal, backdraft process. Thus, women are talking about the courts and men about how one needs to act like a responsible American, but neither is talking about "who" is the government or seeking personal ties to get things done. A contributing factor for the women may, as Jamal suggests, be that the patriarchal system no longer does many things for them. They must

now shop, earn money, deal with civic officials, etc., without the intervention of brothers or other men. Men, meanwhile, may have to work within a more anonymizing marketplace, where role expectations trump predictability by ethnicity, religion, or sect. Regardless, shared economic and social experience found among such ethnic and religious groupings may be contributing to the overriding movement toward institutional rather than predominantly personalistic structures.

26. On the replication of older patterns by new "democratic" parties, see Abukhalil 1997. On the subsequent hindrance presented to further democratization, one observer writes, "This conundrum is created by the fact that, while all the players involved may welcome democratization as one step *closer* to their preferred type of democracy, once they reach a 'pseudo-democratic' stage, any further democratization that does not directly strengthen their own political model is, in their view, a move *away* from democracy. Hence, the situation reaches a stalemate" (Volpi 2004, 1067).

27. I therefore disagree with such assertions as that of the Iranian scholar who writes, "[T]he primary condition for the realization of democracy is the liberation of human beings from the elementary needs and necessities of life. It is true that human beings have always opposed inequity and demanded justice (democracy being a modern manifestation of this perennial human quest), but justice can prevail only where its seekers are not weighed down by poverty and insecurity. It is available to those who have already escaped other forms of slavery. Democracy is desirable for all, but in practice it is not available to all. It requires a certain normative, political, and governmental development that is contingent upon economic development" (Soroush 2000, 45).

CHAPTER TWELVE

1. On religion and gender discrimination, see, e.g., Sunstein 1999. Compare Sunstein on allowing discrimination by religious groups with Nussbaum 1999. See also Schaefer 2003. On circumcision as child abuse, see Brigman 1984–85; J. Rosen 2006, 28. On female genital cutting, see Green and Lim 1998; Shweder 2003, 168–216. On corporal punishment, see Bartman 2002 and Pollard 2003.

2. See *Santa Clara Pueblo v. Martinez*, 436 U.S. 49 (1978) (tribal sovereignty takes precedence over federal discrimination statute even though female marrying out of tribe is treated differently than males marrying out); *Lovelace v. Canada*, Communication No. R.6/24, U.N. Doc. Supp. No. 40 (A/36/40) at 166 (1981) (tribe may not deny status and rights to female who marries outside the tribe).

3. On first-cousin marriage see Grady 2002 and Ottenheimer 1996. On same-sex education see generally Salomone 2003.

4. In response to a group of American academics suggesting the need for democracy, Saudi academics, on October 23, 2002, emphasized that "stability is the basis for rights and freedoms throughout the world," thus drawing a contrast between instability and freedom, which Americans may not so readily see as opposed propositions. See the correspondence on the Web site of the conservative Institute for American Values, http://www.americanvalues.org. On the French controversy about Muslim girls wearing headscarves in school, see Poulter 1997 and Bowen 2006. On the Islamic idea of the right of the poor to support by those who have property, see Glenn 2000, 168. Some are skeptical of even the existence of universal human rights: "Human rights are a very particular concept in the world, a 'contingent, mutable truth and not an eternal one,' and 'exist' only because of an extraordinary congruence of traditions, which occurred nowhere else in the world. . . . Universal rights are simply another form of universalizing the truths of a particular tradition. . . . So rights doctrines eventually end up, as they should, being evaluated against other doctrines, in particular circumstances by particular people" (Glenn 2000, 244–45).

5. The clearest expression of this theory of culture remains Geertz 1973, 1–83.

6. Inclusion in an enlarged category may, of course, reconstitute that category itself, so that greater inclusiveness would result in a new category.

7. See Daley 2000.

8. On the characteristic features of this process, see Wallace 1956.

9. See Toulmin 1972, 71–72.

10. The novelist Barry Unsworth points to the importance of conceptual purity, rather than simple control over others' behavior, when he has his fictionalized Odysseus say, "It's all conceptual! The driving force in human society was not greed or the lust for power, as he had always thought, but the energy generated by juggling with concepts, endlessly striving to make perceptions of reality agree with them, to melt things together, iron out problems, harmonize warring elements, what was the phrase he was looking for? *Eliminate the contradictions.* They would rule the world who knew this and used it" (2002, 155–56; emphasis in original).

11. "[I]n the end, we can't explain why we believe the things we believe or—more to the point—why those who disagree with us should be forced to act as if they believed those things as well" (Campos 1998, 102).

12. See generally Geertz 1973.

13. For the quoted phrase, see Shweder 2005.

14. Article 6(2) of the European Convention on Human Rights, for example, reasserts the presumption of innocence, and national laws have followed suit. See Mundy 1995, 83.

15. Tyler 2000.

16. See generally Sunder 2003.

17. Commonly, too, human rights analysts equate "culture" with static tradition, thus applying a concept of culture that is greatly out-of-date and misleading. See Merry 2003.

18. Cover 1983. See generally Stone 1993, 823–26. Elsewhere Cover (1988) argues that an emphasis on rights alone, as opposed to obligations, is a bad idea. For a recent assessment of Cover's arguments, see the symposium "Nomos and Narrative" 2005.

19. The idea of equivalence is not the same as erasing the differences among the disadvantaged in the name of placing them all on the same level, an approach criticized by Bhabha when he speaks of "the prevailing orthodoxy that establishes 'equivalences' between disadvantaged groups, aggregating 'communities of interest' without doing the hard work of specifying rights and interests, shying away from conflicts within, and between, minorities" (1999, 79). While an emphasis on true equivalence may yield inequality in the eyes of those who would favor strict uniformity, the quest for standards of equivalence may ultimately accomplish greater representation within cultures that do recognize the worth of different categories of persons and may build upon that respect for a reallocation of roles, resources, etc. that is consistent with both their own values and the broad goals sought through international accords. On the Islamic example, see L. Rosen 2000, 153–75.

   An analogy from the academy may be helpful here. Teaching loads commonly vary a good deal from one discipline to another, yet few institutions are prepared to demand exactly the same number of courses from professors regardless of department. When, for example, my own university looked into the issue some years ago, officials eventually gave up on any uniformity because disciplines had such varied expectations. But no one thought to use an equivalency rule—to require each department, say, to show a plan by which the *equivalent* of two courses per semester would be met. Such an approach could have left intact the localized way in which the general precept would have been met while shifting the discussion to a common ground that would have an agreed-upon aspect of equality. One could readily imagine such propositions being applied in the domain of human rights.

20. The conflict may, of course, arise between groups and individuals. As Okin puts it, "[G]ranting group rights without paying attention to the multiple voices of members of a group may impede the kind of change from within that might otherwise occur" (1999b, 118).

21. On the education issue, see Okin 1999a, 2002.

22. For an example of human rights and the treatment of political "crimes" in one Arab nation, see Slyomovics 2005.

23. Aslan 2006, 264. See also the Universal Islamic Declaration of Human Rights, http://www.alhewar.com/ISLAMDECL.html, and the Cairo

Declaration on Human Rights in Islam, http://www.oic-oci.org/english/
article/human.htm (requiring all rights to be consistent with the shari'a).

24. See generally Morgan-Foster 2005. See also An-Na'im 1990 and Baderin
2005.

25. Raz 1999, 99.

26. Krutch 1956, 27.

27. In 1947 the executive board of the American Anthropological Association prepared a statement opposing the United Nations declaration. They
saw the proposed declaration as the imposition of Western precepts on
all peoples. The association's position has been much misunderstood as
a statement of radical relativism when it should more accurately be seen
as an assertion against both imperialism and the view of culture as static
and unitary. American Anthropological Association 1947. See generally
Merry 2003.

28. An-Na'im 1999. For comparisons to human rights concepts in other cultures, see, e.g., Bauer and Bell 1999; Bell, Nathan, and Peleg 2001. On the
relation of cultural rights to human and individual rights, see Mamdani
1999.

29. See generally Note 1986; Levine 2003; Phillips 2003; and Renteln 2003.
On the acceptability of difference in multicultural (particularly Indian–
White) relations, see L. Rosen 1997.

References

Abukhalil, As'ad. 1997. "Change and Democratisation in the Arab World: The Role of Political Parties." *Third World Quarterly* 18(1): 149–63.

Agoumy, Taoufiq A. 1994. "Housing the Urban Poor of Taza, Morocco, and the Impact of the Relocation Process." Ph.D. diss., Princeton University.

Ahmad, Aijazz. 2003. "Madrassas: A Make-Believe World." *Asia Times Online*, January 14.

Ahmad, Zaid. 2003. *The Epistemology of Ibn Khaldun.* London: RoutledgeCurzon.

Ahmed, Akbar S. 2004. *Postmodernism and Islam: Predicament and Promise.* Rev. ed. New York: Routledge.

———. 2005. "Ibn Khaldun and Anthropology: The Failure of Methodology in the Post 9/11 World." *Contemporary Sociology* 34(6): 591–96.

al-A'zami, Muhammad Mustafa. 2003. *The History of the Qur'anic Text from Revelation to Compilation.* Leicester, UK: Islamic Academy.

al-Hujwiri, Ali ibn Uthman. 1976. *Kashf al-Mahjūb.* Translated by R. A. Nicholson. London: Luzac.

al-Kalbî, Hishâm ibn. 1952. *The Book of Idols.* Translated by Nashim Amin Faris. Princeton: Princeton University Press.

Allen, Jessie. 2005. "How Ritual Formality and Doctrinal Formation Help Adjudication Shape the World." S.J.D. diss., Columbia University.

Allen, Terry. 1988. *Five Essays on Islamic Art.* Occidental, CA: Solipsist Press.

American Anthropological Association. 1947. "Statement on Human Rights." *American Anthropologist* 49:539–43.

Ammitzbøll, Pernille, and Lorenzo Vidino. 2007. "After the Danish Cartoon Controversy." *Middle East Quarterly* 14(1): 3–11.

Anderson, Jon W. 1984. "Conjuring with Ibn Khaldun: From an Anthropological Point of View." In *Ibn Khaldun and Islamic Ideology*, edited by Bruce B. Lawrence, 111–21. Leiden: Brill.

Anidjar, Gil. 2002. *"Our Place in Al-Andalus": Kabbalah, Philosophy, Literature in Arab Jewish Letters.* Stanford: Stanford University Press.

An-Naʿim, Abdullahi Ahmed. 1990. "Human Rights in the Muslim World: Socio-political Conditions and Scriptural Imperatives." *Harvard Human Rights Journal* 3:13–52.

———. 1999. "Promises We Should All Keep in Common Cause." In Cohen, Howard, and Nussbaum 1999, 59–64.

Arabi, Oussama. 2004. "The Regimentation of the Subject: Madness in Islamic and Modern Arab Civil Law." In *Standing Trial: Law and the Person in the Modern Middle East*, edited by Baudouin Dupret, 264–93. London: I. B. Tauris.

Arkoun, Mohammed. 1982. *Lectures du Coran.* Paris: G.-P. Maisonneuve et Larose.

Arnold, Thomas W. 1928. *Painting in Islam: A Study of the Place of Pictorial Art in Muslim Culture.* Oxford: Clarendon Press.

Asad, Talal. 1993. *Genealogies of Religion.* Baltimore: Johns Hopkins Press.

Aslan, Reza. 2006. *No God but God.* New York: Random House.

Asser, Martin. 2006. "What the Muhammad Cartoons Portray." *BBC News Online*, February 9. http://news.bbc.co.uk/2/hi/middle_east/4693292.stm.

Associated Press. 2004. "The Sin of Cellphone Cameras." *New York Times*, September 30, A15.

———. 2005. "Exorcism Course Continues at Vatican." *Washington Post*, October 14.

Atherton, J. S. 1954. "Islam and the Koran in *Finnegans Wake*." *Comparative Literature* 6(3): 240–55.

Baali, Fuad. 1992. *Social Institutions: Ibn Khaldun's Social Thought.* Lanham, MD: University Press of America.

Baderin, Mashood A. 2005. *International Human Rights and Islamic Law.* Oxford: Oxford University Press.

Baer, Eva. 1999. "The Human Figure in Early Islamic Art: Some Preliminary Remarks." In *Muqarnas: An Annual on the Visual Culture of the Islamic World*, edited by Gülru Necipoğlu, 32–41. Leiden: Brill.

Bailey, Clinton. 2004. *A Culture of Desert Survival: Bedouin Proverbs from Sinai and the Negev.* New Haven: Yale University Press.

Bakar, Osman. 2005. "Gülen on Religion and Science: A Theological Perspective." *Muslim World* 95(3): 359–72.

Bakhash, Shaul. 1989. "The Politics of Land, Law, and Social Justice in Iran." *Middle East Journal* 43(2): 186–201.

Baljon, J. M. S. 1961. *Modern Muslim Koran Interpretation (1880–1960).* Leiden: E. J. Brill.

Barlas, Asma. 2002. *"Believing Women" in Islam: Unreading Patriarchal Interpretations of the Qurʾān.* Austin: University of Texas Press.

Barr, James. 1978. *Fundamentalism*. Philadelphia: Westminster Press.

Barry, Mike. 2004. *Figurative Art in Medieval Islam and the Riddle of Bihzâd of Herât*. Paris: Flammarion.

Bartman, Angela. 2002. "Spare the Rod and Spoil the Child? Corporal Punishment in Schools around the World." *Indiana International and Comparative Law Review* 13(1): 283–315.

Batnitzky, Leora. 2000. *Idolatry and Representation: The Philosophy of Franz Rosenzweig Reconsidered*. Princeton: Princeton University Press.

Bauer, Jeanne R., and Daniel A. Bell, eds. 1999. *The East Asian Challenge for Human Rights*. Cambridge: Cambridge University Press.

Behdad, S. 1989. "Property Rights in Contemporary Islamic Economic Thought: A Critical Perspective." *Review of Social Economy* 47(2): 185–211.

Bell, Lynda S., Andrew J. Nathan, and Ilan Peleg, eds. 2001. *Negotiating Culture and Human Rights*. New York: Columbia University Press.

Bennet, James. 2005. "The Enigma of Damascus." *New York Times Magazine*, July 10, 28–64.

Benoliel, Sharon. 2003. *Strengthening Education in the Muslim World*. Washington: Agency for International Development, Bureau for Policy and Program Coordination.

Ben-Ze'ev, Efrat and Issam Aburaiya. 2004. "'Middle-Ground' Politics and the Re-Palestinization of Places in Israel." *International Journal of Middle East Studies* 36:639–55.

Bergen, Peter. 2005. "The Madrasa Myth." *New York Times*, June 14, 23.

Besançon, Alain. 2000. *The Forbidden Image: An Intellectual History of Iconoclasm*. Chicago: University of Chicago Press.

Bhabha, Homi K. 1999. "Liberalism's Sacred Cow." In Cohen, Howard, and Nussbaum 1999, 79–84.

Bin Laden, Osama. *Messages to the World: The Statements of Osama bin Laden*. Edited by Bruce Lawrence. New York: Verso, 2005.

Blair, Sheila S., and Jonathan M. Bloom. 1999. "Art and Architecture: Themes and Variations." In *The Oxford History of Islam*, edited by John L. Esposito, 215–67. Oxford: Oxford University Press.

Bland, Kalman P. 2001. *The Artless Jew: Medieval and Modern Affirmations and Denials of the Visual*. Princeton: Princeton University Press.

Bloom, Mia. 2004. "Palestinian Suicide Bombing: Public Support, Market Share, and Outbidding." *Political Science Quarterly* 119(1): 61–88.

———. 2005. "Women are Increasingly Taking a Leading Role in Conflicts by Becoming Terrorists—Specifically by Becoming Suicide Bombers." *Bulletin of the Atomic Scientists* 61(6): 54–62.

Boorstin, Daniel J. 1992. *The Creators*. New York: Random House.

Bowen, John. 2006. *Why the French Don't Like Headscarves: Islam, the State, and Public Space*. Princeton: Princeton University Press.

Box, Laura Chakravarty. 2005. *Strategies of Resistance in the Dramatic Texts of North African Women: A Body of Words*. New York: Routledge.

Brigman, William E. 1984–85. "Circumcision as Child Abuse: The Legal and Constitutional Issues." *Journal of Family Law* 23(3): 337–57.

Brinton, Henry. 2005. "Darwin Goes to Church." *Washington Post*, September 18, B1–5.

Brown, Nathan J. 2002. *Constitutions in a Non-constitutional World: Arab Basic Laws and the Prospects for Accountable Government*. Albany: State University of New York Press.

Brown, Norman O. 1983–84. "The Apocalypse of Islam." *Social Text* 8:155–71.

Bucaille, Maurice. 2003. *The Bible, the Qur'an and Science*. 7th ed. Elmhurst, NY: Tahrike Tarsile Qur'an.

Bukay, David. 2006. "The Religious Foundations of Suicide Bombings." *Middle East Quarterly* 13(4): 26–36.

Bukhari, M. Saleem. 1982. "Squatting and the Use of Land: A Case Study of Land Occupation in Madinah Munawara, Saudi Arabia." *Habitat International* 6(5/6): 555–63.

Bulliet, Richard W. 2004. *The Case for Islamo-Christian Civilization*. New York: Columbia University Press.

Burke, Jason. 2006. *On the Road to Kandahar: Travels through Conflict in the Islamic World*. London: Allen Lane.

Campbell, Caroline, and Alan Chong. 2005. *Bellini and the East*. London: National Gallery Co. Distributed by Yale University Press. Published in conjunction with the exhibition "Gentile Bellini and the East," shown at the Isabella Stewart Gardner Museum, Boston, and the National Gallery, London.

Campos, Paul F. 1998. *Jurismania: The Madness of American Law*. New York: Oxford University Press.

Carlyle, Thomas. 1966 [1841]. *On Heroes, Hero-Worship, and the Heroic in History*. Lincoln: University of Nebraska Press.

Carr, Matthew. 2006. *Unknown Soldiers: How Terrorism Transformed the Modern World*. London: Profile Books.

Carter, Jimmy. 1989. "Rushdie's Book Is an Insult." *New York Times*, March 5, E23.

Carter, M. G. 1998. "Infinity and Lies in Medieval Islam." In *Philosophy and Arts in the Islamic World*, edited by U. Vermeulen and D. De Smet, 233–42. Leuven: Uitgeveru Peeters.

Caton, Steven C. 1990. *"Peaks of Yemen I Summon": Poetry as Cultural Practice in a North Yemeni Tribe*. Berkeley: University of California Press.

———. 2005. *Yemen Chronicle*. New York: Hill and Wang.

Centlivres, Pierre, and Micheline Centlivres-Demont. 2005. "Une étrange rencontre: La photographie orientaliste de Lehnert et Landrock et l'image iranienne du prophète Mahomet." *Etudes Photographiques* 17:4–15.

———. 2006. "The Story of a Picture: Shiite Depictions of Muhammad." *International Institute for the Study of Islam in the Modern World (ISIM) Review* 17:18–19.

Chakravorty, Pinaki. 1995. "The Rushdie Incident as Law and Literature Parable." *Yale Law Journal* 104(8): 2212–47.

Cheddadi, Abdesselam. 1999. *Ibn Khaldûn Revisité*. Casablanca: Les Editions Toubkal.

———. 2002. *Le livre des examples: Ibn Khaldûn*. Paris: Gallimard.

Cilardo, Agostino. 1993. "The Transmission of the Patronate in Islamic Law." In *Miscellanea Arabica et Islamica*, edited by F. DeLong, 31–52. Leuven: Uitgeverij Peeters en Departement Orientalistiek.

Clarence-Smith, W. G. 2006. *Islam and the Abolition of Slavery*. New York: Oxford University Press.

Clark, Wesley K. 2005. "The Next Iraq Offensive." *New York Times*, December 6, 27.

Cohen, Joshua, Matthew Howard, and Martha C. Nussbaum, eds. 1999. *Is Multiculturalism Bad for Women?* Princeton: Princeton University Press.

Collins, Francis. 2006. *The Language of God: A Scientist Presents Evidence for Belief*. New York: Free Press.

Cook, David. 2007. *Martyrdom in Islam*. Cambridge: Cambridge University Press.

Cook, Michael A. 2000. *Commanding Right and Forbidding Wrong in Islamic Thought*. Cambridge: Cambridge University Press.

Cooperson, Michael. 2001. "Images without Illustrations: The Visual Imagination in Classical Arabic Biography." In *Islamic Art and Literature*, edited by Oleg Grabar and Cynthia Robinson, 7–20. Princeton: Markus Weiner Publishers.

Cornell, Vincent. 1995. "The Qur'ān as Scripture." In *The Oxford Encyclopedia of the Modern Islamic World*, edited by John L. Esposito, 3:387–94. Oxford: Oxford University Press.

Cover, Robert M. 1983. "The Supreme Court, 1982 Term—Foreword: Nomos and Narrative." *Harvard Law Review* 97(1): 4–68.

———. 1988. "Obligation: A Jewish Jurisprudence of the Social Order." *Journal of Law and Religion* 5:65–74.

Crapanzano, Vincent. 1975. "Saints, Jnun, and Dreams: An Essay in Moroccan Ethnopsychology." *Psychiatry* 38(2): 145–59

Creswell, K. A. C. 2002. "The Lawfulness of Painting in Early Islam" [revised from 1932 publication]. In *Early Islamic Art and Architecture*, edited by Jonathan Bloom, 101–108. Aldershot, UK: Ashgate.

Crone, Patricia. 2001. "*SHŪRĀ* as an Elective Institution." *Quaderni di Studi Arabi* 19:3–39.

Crone, Patricia, and Michael Cook. 1977. *Hagarism: The Making of the Islamic World*. Cambridge: Cambridge University Press.

Crosby, Alfred W. 1997. *The Measure of Reality: Quantification and Western Society, 1250–1600*. Cambridge: Cambridge University Press.

Cuisenier, Jean. 1976. "The Domestic Cycle in the Traditional Family Organisation in Tunisia." In *Mediterranean Family Structures*, edited by J. G. Peristiany, 137–55. Cambridge: Cambridge University Press.

Dale, Stephen Frederic. 2006. "Ibn Khaldun: The Last Greek and the First *Annaliste* Historian." *International Journal of Middle East Studies* 38(3): 431–51.

Daley, Suzanne. 2000. "French Farmer Is Sentenced to Jail for Attack on McDonald's." *New York Times*, September 14, A13.

Dallal, Ahmad. 1999. "Science, Medicine, and Technology: The Making of a Scientific Culture." In *The Oxford History of Islam*, edited by John L. Esposito, 154–213. Oxford: Oxford University Press.

Dalrymple, William. 2005. "Inside the Madrasas." *New York Review of Books*, December 1, 16–20.

Darwish, Mahmud. 2002. "A Love Story between an Arab Poet and His Land." *Journal of Palestine Studies* 31(3): 67–79.

Daube, David. 1951. "The Scales of Justice." *Juridical Review* 43(2): 109–29.

Davis, Joyce M. 2003. *Martyrs: Innocence, Vengeance, and Despair in the Middle East*. New York: Palgrave Macmillan.

Decroux, Paul. 1977. *Droit Foncier Marocain*. Rabat: Editions La Porte.

Dehlevi, Ahmad Sa'eed. 1990. *What Happens after Death?* 2d rev. ed. Delhi: Dini Book Depot.

Delong-Bas, Natana J. 2004. *Wahhabi Islam: From Revival and Reform to Global Jihad*. New York: Oxford University Press.

Dhaouadi, Mahmoud. 2005. "The *Ibar*: Lessons of Ibn Khaldun's Umran Mind." *Contemporary Sociology* 34(6): 585–91.

Donahue, Charles J. 1980. "The Future of the Concept of Property Predicted from Its Past." In *Property*, edited by J. R. Pennock and J. W. Chapman, 28–68. New York: New York University Press.

Douglas, Allen, and Fedwa Malti-Douglas. 1994. *Arab Comic Strips: Politics of an Emerging Mass Culture*. Bloomington: Indiana University Press.

Dresch, Paul. 1990. "Imams and Tribes: The Writing and Acting of History in Upper Yemen." In *Tribes and State Formation in the Middle East*, edited by Philip S. Khoury and Joseph Kostiner, 252–87. Berkeley: University of California Press.

Drieskens, Barbara. 2004. "The Misbehaviour of the Possessed: On Spirits, Morality and the Person." In *Standing Trial: Law and the Person in the Modern Middle East*, edited by Baudouin Dupret, 140–69. London: I. B. Tauris.

———. 2006. *Living with Djinns: Understanding and Dealing with the Invisible in Cairo*. London: Saqi Books.

———. 2008. "What to Do with Djinns in Legal Stories?" In *Narratives of Truth in Islamic Law*, edited by Baudouin Dupret. New York: Palgrave Macmillan.

Dundes, Alan. 2003. *Fables of the Ancients? Folklore in the Qur'an*. Lanham, MD: Rowman & Littlefield Publishers, Inc.

Dupret, Baudouin. 2003. "The Person in an Egyptian Context: An Ethnomethodological Analysis of Courtroom Proceedings." *International Journal for the Semiotics of Law* 16(1): 15–44.

Ehrman, Bart D. 2005. *Misquoting Jesus: The Story behind Who Changed the Bible and Why*. New York: HarperCollins Publishers.

Einstein, Albert. 1954. *Ideas and Opinions*. New York: Dell.

El Kadi, Omar Mokhtar [Omar Mukhtar Qadi]. 1996. *Sculpture and the Making of Statues from an Islamic Point of View*. [Rabat]: Islamic Educational, Scientific and Cultural Organization.

Erlanger, Steven. 2006. "Into the West Bank Abyss: From Student to Suicide Bomber." *New York Times*, January 20, A3.

Ettinghausen, Richard. 1956. "Early Realism in Islamic Art." *Studi Orientalistici in Onore di Giorgio Levi Della Vida* 1:250–73. Rome: Instituto per l'Oriente.

————. 1981. "World Awareness and Human Relationships in Iranian Painting." In *Highlights of Persian Art*, edited by Richard Ettinghausen and Ehsan Yarshater, 243–71. New York: Wittenborn Art Books.

Euben, J. Peter. 1977. "Creatures of a Day: Thought and Action in Thucydides." In *Political Theory and Praxis: New Perspectives*, edited by Terence Ball, 28–56. Minneapolis: University of Minnesota Press.

Euben, Roxanne L. 1999. *Enemy in the Mirror: Islamic Fundamentalism and the Limits of Modern Rationalism*. Princeton: Princeton University Press.

Feldman, Noah. 2004. *What We Owe Iraq: War and the Ethics of Nation Building*. Princeton: Princeton University Press.

Fendrich, Laurie. 2005. "The Lie of the Portrait." *Chronicle of Higher Education* (*The Chronicle Review*), November 11, B10–11.

Fergany, Nader, et al. 2002. *Arab Human Development Report 2002*. New York: United Nations Development Programme, Regional Bureau for Arab States.

Fischer, A. 1987. "Kāhin." In *E. J. Brill's First Encyclopaedia of Islam, 1913–1936*, 4:624–26. Leiden: E. J. Brill.

Fisher, Ian. 2001. "Europe's Muslims Seek a Path amid Competing Cultures." *New York Times*, December 8, B1.

Fisher, Michael M. J., and Mehdi Abedi. 1990. *Debating Muslims: Cultural Dialogues in Postmodernity and Tradition*. Madison: University of Wisconsin Press.

Folsach, Kjeld von. 1996. "The Prohibition against Images and Its Consequences for Islamic Art." In *Sultan, Shah, and Great Mughal: The History and Culture of the Islamic World*, edited by Kjeld von Folsach et al., 79–95. Copenhagen: National Museum.

Forest, James J. F. 2005. *The Making of a Terrorist: Recruitment, Training, and Root Causes*. 3 vols. New York: Praeger.

Foucault, Michel. 1973. *Madness and Civilization: A History of Insanity in the Age of Reason*. New York: Vintage.

Freamon, Bernard K. 2006. "Conceptions of Equality and Slavery in Islamic Law: Tribalism, Piety, and Pluralism." S.J.D. diss., Columbia University.

Freeman, Ira Henry. 1955. "Mohammed Quits Pedestal Here on Moslem Plea after 50 Years." *New York Times*, April 9, 1.

Fried, Morton H. 1966. "On the Concepts of 'Tribe' and 'Tribal Societies.'" *Transactions of the New York Academy of Sciences* 28(4): 527–40.

Friedman, Thomas L. 1989. *From Beirut to Jerusalem*. New York: Farrar Straus Giroux.

———. 2001. "Hama Rules." *New York Times*, September 21, A35.

———. 2002. "The Hard Truth." *New York Times*, April 3, A19.

———. 2004. "Tilting the Playing Field." *New York Times*, May 30, 9.

———. 2005. "Ballots and Boycotts." *New York Times*, January 13, A35.

Gallaire, Fatima. 1990. *Les Co-épouses*. Paris: Éditions Quatres-Vents.

Gardet, Louis. 1965. "Fitna." In *The Encyclopedia of Islam*, new ed., vol. 2, edited by Bernard Lewis, Ch. Pellat, and J. Schacht, 930–31. Leiden: E. J. Brill.

———. 1976. "Moslem Views of Time and History." In *Cultures and Time*, edited by Louis Gardet et al., 197–227. Paris: Unesco Press.

Gätje, Helmut. 1976. *The Qur'ān and its Exegesis*. Berkeley: University of California Press.

Geertz, Clifford. 1968. *Islam Observed*. New Haven: Yale University Press.

———. 1973. *The Interpretation of Cultures*. New York: Basic Books.

Geertz, Clifford, Hildred Geertz, and Lawrence Rosen. 1979. *Meaning and Order in Moroccan Society*. New York: Cambridge University Press.

Gelder, Lawrence Van. 2006. "Bookstores Bar Magazine with Muhammad Cartoons." *New York Times*, April 1, A18.

Gellner, Ernest. 1981. *Muslim Society*. Cambridge: Cambridge University Press.

Gerber, Haim. 1999. *Islamic Law and Culture*. Leiden: E. J. Brill.

Gerges, Fawas A. 2005. *The Far Enemy: Why Jihad Went Global*. New York: Cambridge University Press.

Ghabin, Ahmad Y. 1998. "The Quranic Verses as a Source for Legitimacy or Illegitimacy of the Arts in Islam." *Der Islam* 75(2): 193–225.

Giddens, Anthony. 1990. *The Consequences of Modernity*. Stanford: Stanford University Press.

Gilsenan, Michael. 1996. *Lords of the Lebanese Marches: Violence and Narrative in an Arab Society*. Berkeley: University of California Press.

———. 2000. "Signs of Truth: Enchantment, Modernity and the Dreams of Peasant Women." *Journal of the Royal Anthropological Institute*, n.s., 6(4): 597–615.

Gimaret, D. 1993. "Muʿtazila." In *The Encyclopaedia of Islam*, new ed., vol.7, edited by C. E. Bosworth et al., 783–93. Leiden: E. J. Brill.

———. 1997. "Shirk." In *The Encyclopaedia of Islam*, new ed., vol. 9, edited by C. E. Bosworth et al., 484–86. Leiden: E. J. Brill.

Gittes, Katherine S. 1991. *Framing the Canterbury Tales: Chaucer and the Medieval Frame Narrative*. New York: Greenwood Press.

Glenn, H. Patrick. 2000. *Legal Traditions of the World*. Oxford: Oxford University Press.

Goitein, S. D. 1967–83. *A Mediterranean Society*. 4 vols. Berkeley: University of California Press.

Goldberg, Mark Leon. 2006. "Continental Drift: Demagogues and the Dangerous Tide of Anti-immigrant Populism." *The American Prospect* 17(5): 15–17.

Goldman, Shalom. 1995. *The Wiles of Women/The Wiles of Men: Joseph and Potiphar's Wife in Ancient Near Eastern, Jewish, and Islamic Folklore*. Albany: State University of New York Press.

Gombrich, Erich H. 1969. *Art and Illusion: A Study in the Psychology of Pictorial Representation*. Princeton: Princeton University Press.

Goody, Jack. 1962. *Death, Property and the Ancestors: A Study of the Mortuary Customs of the LoDagaa of West Africa*. Stanford: Stanford University Press.

Gould, Stephen Jay. 1985. *The Flamingo's Smile*. New York: W. W. Norton.

Grady, Denise. 2002. "Few Risks Seen to the Children of 1st Cousins." *New York Times*, April 4, A1.

Graham, William A. 1979. *Divine Word and Prophetic Word in Early Islam*. Leiden: Mouton.

———. 1984. "The Earliest Meaning of 'Qur'ān.'" *Die Welt des Islams*, n.s., 23–24: 361–77.

Green, Kate, and Hilary Lim. 1998. "What Is This Thing about Female Circumcision? Legal Education and Human Rights." *Social and Legal Studies* 7(3): 339–64.

Gregg, Gary S. 2005. *The Middle East: A Cultural Psychology*. New York: Oxford University Press.

Grey, Thomas C. 1980. "The Disintegration of Property." In *Property*, edited by J. R. Pennock and J. W. Chapman, 69–85. New York: New York University Press.

Grossman, Andrew. 2003–4. "'Islamic Land': Group Rights, National Identity and Law." *UCLA Journal of Islamic and Near Eastern Law* 3:53–89.

Grunebaum, Gustave E. von. See Von Grunebaum, Gustave E.

Gülen, M. Fetullah. 1997. *Understanding and Belief: The Essentials of Islamic Faith*. Konak-Izmir, Turkey: Kaynak Publishing.

Günther, Sebastian. 2002. "Muhammad, the Illiterate Prophet: An Islamic Creed in the Qur'an and Qur'anic Exegesis." *Journal of Qur'anic Studies* 4(1): 1–26.

———. 2008. "The Ten Commandments and the Quran." In *The Ten Commandments and Their Appropriations in Judaism, Christianity, and Islam*, edited by Leonard V. Kaplan and Charles L. Cohen. Lanham, MD: Lexington Books.

Hafez, Mohammed M. 2006. *Manufacturing Human Bombs: The Making of Palestinian Suicide Bombers*. Washington, DC: United States Institute of Peace Press.

———. 2007. *Suicide Bombers in Iraq*. Washington, DC: U.S. Institute for Peace.

Hamdy, Sherine. 2006. "Science and Modern Islamic Discourses." In *Encyclopedia of Women and Islamic Cultures*, vol. 3, edited by Suad Joseph, 360–65. Leiden: Brill.

Hammoudi, Abdellah. 1997. *Master and Disciple: The Cultural Foundations of Moroccan Authoritarianism*. Chicago: University of Chicago Press.

———. 2006. *A Season in Mecca: Narrative of a Pilgrimage*. New York: Hill and Wang.

Hampshire, Stuart. 2000. *Justice Is Conflict*. Princeton: Princeton University Press.

Hann, C. M. 1996. "Property." In *Encyclopedia of Social and Cultural Anthropology*, edited by A. Barnard and J. R. Spencer, 453–54. London: Routledge.

———, ed. 1998. *Property Relations: Renewing the Anthropological Tradition*. Cambridge: Cambridge University Press.

Harris, J. W. 1996. *Property and Justice*. Oxford: Oxford University Press.

Hashim, Ahmed S. 2006. *Insurgency and Counterinsurgency in Iraq*. Ithaca: Cornell University Press.

Hassan, Nasra. 2006. "Suicide Terrorism." In *The Roots of Terrorism*, edited by Louise Richardson, 29–42. New York: Routledge.

Hawting, G. R. 1999. *The Idea of Idolatry and the Emergence of Islam: From Polemic to History*. New York: Cambridge University Press.

Hecht, Jennifer Michael. 2004. *Doubt: A History*. New York: Harper San Francisco.

Heffelfinger, Christopher, ed. 2005. *Unmasking Terror: A Global Review of Terrorist Activities*. Vol. 2. Washington, DC: The Jamestown Foundation.

Hefner, Robert W., ed. 2005. *Remaking Muslim Politics: Pluralism, Contestation, Democratization*. Princeton: Princeton University Press.

Hegasy, Sonja. 1997. *Staat, Öffentlichkeit und Zivilgesellschaft in Marokko. Die Potentiale der Sozio-kulturellen Opposition*. Politik, Wirtschaft und Gesellschaft des Vorderen Orients. Hamburg: Deutsches Orient-Institute.

———. 2007. "Young Authority: Quantitative and Qualitative Insights into Youth, Youth Culture, and State Power in Contemporary Morocco." *Journal of North African Studies* 12(1): 19–36.

Hermassi, Elbaki. 1984. "La société tunisienne au miroir islamiste." *Maghreb-Machrek* 103:31–33.

Hillenbrand, Richard. 1999. *Islamic Art and Architecture*. London: Thames & Hudson.

Himmich, Bensalem. 2001. *The Polymath*. Cairo: American University of Cairo Press.

Hirschkind, Charles. 1995. "Heresy or Hermeneutics: The Case of Nasr Hamid Abu Zayd." *Stanford Humanities Review* 5:35–48.

Hodgson, Marshall G. S. 1974. *The Venture of Islam*. Vol. 2. Chicago: University of Chicago Press.

Hoffman, Valerie J. 1995. "Muslim Fundamentalists: Psychosocial Profiles." In *Fundamentalisms Comprehended*, edited by Martin E. Marty and R. Scott Appleby, 199–230. Chicago: University of Chicago Press.

Hofmann, Murad Wilfried. 2004. Review of *The History of the Qur'anic Text from Revelation to Compilation*, by Muhammad Mustafa Al-A'zami. *Muslim World Book Review* 24(4): 20–22.

Hohfeld, Wesley Newcomb. 1919. *Fundamental Legal Conceptions as Applied in Judicial Reasoning and Other Essays*. New Haven: Yale University Press.

Holmes, Stephen. 2005. "Al-Qaeda, September 11, 2001." In *Making Sense of Suicide Missions*, edited by Diego Gambetta, 131–72. Oxford: Oxford University Press.

Hoodbhoy, Pervez. 1991. *Islam and Science: Religious Orthodoxy and the Battle for Rationality*. London: Zed Books.

———. 2002. Muslims and the West after September 11." *Free Inquiry* 22(2): 32–36.

———. 2006. "Pakistan: Waiting for Enlig[h]tenment." July 24. http://sacw .insaf.net/peace/Hoodbhoy24072006.html.

Hopkins, Nicholas S. 1990. "Engels and Ibn Khaldun." *Alif: Journal of Comparative Poetics* 10:9–18.

Hourani, Albert. 1991. *A History of the Arab Peoples.* Cambridge: Harvard University Press.

Huff, Toby E. 2003. *The Rise of Early Modern Science: Islam, China, and the West.* 2d ed. Cambridge: Cambridge University Press.

Ibn Khaldun. 1952. *Ibn Khaldun and Tamerlane, Their Historic Meeting in Damascus, 1401 A.D. (803 A.H.): A Study Based on Arabic Manuscripts of Ibn Khaldun's "Autobiography."* Translated by Walter J. Fischel. Berkeley: University of California Press.

———. 1967. *The Muqaddimah: An Introduction to History.* Translated by Franz Rosenthal. 3 vols. 2d ed. Princeton: Princeton University Press.

———. 1984. *Le Voyage d'Occident et d'Orient: Autobiographie de Ibn Khaldûn.* 2d ed. Edited by Abdesslam Cheddadi. Paris: Sindbad.

———. 1987. *An Arab Philosophy of History: Selections from the Prolegomena of Ibn Khaldun of Tunis (1332–1406).* Translated by Charles Issawi. Princeton: Darwin Press.

Ibn Warraq. 2002a. "Virgins? What Virgins?" 2002. *The Guardian* (London), January 12.

———, ed. 2002b. *What the Koran Really Says.* Amherst, NY: Prometheus Books.

———. 2006. "Representation of the Human Form in Islam." *Free Inquiry* 26(3): 13.

Irwin, Robert. 1996. "The Emergence of the Islamic World System, 1000–1500." In *The Cambridge Illustrated History of the Islamic World*, edited by Francis Robinson, 32–61. Cambridge: Cambridge University Press.

———. 1997. "Toynbee and Ibn Khaldun." *Middle Eastern Studies* 33: 461–79.

'Isa, Ahmad Muhammad. 1955. "Muslims and Taswir." *Muslim World* 45(3): 250–68.

IslamOnline.net. 2003. "Theory of Evolution from an Islamic Perspective." Fatwa Bank, September 9. http://www.islamonline.net/servlet/Satellite? pagename=IslamOnline-English-Ask_Scholar/FatwaE/FatwaE&cid= 1119503547388.

Izutsu, Toshihiko. 1959. *The Structure of Ethical Terms in the Koran.* Tokyo: Keio Institute.

———. 1964. *God and Man in the Koran.* Tokyo: The Keio Institute of Cultural and Linguistic Studies.

———. 1966. *Ethico-Religious Concepts in the Qur'an.* Montreal: McGill University Press.

Jamal, Amaney. 2005. "Mosques, Collective Identity and Gender Differences among Arab American Muslims." *Journal of Middle East Women's Studies* 1(1): 53–78.

REFERENCES

Jameelah, Maryam. 1983. *Modern Technology and the Dehumanization of Man.* Lahore: El-Matbaat-ul-Arabia.

James, William. 1918. *The Principles of Psychology.* New York: H. Holt and Co.

Johns, Jeremy. 2005. "The Language of Islamic Art." *Oxford Today* 17(3): 13–15.

Johnstone, Steven. 2003. "Women, Property, and Surveillance in Classical Athens." *Classical Antiquity* 22(2): 247–74.

Kakutani, Michiko. 2005. "Ordinary but for the Evil They Wrought." Review of *Perfect Soldiers*, by Terry McDermott. *New York Times*, May 20, E35.

Kamali, Mohammad Hashim. 1993. "Freedom of Expression in Islam: An Analysis of *Fitnah.*" *American Journal of Islamic Social Science* 10(2): 178–201.

———. 2002. *Freedom, Equality and Justice in Islam.* Cambridge, UK: Islamic Texts Society.

Karimi, Nasser. 2006. "Iran Opens Exhibit of Cartoons Mocking Holocaust." Associated Press, *Bangor (ME) Daily News*, August 16, A2.

Kassem, Hammond. 1972. "The Idea of Justice in Islamic Philosophy." *Diogenes* 79:81–108.

Keddie, Nikki. 1968. *An Islamic Response to Imperialism: Political and Religious Writings of Sayyid Jamal ad-Din "al-Afghani."* Berkeley: University of California Press.

Kelly, Tobias. 2004. "Returning Home? Law, Violence, and Displacement among West Bank Palestinians." *POLAR: Political and Legal Anthropology Review* 27(2): 95–112.

Kepel, Gilles. 1993. *The Revenge of God: The Resurgence of Islam, Christianity and Judaism in the Modern World.* London: Polity Press.

Khadduri, Majid. 1984. *The Islamic Conception of Justice.* Baltimore: Johns Hopkins Press.

Khalidi, Tarif. 2001. *The Muslim Jesus: Sayings and Stories in Islamic Literature.* Cambridge: Harvard University Press.

Khatibi, Abdelkébir. 1984. "Possession d'Iblis." *Sindbad* 36: 16–26.

Khuri, Fuad I. 1990. *Tents and Pyramids: Games and Ideology in Arab Culture from Backgammon to Autocratic Rule.* London: Saqi Books.

———. 2007. *An Invitation to Laughter: A Lebanese Anthropologist in the Arab World.* Chicago: University of Chicago Press.

Kifner, John. 2006. "Images of Muhammad, Gone for Good." *New York Times*, February 12, 4.

Kimhi, Shaul, and Shemuel Even. 2004. "Who Are the Palestinian Suicide Bombers?" *Terrorism and Political Violence* 16(4): 815–40.

Klausen, Jytte. 2005. *The Islamic Challenge: Politics and Religion in Western Europe.* Oxford: Oxford University Press.

Koning, Danielle. 2006. "Anti-evolutionism among Muslim Students." *ISIM (International Institute for the Study of Islam in the Modern World) Review* 18:48–49.

Kotek, Joël, and Dan Kotek. 2003. *Au nom de antisionisme: L'image des Juifs et d'Israël dans la caricature depuis la seconde Intifada.* Brussels: Editions Complexe.

Krueger, Alan B. 2007. *What Makes a Terrorist: Economics and the Roots of Terrorism*. Princeton: Princeton University Press.

Krutch, Joseph Wood. 1956. "The Search for a Rule of Life." *Saturday Review* 39:26–27.

Kühnel, Ernst. 1977. *The Arabesque: Meaning and Transformation of an Ornament.* Translated by Richard Ettinghausen. Graz: Verlag fur Sammler.

Lacoste, Yves. 1984. *Ibn Khaldun: The Birth of History and the Past of the Third World*. London: Verso.

Lakhsassi, Abderrahmane. 1996. "Ibn Khaldūn." In *History of Islamic Philosophy*, edited by Seyyed Hossein Nasr and Oliver Leaman, 1:350–64. London: Routledge.

Langer, Suzanne K. 1957. *Philosophy in a New Key: A Study in the Symbolism of Reason, Rite and Art*. Cambridge: Harvard University Press.

Latour, Bruno. 1987. *Science in Action*. Cambridge: Harvard University Press.

———. 1999. *Pandora's Hope: Essays on the Reality of Science Studies*. Cambridge: Harvard University Press.

Lazare, Daniel. 2004. "The Gods Must Be Crazy." *The Nation*, November 15, 29–36.

Leaman, Oliver. 1985. *An Introduction to Medieval Islamic Philosophy*. Cambridge: Cambridge University Press.

———. 2004. *Islamic Aesthetics: An Introduction*. Notre Dame: University of Notre Dame Press.

Leemhuis, Fred. 1993. "Epouser un Djinn? Passé et Present." *Quaderni di Studi Arabi* 11: 179–92.

Lester, Toby. 1999. "What Is the Koran?" *Atlantic Monthly*, January, 43–56.

Leveau, Rémy. 1985. "Public Property and Control of Property Rights: Their Effects on Social Structure in Morocco." In *Property, Social Structure, and the Modern Middle East*, edited by Ann Elizabeth Mayer, 61–84. Albany: State University of New York Press.

Levine, K. L. 2003. "Negotiating Boundaries of Crime and Culture: A Sociological Perspective on Cultural Defense Strategies." *Law and Social Inquiry* 28(1): 39–85.

Lewis, Bernard, ed. 1974. *Islam from the Prophet Muhammad to the Capture of Constantinople*. Vol. 2, *Religion and Society*. New York: Harper & Row.

———, ed. 1976. *Islam and the Arab World: Faith, People, Culture*. New York: Knopf.

———. 1988. *The Political Language of Islam*. Chicago: University of Chicago Press

———. 1990. *Race and Slavery in the Middle East*. New York: Oxford University Press.

———. 2000. *A Middle East Mosaic*. New York: Random House.

———. 2002. *What Went Wrong? Western Impact and Middle East Response*. New York: Oxford University Press.

———. 2006. "The New Anti-Semitism." *American Scholar* 75(1): 25–36.

Liebesny, Herbert. J. 1975. *The Law of the Near and Middle East*. Albany: State University of New York Press.

Livingston, John W. 1995. "Muhammad 'Abduh on Science." *Muslim World* 85(3–4): 215–34.

Lowie, Robert H. 1940. *An Introduction to Cultural Anthropology*. New York: Farrar & Rinehart.

Lu, Peter J., and Paul J. Steinhardt. 2007. "Decagonal and Quasi-Crystalline Tilings in Medieval Islamic Architecture." *Science* 315:1106–1110.

Luccioni, J. 1982. *Les Fondations Pieuses: "Habous" au Maroc*. Rabat: Imprimerie Royale.

Luxenberg, Christoph. 2000. *Die Syro-Aramäische Lesart des Koran: Ein Beitrag zur Entschlüsselung der Koransprache*. Berlin: Verlag Das Arabische Buch.

Macdonald, D. B., and H. Massé. 1991. "Djinn." In *The Encyclopedia of Islam*, new ed., vol. 2, edited by C. E. Bosworth et al., 546–48. Leiden: E. J. Brill.

MacFarquhar, Neil. 2006. "In Tiny Arab State, Web Takes on Ruling Elite." *New York Times*, January 15, 1.

———. 2007. "New Translation Prompts Debate on Islamic Verse." *New York Times*, March 25, 23.

Maddy-Weitzman, Bruce. 2005. "Women, Islam, and the Moroccan State: The Struggle over the Personal Status Law." *Middle East Journal* 59(3): 393–410.

Mahdi, Muhsin. 1957. *Ibn Khaldun's Philosophy of History: A Study in the Foundation of the Science of Culture*. Chicago: University of Chicago Press.

———. 1968. "Ibn Khaldun." In *International Encyclopedia of the Social Sciences*, edited by David L. Sills, 7:53–57. New York: Macmillan.

Maher, Vanessa. 1974. *Women and Property in Morocco*. Cambridge: Cambridge University Press.

Mahmoud, Mohamed. 1998. "Mahmud Muhammad Taha's Second Message of Islam and His Modernist Project." In *Islam and Modernity: Muslim Intellectuals Respond*, edited by John J. Cooper, 105–28. London: I. B. Tauris.

Makdisi, John. 1985. "An Objective Approach to Contractual Mistake in Islamic Law." *Boston University International Law Journal* 3:325–44.

Makiya, Kanan. 2005. "Present at the Disintegration." *New York Times*, December 11, WK 13.

Mamdani, Mahmoud. 1999. "Historicizing Power and Responses to Power: Indirect Rule and Reform." *Social Research* 66(3): 859–86.

Maning, Frank E. 2001. *Old New Zealand and Other Writings*. London: Leicester University Press.

Manji, Irshad. 2004. *The Trouble with Islam: A Muslim's Call for Reform in Her Faith*. New York: St. Martin's Press.

Markon, Jerry. 2005. "Muslim Lecturer Sentenced to Life." *Washington Post*, July 14, B1.

Marozzi, Justin. 2006. *Tamerlane: Sword of Islam, Conqueror of the World*. New York: Da Capo Press.

Martin, Richard C. 1982. "Understanding the Quran in Text and Context." *History of Religions* 21(4): 361–84.

McDermott, Terry. 2005. *Perfect Soldiers: The Hijackers: Who They Were, Why They Did It*. New York: HarperCollins.

Meeker, Michael E. 1979. *Literature and Violence in North Arabia*. New York: Cambridge University Press.

Mehdi, Rubya. 2001. *Gender and Property Law in Pakistan*. Copenhagen: DJOF Publishing.

Melikian-Chirvani, Assadullah Souren. 1987. "L'Islam, le verbe et l'image." In *Nicée II,787–1987: Douze siècles d'images réligieuses*, edited by François Boespflug and Nicolas Lossky, 89–117. Paris: Cerf.

Mernissi, Fatima. 1991. *The Veil and the Male Elite: A Feminist Interpretation of Women's Rights in Islam*. Reading, MA: Addison-Wesley Publishing Co.

Merry, Sally E. 2003. "Human Rights Law and the Demonization of Culture (and Anthropology Along the Way)." *POLAR: Political and Legal Anthropology Review* 26(1): 55–76.

Messier, Ronald A. 2001. "Re-thinking the Almoravids, Re-thinking Ibn Khaldun." In *North Africa, Islam and the Mediterranean World: From the Almoravids to the Algerian War*, edited by Julia Clancy-Smith, 59–80. London: Frank Cass.

Metlitzki, Dorothee. 1977. *The Matter of Araby in Medieval England*. New Haven: Yale University Press.

Montagu, M. F. Ashley, ed. 1956. *Toynbee and History: Critical Essays and Reviews*. Boston: Porter Sargent Publisher.

Morgan-Foster, Jason. 2005. "Third Generation Rights: What Islamic Law Can Teach the International Human Rights Movement." *Yale Human Rights and Development Law Journal* 8:67–116.

Mottahedeh, Roy P. 1976. "The Shuʿûbiyah Controversy and the Social History of Early Islamic Iran." *International Journal of Middle East Studies* 7:161–82.

Mundy, Roderick. 1995. "What Do the French Think of Their Jury? Views from Poitiers and Paris." *Legal Studies* 15(1): 65–87.

Murphy, Caryle. 2006. "Area Muslims React with Tempered Anger." *Washington Post*, February 5, A15.

Nachi, Mohamed. 2004. "The Articulation of 'I,' 'We' and the 'Person': Elements for an Anthropological Approach within Western and Islamic Contexts." In *Standing Trial: Law and the Person in the Modern Middle East*, edited by Baudouin Dupret, 39–65. London: I. B. Tauris.

Nasr, Seyyed Hossein. 1976. *Islamic Science: An Illustrated Study*. London: World of Islam Festival.

———. 1987. *Science and Civilisation in Islam*. 2d ed. Cambridge: Islamic Texts Society.

———. 1994. *Religion and the Order of Nature*. Oxford: Oxford University Press.

Nasr, Vali. 2005. "The Rise of 'Muslim Democracy.' " *Journal of Democracy* 16(2): 13–27.

Negus, Michael Robert. 1995. "The Concept of Islamic Science and the Thought Patterns of the Islamic Scientist." *Muslim Education Quarterly* 12(4): 30–36.

Nelson, Kristina. 2001. *The Art of Reciting the Qur'an.* New ed. Cairo: American University of Cairo Press.

Newcomb, Rachel. 2004. *"Singing to Many Audiences": Negotiations of Gender, Identity, and Social Space in Fes, Morocco.* Ph.D. diss., Princeton University.

"Nomos and Narrative." 2005. Symposium in the *Yale Journal of Law and the Humanities* 17:1–105.

Noorani, Yaseen. 2004. "Heterotopia and the Wine Poem in Early Islamic Culture." *International Journal of Middle East Studies* 36(3): 345–66.

Note. 1986. "The Cultural Defense in the Criminal Law." *Harvard Law Review* 99(4): 1293–1311.

Nussbaum, Martha. 1999. "A Plea for Difficulty." In Cohen, Howard, and Nussbaum 1999, 105–14.

Okin, Susan M. 1999a. "Is Multiculturalism Bad for Women? In Cohen, Howard, and Nussbaum 1999, 9–24.

———. 1999b. "Reply." In Cohen, Howard, and Nussbaum 1999, 117–31.

———. 2002. "'Mistresses of Their Own Identity': Group Rights, Gender, and Realistic Rights of Exit." *Ethics* 112(2): 205–30.

Oliver, Anne Marie, and Paul F. Steinberg. 2005. *The Road to Martyrs' Square: A Journey into the World of the Suicide Bomber.* New York: Oxford University Press.

Olschki, Leonardo. 1951. "Mohammedan Eschatology and Dante's Other World." *Comparative Literature* 3(1): 1–17.

Ottenheimer, Martin. 1996. *Forbidden Relatives: The American Myth of Cousin Marriage.* Urbana: University of Illinois Press.

Overbye, Dennis. 2001. "How Islam Won, and Lost, the Lead in Science." *New York Times*, October 30, F1.

Palacios, Miguel Asin. 1977. *Islam and the Divine Comedy.* Translated by Harold Sunderland. Lahore: Quasain.

Pamuk, Orhan. 2001. *My Name Is Red.* Translated by Erdag M. Göknar. New York: Knopf.

Pandolfo, Stephania. 1989. "Detours of Life: Space and Bodies in a Moroccan Village." *American Ethnologist* 16(1): 3–23.

———. 1997. *Impasse of the Angels.* Chicago: University of Chicago Press.

Papadopoulo, Alexandre. 1979. *Islam and Muslim Art.* London: Thames and Hudson.

Pape, Robert Anthony. 2005. *Dying to Win: The Strategic Logic of Suicide Terrorism.* New York: Random House.

Parcheminal, Hervé. 1985. *La Copropriété en Droit Marocain.* Casablanca: Les Editions Maghrébines.

Paret, R. 1986. "Ḳirā'a." In *The Encyclopaedia of Islam*, new ed., vol. 5, edited by C. E. Bosworth et al., 127–29. Leiden: E. J. Brill.

Patai, Raphael. 2002. *The Arab Mind.* Rev. ed. New York: Hatherleigh Press.

Patterson, Orlando. 1982. *Slavery and Social Death: A Comparative Study.* Cambridge: Harvard University Press.

Paulo, John Allen. 1996. "Dangerous Abstractions," *New York Times,* April 7, sec. 4, 11.

Peckham, Morse. 1965. *Man's Rage for Chaos: Biology, Behavior and the Arts.* Philadelphia: Chilton Books.

Pennock, J. Roland, and John W. Chapman, eds. 1980. *Property.* Nomos 22. New York: New York University Press.

Pettit, Philip. 2004. "Depoliticizing Democracy." *Ratio Juris* 17(1): 52–65.

Phillips, Anne. 2003. "When Culture Means Gender: Issues of Cultural Defense in the English Courts." *Modern Law Review* 66(4): 510–31.

Pipes, Daniel, and Lars Hedegaard. 2002. "Muslim Extremism: Denmark's Had Enough." *National Post* (Toronto), August 27, A14.

Pipes, Richard. 1999. *Property and Freedom.* New York: Alfred A. Knopf.

Planhol, Xavier de. 1959. *The World of Islam.* Ithaca: Cornell University Press.

Pollard, Deana A. 2003. "Banning Child Corporal Punishment." *Tulane Law Review* 77:575–656.

Potok, Chaim. 1972. *My Name Is Asher Lev.* New York: Ballantine Books.

Pottage, Alain. 1994. "The Measure of Land." *Modern Law Review* 57(3): 361–84.

Poulter, Sebastian. 1997. "Muslim Headscarves in School: Contrasting Legal Approaches in England and France." *Oxford Journal of Legal Studies* 17(1): 43–74.

Pound, Roscoe. 1954. *Introduction to the Philosophy of Law.* New Haven: Yale University Press.

Power, Carla. 2007. "A Secret History." *New York Times Magazine,* February 25, 22–23.

Powers, Paul R. 2006. *Intent in Islamic Law: Motive and Meaning in Medieval Sunni Fiqh.* Leiden: Brill.

Qadir, C. A. 1988. *Philosophy and Science in the Islamic World.* London: Routledge.

Qutb, Sayyid. 1953. *Social Justice in Islam.* Washington: American Council of Learned Societies.

Rahman, Fazlur. 1958. *Prophecy in Islam: Philosophy and Orthodoxy.* London: George Allen & Unwin Ltd.

———. 1966. "The Status of the Individual in Islam." *Islamic Studies* 5:319–30.

———. 1979. *Islam.* 2d ed. Chicago: University of Chicago Press.

———. 1983. "Some Key Ethical Concepts of the Qur'ān." *Journal of Religious Ethics* 11(2): 170–85.

Raman, B. 2004. "Pakistan and Dangers of Nuclear Jihad." *South Asia Analysis Group, Paper no. 904,* January 27, 2. http://www.saag.org/papers10/paper904.html.

Ramic, Sukri (Husejn). 2003. *Language and the Interpretation of Islamic Law.* Cambridge, UK: Islamic Texts Society.

Randal, Jonathan. 2004. *Osama: The Making of a Terrorist*. New York: Knopf.

Rawls, John. 1999. *A Theory of Justice*. Rev. ed. Cambridge: Harvard University Press.

Raz, Joseph. 1999. "How Perfect Should One Be? And Whose Culture Is?" In Cohen, Howard, and Nussbaum 1999, 95–99.

Reagan, Ronald. 1993. "There They Go Again." *New York Times*, February 18, 23.

Renteln, Alison Dundes. 2003. *The Cultural Defense*. New York: Oxford University Press.

Reuter, Christopher 2004. *My Life Is a Weapon: A Modern History of Suicide Bombing*. Princeton: Princeton University Press.

Reynolds, Gabriel Said. 2004. "A Reflection on Two Qur'anic Words (Iblis and Judi) with Attention to the Theories of A. Mingana." *Journal of the American Oriental Society* 124(4): 675–89.

Ricoeur, Paul. 2000. *The Just*. Chicago: University of Chicago Press.

Riexinger, Martin. 2002. "The Islamic Creationism of Harun Yahya." *ISIM (International Institute for the Study of Islam in the Modern World) Newsletter* 11:5.

Rippin, Andrew. 2001. *The Qur'an and Its Interpretive Traditions*. Aldershot, UK: Ashgate Variorum.

———. 2005. "Tafsīr." In *Encyclopedia of Religion*, 2d ed., edited by Lindsay Jones, 13:8949–57. Detroit: Thomson Gale.

Robinson, Francis. 2006. " 'Hero of Islam?' " Review of *The Muqaddimah*, by Ibn Khaldun, translated by Franz Rosenthal. *Times Literary Supplement*, February 17, 11.

Rose, Carol. 1985. "Possession as the Origin of Property." *University of Chicago Law Review* 52(1): 73–88.

Rose, Flemming. 2006a. "A Right to Offend?" *Time*, February 13, 48.

———. 2006b. "Why I Published Those Cartoons." *Washington Post*, February 19, B1.

Rosen, Jeffrey. 2006. "Is Ritual Circumcision Religious Expression?" *New York Times Magazine*, February 5, 28.

Rosen, Lawrence. 1979. "Social Identity and Points of Attachment: Approaches to Social Organization." In Geertz, Geertz, and Rosen 1979, 19–122.

———. 1984. *Bargaining for Reality: The Structure of Social Relations in a Moroccan City*. Chicago: University of Chicago Press.

———. 1989. *The Anthropology of Justice: Law as Culture in Islamic Society*. Cambridge: Cambridge University Press.

———. 1997. "The Right to Be Different: Indigenous Peoples and the Quest for a Unified Theory." *Yale Law Journal* 107(1): 227–59.

———. 2000. *The Justice of Islam*. Oxford: Oxford University Press.

———. 2002. *The Culture of Islam*. Chicago: University of Chicago Press.

———. 2005. "Homesick Everywhere." *London Review of Books*, August 4, 3–5.

———. Forthcoming. "Character and Caricature: The Danish Cartoon Controversy and the Meaning of the Prophet Muhammad." In *The Ten Command-*

ments and Their Appropriation in Judaism, Christianity, and Islam, edited by Leonard V. Kaplan and Charles L. Cohen. Lanham, MD: Lexington Books.

Rosenthal, Franz. 1960. *The Muslim Concept of Freedom, Prior to the Nineteenth Century.* Leiden: E. J. Brill.

———. 1968. *A History of Muslim Historiography.* Leiden: E. J. Brill.

———. 1970. *Knowledge Triumphant: The Concept of Knowledge in Medieval Islam.* Leiden: E. J. Brill.

———. 1971. *Four Essays on Art and Literature in Islam.* Leiden: E. J. Brill.

———. 1975. *Gambling in Islam.* Leiden: E. J. Brill.

———. 1984. "Ibn Khaldun in His Time." In *Ibn Khaldun and Islamic Ideology*, edited by Bruce B. Lawrence, 14–26. Leiden: Brill.

———. 1987. "Ibn Khaldun." In *The Encyclopedia of Religion*, edited by Mircea Eliade, 6:565–67. New York: The Macmillan Company.

Rosenzweig, Franz. 2005. *The Star of Redemption.* Translated by Barbara E. Galli. Madison: University of Wisconsin Press.

Rothenberg, Celia E. 2004. *Spirits of Palestine: Gender, Society, and Stories of the Jinn.* Lanham, MD: Lexington Books.

Rouse, Carolyn M. 2004. *Engaged Surrender: African American Women and Islam.* Berkeley: University of California Press.

Roy, Olivier. 2004. *Globalised Islam: The Search for a New Ummah.* London: Hurst.

Ruggles, D. Fairchild. 2000. *Gardens, Landscape, and Vision in the Palaces of Islamic Spain.* University Park: Pennsylvania State University Press.

Rushdie, Salman. 1991. "In Good Faith." In *Imaginary Homelands*, 393–414. London: Granta.

Ruthven, Malise. 1984. *Islam in the World.* London: Penguin.

———. 1994. "Was Weber Wrong?" *London Review of Books*, August 18, 20.

———. 2004. *Fundamentalism: The Search for Meaning.* Oxford: Oxford University Press.

Ryan, Alan. 1984. *Property and Political Theory.* Oxford: Basil Blackwell.

Sabra, A. I. 1976. "The Scientific Enterprise." In *Islam and the Arab World*, edited by Bernard Lewis, 181–200. New York: Alfred A. Knopf.

Sachs, Susan. 2000. "With Trepidation, Saudi Arabia Meets the World." *New York Times*, December 10, 22.

Sageman, Marc. 2004a. "Understanding Terror Networks." *Foreign Policy Research Institute, E-Notes*, November 1.

———. 2004b. *Understanding Terror Networks.* Philadelphia: University of Pennsylvania Press.

Salam, Abdus. 1989a. *Renaissance of Sciences in Islamic Countries.* Teaneck, NJ: World Scientific.

———. 1989b. *Science in the Third World, The First Edinburgh Medal Address.* Edinburgh: Edinburgh University Press.

———. 1991. Foreword to *Islam and Science: Religious Orthodoxy and the Battle for Rationality*, by Pervez Hoodbhoy. London: Zed Books.

———. [1996]. "The Future of Science in Islamic Countries." Statement prepared for inclusion in a volume presented to the Islamic Summit held in Kuwait in January 1987. http://www.alislam.org/library/salam-2.html.

Salomone, Rosemary C. 2003. *Same, Different, Equal: Rethinking Single-Sex Schooling.* New Haven: Yale University Press.

Sardar, Ziauddin. 1989. *Explorations in Islamic Science.* London: Mansell.

Schacht, Joseph. 1964. *An Introduction to Islamic Law.* Oxford: Clarendon Press.

Schaefer, Naomi. 2003. "Women at Religious Colleges—Subordination or Secularization?" *Public Interest,* no. 152 (summer): 81–99.

Schillinger, Liesl. 2006. Review of *The Courtier and the Heretic,* by Matthew Stewart. *New York Times Book Review,* February 26, 17.

Schmitt, Eric. 2003. "How Army Sleuths Stalked the Adviser Who Led to Hussein." *New York Times,* December 20, 1.

Sells, Michael Anthony. 1999. *Approaching the Qur'ān: The Early Revelations.* Ashland, OR: White Cloud Press.

Sen, Amartya. 1992. *Inequality Reexamined.* Cambridge: Harvard University Press.

Serjeant, R. B. 1954. "Hud and Other Pre-Islamic Prophets of Hadramawt." *Le Muséon* 47:121–79.

Shadid, Anthony. 2005. *Night Draws Near: Iraq's People in the Shadow of America's War.* New York: Henry Holt and Company.

Shadid, Anthony, and Kevin Sullivan. 2006. "Anatomy of the Cartoon Protest Movement." *Washington Post,* February 16, A1.

Shah, Tahir. 2006. *The Caliph's House: A Year in Casablanca.* New York: Bantam.

Shahid, Irfan. 1965. "A Contribution to Koranic Exegesis." In *Arabic and Islamic Studies in Honor of Hamilton A. R. Gibb,* edited by George Makdisi, 563–80. Cambridge: Harvard University Press.

Shapiro, Ari. 2000. "A Curse on All Our Houses: The Ethics of Ownership in the Czech Republic." Ph.D. diss., Princeton University.

Shweder, Richard A. 2003. *Why Do Men Barbeque? Recipes for Cultural Psychology.* Cambridge: Harvard University Press.

———. 2005. "Cliff Notes: The Pluralism of Clifford Geertz." In *Clifford Geertz and His Colleagues,* edited by Jerome Bruner and Richard A. Shweder, 1–9. Chicago: University of Chicago Press.

Siino, François. 2004. *Science et Pouvoir dans la Tunisie Contemporaine,* Paris: Editions Karthala.

Sikand, Yoginder. 2006. *Bastions of the Believers: Madrasas and Islamic Education in India.* London: Penguin Group.

Silverstein, Theodore. 1952. "Dante and the Legend of the Mi'raj." *Journal of Middle Eastern Studies* 11(1): 89–110.

Singer, Joseph William. 2000. *Entitlement: The Paradoxes of Property.* New Haven: Yale University Press.

Slackman, Michael. 2006. "Beneath the Rage in the Mideast." *New York Times,* February 12, WK1.

Slyomovics, Susan. 2005. *The Performance of Human Rights in Morocco.* University of Pennsylvania Press.

Smirnov, A. 1996. "Understanding Justice in an Islamic Context: Some Points of Contrast with Western Theories." *Philosophy East and West* 46(3): 337–50.

Smith, Craig S., and Ian Fisher. 2006. "Temperatures Rise over Cartoons Mocking Muhammad." *New York Times*, February 3, 3.

Solomon, Andrew. 2006. "Letter from Libya: Circle of Fire." *New Yorker*, May 8, 44–61.

Sonnert, Gerhard. 2005. *Einstein and Culture.* Amherst, N.Y.: Humanity Books.

Sorek, Tamir. 2002. "Memory and Identity: The Land Day Monument." *ISIM (International Institute for the Study of Islam in the Modern World) Newsletter* 10:17.

Soroush, 'Abdolkarim. 2000. *Reason, Freedom, and Democracy in Islam.* New York: Oxford University Press.

Spellberg, Denise A. 1996. "Writing the Unwritten Life of the Islamic Eve: Menstruation and the Demonization of Motherhood." *International Journal of Middle East Studies* 28:305–24.

Spiegelman, Art. 2006. "Drawing Blood: Outrageous Cartoons and the Art of Outrage." *Harper's*, June, 43–51.

Stern, Jessica. 2001. "Meeting with the Muj." *Bulletin of the Atomic Scientists* 57(1): 42–50

——— 2003. *Terror in the Name of God: Why Religious Militants Kill.* New York: HarperCollins.

Stewart, Frank Henderson. 1994. *Honor.* Chicago: University of Chicago Press.

Stewart, Matthew. 2006. *The Courtier and the Heretic: Leibniz, Spinoza, and the Fate of God in the Modern World.* New York: Norton.

Stille, Alexander. 2002. "Scholars Are Quietly Offering New Theories of the Koran." *New York Times*, March 2, A1.

Stone, Suzanne Last. 1993. "In Pursuit of the Counter-text: The Turn to the Jewish Legal Model in Contemporary American Legal Theory." *Harvard Law Review* 106(4):813–94.

Strathern, Marilyn. 1988. *The Gender of the Gift: Problems with Women and Problems with Society in Melanesia.* Berkeley: University of California Press.

———. 1996. "Cutting the Network." *Journal of the Royal Anthropological Institute*, n.s., 2:517–35.

———. 1999. *Property, Substance and Effect.* London: The Athlone Press.

———. 2004. "Losing (out on) Intellectual Resources." In *Law, Anthropology, and the Constitution of the Social: Making Persons and Things*, edited by Alain Pottage and Martha Mundy, 201–33. Cambridge: Cambridge University Press.

Stroumsa, Sarah. 1999. *Freethinkers of Medieval Islam.* Leiden: Brill.

Sunder, Madhavi. 2003. "Piercing the Veil." *Yale Law Journal* 112(6): 1399–1472.

Sunstein, Cass. 1999. "Should Sex Equality Law Apply to Religious Institutions?" In Cohen, Howard, and Nussbaum 1999, 85–94.

Taha, Mahmoud Muhammad. 1987. *The Second Message of Islam*. Translated by Abdullahi Ahmed An-Naʿim. Syracuse: Syracuse University Press.

Talbi, M. 1971. "Ibn Khaldûn." In *Encyclopaedia of Islam*, new ed., vol. 3, edited by C. E. Bosworth et al, 825–31. Leiden: E. J. Brill.

Taseer, Aatish. 2005. "A British Jihadist." Interview with Hassan Butt. *Prospect*, August, 18–24.

Tayob, Abdulkader I. 1995. "Muhammad: Role of the Prophet in Muslim Thought and Practice." *The Oxford Encyclopedia of the Modern Islamic World*, vol. 3, edited by John L. Esposito, 164–66. Oxford: Oxford University Press.

Toulmin, Stephen Edelston. 1972. *Human Understanding*. Princeton: Princeton University Press.

Toynbee, Arnold J. 1935. *A Study of History*. 2d ed. Vol. 3. Oxford: Oxford University Press.

———. 1954. *A Study of History*. 2d ed. Vol. 10. Oxford: Oxford University Press.

Tritton, A. S. 1972. "The Speech of God." *Studia Islamica* 36:5–22.

Tyler, Tom R. 2000. "Multiculturalism and the Willingness of Citizens to Defer to Law and to Legal Authorities." *Law and Social Inquiry* 25:983–1016.

United Nations Development Programme. 2003. *Arab Human Development Report 2003: Building a Knowledge Society*. New York: United Nations Development Programme, Regional Bureau for Arab States.

———. 2004. *Arab Human Development Report 2004: Towards Freedom in the Arab World*. New York: United Nations Development Programme, Regional Bureau for Arab States.

Unsworth, Barry. 2002. *The Song of the Kings*. London: Hamish Hamilton.

Venema, Bernhard, and Ali Mguild. 2003. "Access to Land and Berber Ethnicity in the Middle Atlas, Morocco." *Middle Eastern Studies* 39(4): 35–53.

Viorst, Milton. 2006. "The Education of Ali Al-Timimi." *Atlantic Monthly*, June, 69–78.

Volpi, Frédéric. 2004. "Pseudo-Democracy in the Muslim World." *Third World Quarterly* 25(6): 1061–1078.

Von Grunebaum, Gustave E. 1953. *Medieval Islam*. Chicago: University of Chicago Press.

———. 1955. *Islam: Essays in the Nature and Growth of a Cultural Tradition*. Menasha, WI: American Anthropological Association.

Wadud, Amina. 1999. *Qurʾan and Woman: Rereading the Sacred Text from a Woman's Perspective*. Oxford: Oxford University Press.

Wallace, Anthony F. C. 1956. "Revitalization Movements." *American Anthropologist* 58: 264–81.

Wansbrough, John. 2004. *Quranic Studies: Sources and Methods of Scriptural Interpretation*. Exp. ed. Amherst, NY: Prometheus Books.

Wensinck, A. J., and Charles Pellat. 1971. "Hud." In *The Encyclopaedia of Islam*, new ed., vol. 3, edited by Bernard Lewis et al., 537–38. Leiden: E. J. Brill.

Werbner, Pnina. 1996. "Allegories of Sacred Implication." *Current Anthropology* 37:S55–S86.

Wheeler, Brannon M. 2002. *Prophets in the Quran: An Introduction to the Quran and Muslim Exegesis.* London: Continuum.

Whishaw, Bernhard, and Ellen M. Whishaw. 1910. "Animate Life in Early Arabic Art." *The Nineteenth Century and After* 67:1068–76.

Wicker, Brian, ed. 2006. *Witnesses to Faith? Martyrdom in Christianity and Islam.* Aldershot, UK: Ashgate.

Wiktorowicz, Quintan. 2005. *Radical Islam Rising: Muslim Extremism in the West.* Lanham, MD: Rowman & Littlefield Publishers, Inc.

Wilford, John Noble. 2007. "In Medieval Architecture, Signs of Advanced Math." *New York Times,* February 27, F2.

Williams, John Alden. 1962. *Islam.* New York: George Braziller.

———. 1995. "Fitnah." In *The Oxford Encyclopedia of the Modern Islamic World,* vol. 2, edited by John Esposito, 26–28. Oxford: Oxford University Press.

Wilson, Scott. 2005. "Clampdown at Gaza—Egypt Border Crossing Ends Days of Chaos." *Washington Post,* September 18, A27.

Wiltz, Teresa. 2006. "Funny, He Doesn't Look Jamaican: Chart-Topping Matisyahu Wants to Be More Than Just a Hassidic Reggae Superstar." *Washington Post,* February 19, N4.

Winter, Tim. 2006. "A Sense of Awe." *Prospect,* March, 20–21.

Wolf, Eric R. 1951. "The Social Organization of Mecca and the Origins of Islam." *Southwestern Journal of Anthropology* 7(4): 329–56.

Wolfson, Harry A. 1959. "Ibn Khaldûn on Attributes and Predestination." *Speculum* 34(4): 585–97.

Wolin, Sheldon. 1968. "Political Theory: Trends and Goals." In *The International Encyclopedia of the Social Sciences,* edited by David L. Sills, 12:318–31. New York: Macmillan.

Wright, Lawrence. 2006. *The Looming Tower: Al-Qaeda and the Road to 9/11.* New York: Alfred A. Knopf.

Yahya, Harun. 2000. *The Evolution Deceit.* Istanbul: Okur Publishing.

———. 2001. *The Disasters Darwinism Brought to Humanity.* Scarborough, Canada: Al-Attique Publishers.

———. 2007. *Atlas of Creation.* Istanbul: Global Publishing.

Yared, Aida. 1990. " 'In the Name of Annah': Islam and *Salam* in Joyce's *Finnegans Wake.*" *James Joyce Quarterly* 35(2–3): 401–38.

Younis, Yahia O. 2000. "Possession and Exorcism: An Illustrative Case." *Arab Journal of Psychiatry* 11(1): 56–59.

Ziadat, Adel A. 1986. *Western Science in the Arab World—The Impact of Darwinism, 1860–1930.* New York: St. Martin's Press.

Ziadeh, Farhat J. 1957. "Equality (*kafaʾah*) in the Muslim Law of Marriage." *American Journal of Comparative Law* 6(4): 503–17.

———. 1985–86. "Shufʾah: Origins and Modern Doctrine." *Cleveland State Law Review* 34:35–46.

Index